EVANGELICAL EXODUS

EVANGELICAL EXODUS

Evangelical Seminarians
and
Their Paths to Rome

Edited by Douglas M. Beaumont

IGNATIUS PRESS   SAN FRANCISCO

Cover art:
The Calling of Andrew and Peter (fresco)
by Giusto di Giovanni de' Menabuoi
Scrovegni Chapel, Padua, Italy
Photograph © Bridgeman Images

Cover design by John Herreid

© 2016 by Ignatius Press, San Francisco
All rights reserved
ISBN 978-1-62164-042-4
Library of Congress Control Number 2015942047
Printed in the United States of America ∞

To the Dumb Ox:
May our speech one day approach the majesty of your silence.

Saint Thomas Aquinas,
pray for us.

In quibus natus sum,
a me rémovens ténebras,
peccátum scílicet et ignorántiam.

CONTENTS

FOREWORD

From "Historic Christianity" to the Christianity of History

I remember distinctly the moment I knew that I had to return to the Catholic Church, in which I had been baptized and confirmed as a youngster. It was in mid-March 2007, only four months after I had been elected the fifty-eighth president of the Evangelical Theological Society, an academic society of about 4,200 members at the time. After decades of assimilating Catholic thought in my spiritual pilgrimage without realizing it, and with the help of some Catholic friends who posed to me just the right questions with just the right degree of gentle prodding, I had been brought to the outer bank of the Tiber. But what finally forced me to take my first steps on the bridge that traversed those seemingly foreboding waters was a passage authored by the renowned Reformed historical theologian Carl Trueman in his review of the book *Is the Reformation Over?* In it Trueman writes:

> Every year I tell my Reformation history class that Roman Catholicism is, at least in the West, the default position. Rome has a better claim to historical continuity and institutional unity than any Protestant denomination, let alone the strange hybrid that is Evangelicalism; in the light of these facts, therefore, we need good, solid reasons for not being Catholic; not being a Catholic should, in other words, be a positive act of will and commitment, something we need to get out of bed determined to do each and every day. It would seem, however, that ... many who call themselves Evangelical really lack any good reason for such an act of will; and the obvious conclusion, therefore, should be that they do the decent thing and rejoin the Roman Catholic Church. I cannot go down that path myself, primarily because of my view of justification by faith and because of my ecclesiology;

but those who reject the former and lack the latter have no real basis upon which to perpetuate what is, in effect, an act of schism on their part. For such, the Reformation is over; for me, the fat lady has yet to sing; in fact, I am not sure at this time that she has even left her dressing room.[1]

After reading that paragraph, I felt as if I had been punched in the nose. I realized at that instant that I was in schism with the Catholic Church, and for that reason, the burden was on me and not on the Church to provide an account of my present state of noncommunion. At that moment, my Christian faith ceased to be something that I chose and became something that chose me. It was, as Doug Beaumont notes in his introduction to this wonderful collection, a paradigm shift, a radical reorientation of where one stands in relation to the universal Church. I no longer saw myself standing before an ecclesial buffet of fragmented Western Christendom, eagerly seeking to select those beliefs that conformed to my theological predilections. I found myself under a creed I did not invent rather than a confession that was under my control.

For those who have not taken this sort of journey, who have not ventured outside the confines of Evangelical culture, doctrine, and spirituality, the very idea of being at a crossroads with Catholicism seems almost counterintuitive. The contributors to this volume, including the author of this foreword, were at one time in that very same state of bewilderment when reports of friends and acquaintances drifting to Rome reached our eyes and ears. Why entertain Catholicism, we thought, when some of its essential beliefs—especially on matters over which Evangelical Protestants part ways with Catholics—are "unbiblical" and not part of "historic Christianity"? After all, as we were told by some of the leading lights of Evangelicalism, the Reformation had simply restored what had been believed by the ancient Church but had been corrupted by the "Roman Communion" of the Middle Ages. True Christianity was like a pristine ocean vessel that had over the years acquired all these Catholic barnacles that impeded the ship from smoothly reaching its eternal

---

[1] Carl Trueman, review of *Is the Reformation Over?*, by Mark Noll and Carolyn Nystrom, *Reformation 21* (November 2005), http://www.reformation21.org/shelf-life/is-the-reformation-over.php.

destination. In contrast, "historic Christianity", as our Evangelical friends are fond of saying, consists of just a few basic doctrines, easily derived from the Church's only authority, an inerrant Bible. All the other doctrines over which Christians disagree—e.g., the nature of the sacraments, ecclesiology, women's ordination, the precise nature of the Incarnation, whether God is inside or outside time, whether one can lose one's salvation—are either nonessential or, in the case of certain "Catholic" doctrines such as praying for the dead and to the saints, unbiblical.

What the contributors to this volume discovered in their journeys is that this narrative, though having sustained them for many years and having kept them from entertaining Catholicism, could not withstand the scrutiny of historical analysis. Speaking for myself, it was a jarring experience to learn that there were serious problems with the "historic Christianity" story I had uncritically believed for decades as an Evangelical Protestant. Take, for example, the use of the early Church Fathers in the work of Norman L. Geisler, the founder of Southern Evangelical Seminary, the institution that connects all the contributors to this book. In volume 3 of his *Systematic Theology*, Geisler argues that the Reformers' understanding of the doctrine of justification can be found in the early Church Fathers. To make his case, he conscripts a few quotations from several of them,[2] including these from the homilies of Saint John Chrysostom (ca. A.D. 344/354–A.D. 407):

> In order then that the greatness of the benefits bestowed may not raise you too high, observe how he brings you down: "by grace you have been saved", says he, "through faith"; Then, that, on the other hand, our free will be not impaired, he adds also our part in the work, and yet again cancels it, and adds, "And that not of ourselves".[3]
>   For this is [the righteousness] "of God" when we are justified not by works (in which case it were necessary that not a spot even should be found) but by grace, in which case all sin is done away.[4]

[2] The following quotations from Saint John Chrysostom are employed by Norman L. Geisler in his *Systematic Theology*, vol. 3, *Sin, Salvation* (Grand Rapids: Baker Book House, 2004), 289–90. However, for the sake of continuity between the two sets of quotations, I am using the version published on the New Advent Catholic website (http://newadvent.org/fathers/).

[3] Saint John Chrysostom, *Homily 4 on Ephesians.*

[4] Saint John Chrysostom, *Homily 11 on 2 Corinthians.*

These comments do indeed sound like what one would find in the sermons of a Calvin or a Luther. Yet, Saint John Chrysostom published many other homilies, two of which contain these words:

> Let us then give them aid and perform commemoration for them. For if the children of Job were purged by the sacrifice of their father, why do you doubt that when we too offer for the departed, some consolation arises to them? [For] God is wont to grant the petitions of those who ask for others. And this Paul signified saying that "in a manifold Person your gift toward us bestowed by many may be acknowledged with thanksgiving on your behalf" (2 Cor 1:11). Let us not then be weary in giving aid to the departed, both by offering on their behalf and obtaining prayers for them: for the common Expiation of the world is even before us.[5]
>
> Mourn for those who have died in wealth, and did not from their wealth think of any solace for their soul, who had power to wash away their sins and would not. Let us all weep for these in private and in public, but with propriety, with gravity, not so as to make exhibitions of ourselves; let us weep for these, not one day, or two, but all our life. Such tears spring not from senseless passion, but from true affection. The other sort are of senseless passion. For this cause they are quickly quenched, whereas if they spring from the fear of God, they always abide with us. Let us weep for these; let us assist them according to our power; let us think of some assistance for them, small though it be, yet still let us assist them. How and in what way? By praying and entreating others to make prayers for them, by continually giving to the poor on their behalf.[6]

In these passages Saint John is asking his readers to pray for the dead, that through their prayers and works of charity the dead may be assisted in their purification in the afterlife. This, of course, sounds an awful lot like the Catholic Church's doctrine of purgatory, which is rejected as "unbiblical" almost universally by Evangelicals such as Geisler.[7] If we set aside the biblical question, it is clear that if Saint John believed in purgatory (or at least some primitive understanding of it), he was not an advocate of the pristine "historic Christianity" that its champions claim had largely vanished from both the

---

[5] Saint John Chrysostom, *Homily 41 on 1 Corinthians*.

[6] Saint John Chrysostom, *Homily 3 on Philippians*.

[7] There are, of course, exceptions, including the Evangelical philosopher Jerry Walls, author of *Purgatory: The Logic of Total Transformation* (New York: Oxford University Press, 2012).

Western and Eastern Churches until the second decade of the sixteenth century.

There is a reason why Blessed John Henry Cardinal Newman once
wrote, "To be deep in history is to cease to be a Protestant."[8] As the
contributors to this book began to encounter more non-Catholic
accounts of Church history and doctrine that were similar to the one
I sketched above, we began connecting the dots. We asked ourselves
questions like: "If the so-called Catholic practices and beliefs rejected
by contemporary Evangelicals were widely and uncontroversially
practiced and believed deep in Church history by the very same people who gave us the ecumenical creeds and the canon of Scripture
on which all Christians—Protestants and Catholics—claim to rely,
why aren't the 'Catholic' beliefs and practices just as Christian as the
creeds and Scripture?" As questions like this began to accumulate, it
became impossible for us to provide a coherent account of the origin
and development of Christianity (that the early creeds and the fix-
ation of the scriptural canon were guided by the Holy Spirit) while
claiming that the "true meaning" of Jesus' religion—"historic Christianity", a sola scriptura faith devoid of sacraments, priests, bishops,
and authoritative tradition—plays no visible or essential role in that
development. It was clear to us that those practices, beliefs, and cleri-
cal offices that we would today say are "Catholic" were no less a part
of the early Church's doctrinal and liturgical mosaic than those beliefs
we had thought were the entirety of historic Christianity.

In the chapters that follow you will be introduced, by way of
their personal journeys, to some very impressive young men, all
of whom are connected by their association with Southern Evangelical Seminary (SES) as either students or members of the faculty.
You may be thinking: How is it possible that such an august group
of Catholic converts can arise from one small Evangelical seminary in
one geographical region of the United States over only a few short
years? One of the reasons, and certainly a very important one, was the
type of theological formation that drew many of them to SES. As is
well known in the Evangelical world, SES founder Norman Geisler
is a self-described Evangelical Thomist,[9] a follower of Saint Thomas

---

[8] John Henry Newman, *An Essay on the Development of Christian Doctrine*, 6th ed. (Notre
Dame, Ind.: University of Notre Dame Press, 1989; repr. of 1878 ed.), 8.

[9] Norman L. Geisler, *Thomas Aquinas: An Evangelical Appraisal* (Grand Rapids: Baker Book
House, 1991).

Aquinas (1225–1274), perhaps the most important Catholic thinker of the second millennium. What Geisler found in Saint Thomas was a theologian whose views on God, faith and reason, natural theology, epistemology, metaphysics, and anthropology were congenial to his Evangelical faith.

Although Geisler, of course, rejects those parts of Aquinas' thought that embrace distinctly Catholic doctrines, his love of the Angelic Doctor inspired his students to investigate Saint Thomas' body of work with greater depth and less antipathy to Catholicism. What those students discovered is that Aquinas' Catholicism was not some time-bound product of the medieval Church, but a wealth of theological insights in perfect continuity with his predecessors, such as Saint Augustine (354–430), and with his successors, such as those at the Council of Trent (1545–1563). What they also discovered is that one cannot easily isolate the "Evangelical-friendly Aquinas" from the "Dominican friar Saint Thomas." There was no "historic Thomas" with "Catholic barnacles". There was just Saint Thomas Aquinas, the Catholic priest.

There was, however, more to the students' being drawn to Catholicism than just accepting a collection of compelling arguments and historical insights. It was, as you shall see, about something alluringly Evangelical: following Jesus—but not as a conclusion to an argument, and not even as a "personal Savior", as if we were nothing but a mere assembly of isolated souls, each with a free ticket to heaven, but rather as a living Lord whom we encounter in every aspect of his universal Church, which includes the Eucharist, the confessional, the saints, our penance, the Liturgy of the Hours, the Magisterium, our fellow parishioners, and the beauty and charity of the Church's various edifices and institutions.

For this reason, as you read the stories in this wonderful collection, keep in mind the words of G. K. Chesterton: "When [the convert] has entered the Church, he finds that the Church is much larger inside than it is outside."[10]

Soli Deo Gloria.

Francis J. Beckwith
Professor of Philosophy and Church-State Studies
Baylor University

[10] G. K. Chesterton, *The Catholic Church and Conversion* (New York: Macmillan, 1926), 49.

INTRODUCTION

Evangelical Catholics?

Apologia Pro Libro

At the beginning of some older books, you will sometimes find a brief apology in which the author explains his reason for writing. This apology is, of course, not a confession indicating sorrow over the writing but rather a justification for the writing. That is the original meaning of *apology*—from the Greek *apologia*, which means something like an explanation offered in defense (as one might hear from a defendant in a court of law). It is the word the apostle Peter used in his first epistle when he commanded Christians, "[A]lways be prepared to *make a defense* to anyone who asks you for a reason for your faith" (1 Pet 3:15, ESV; emphasis added).

This word *apology* is especially relevant to the authors of this book, as all are alumni of Southern Evangelical Seminary—a conservative Evangelical[1] school whose mission is to "evangelize the world and to defend the historic Christian Faith".[2] Thus, it is doubly appropriate to begin this book with an explanation of the seminary's existence.

While many of us were discerning converting to the Catholic Church, we were helped immensely by reading religious conversion

---

[1] The term *Evangelical* is capitalized in this book to set it off as a reference to Evangelicalism and not merely a description. Confusion can enter in here because the suffix *ism* usually implies a system, just as *ist* denotes one of its members. *Evangelicalist*, however, is not used. To be "evangelical" simply means to believe in the need for personal conversion to Christianity according to the gospel. *Evangelicalism* comprises nondenominational Christians of many kinds, often united more by a common culture than by a particular set of theological beliefs. Hence, just as a person can be rational without being a rationalist, or admire science without embracing scientism, a person can be evangelical without being an Evangelical or part of Evangelicalism.

[2] See "Purpose and Philosophy of Education", Southern Evangelical Seminary website, accessed August 6, 2014, http://ses.edu/about-us/purpose-and-philosophy-of-education.

stories.[3] Notable converts who have published their stories of coming into full communion with the Catholic Church include John
Henry Newman, Scott Hahn, David Currie, Thomas Howard, Francis Beckwith, and Patrick Madrid.[4] Conversion stories always garner
interest, and that is one justification for adding another conversion
book to the mix.

What makes this book unique is that although it is a collection of
different stories by different authors, the stories all serve to tell something of a single story—why many seminary-educated Evangelicals
are coming home to Rome. This, then, is a second reason to make
these stories known. A third and final reason is that it may serve as
a needed corrective to much of the spurious speculation that some
of our friends, colleagues, and students have been exposed to (and,
sometimes, engaged in) over the years.[5] This movement from conservative Evangelicalism to Catholicism is not limited to this school;
in fact, some refer to the phenomenon as an exodus.[6]

Southern Evangelical Seminary's Catholic Connection

Southern Evangelical Seminary was cofounded in 1992 by Ross
Rhoads and Norman Geisler. Rhoads was an evangelist and (then)

---

[3] When people become Catholic they often describe it as "coming into full communion
with the Catholic Church". This might sound like an obtuse description of the event, but
it is actually both accurate and important in its details. This is because Catholics consider
all validly baptized Christians to be "in the Church" even if they are not members of the
Catholic Church. In fact, to whatever degree a given Christian group affirms the truths of
the faith, to that degree it can be considered "in communion" with the Catholic Church.
Thus, a validly baptized Christian who becomes Catholic is actually moving from partial to
full communion—not converting (talk of conversion should technically be reserved for non-
Christians becoming Catholics). However, due to the popular usage of the term *convert*, the
awkwardness of the more precise terminology, and the fact that becoming Catholic is, for an
Evangelical, nearly as dramatic as that of a pagan, it will be used throughout this book.

[4] *Apologia pro Vita Sua*; *Rome Sweet Home*; *Born Fundamentalist, Born Again Catholic*; *Evangelical Is Not Enough*; *Return to Rome: Confessions of an Evangelical Catholic*; and *Surprised by
Truth*, respectively.

[5] See, for example, Norman L. Geisler, "Why Roman Catholics Are Leaving the Church
in Mass", Dr. Normal L. Geisler, January 6, 2011, accessed May 28, 2015, http://www
.normgeisler.com/.

[6] E.g., "The last part of the twentieth century has seen thousands of Catholics convert to
Protestant Evangelicalism. Conversely, of late, a number of Evangelical intellectuals have

pastor of Calvary Church in Charlotte, North Carolina—SES' first home. Geisler was a longtime seminary professor and popular Christian apologist. The two concerns for evangelism and apologetics were to be combined into a single twofold vision for the seminary. SES' mission statement was "to evangelize the world and to defend the historic Christian Faith".[7] Rhoads was to serve as the first president, and Norman Geisler the first dean. Some of Geisler's colleagues and previous students were brought on as faculty, and Geisler eventually took over as seminary president. In 1997 SES relocated to McKee Road Baptist Church in Matthews, North Carolina, and really began to grow.

In 2003 SES moved into its own building on a piece of donated property just down the road in Matthews. At that time SES also started its own church, which met on the seminary grounds. It was during these years that most of the authors of this book were enrolling in, graduating from, and even working for SES. We came to SES for various reasons. Some of us "early adopters" left jobs, ministries, and our families and friends thousands of miles away to come to a school that was housed in two trailers in the gravel parking lot of a small church. That SES gathered hundreds of students in such a state is a testimony to the dedication of these students to the kind of academic apologetics training that was, at the time, not available anywhere else.

That SES is an unusual seminary is clear. First, it is completely independent of any university, denomination, or church. Second, SES' doctrine is a mix of generic Protestant affirmations combined with nineteenth-century Dispensationalism and twentieth-century innovations such as Free Grace theology. In addition to this already eclectic theological mix is the school's commitment to classical apologetics and medieval philosophy (specifically that of Saint Thomas Aquinas) and its inclusion of several faculty over the years who have

---

gone the other way, deciding that 'Rome is home.' We will investigate this ecclesiastical relocation and suggest some reasons why.... There are Roman Catholic leaders, both lay and clergy, who view this exodus as an indication of a lack of emphasis on evangelism in Catholic catechesis." Ralph E. MacKenzie, "Why Some Evangelicals Become Roman Catholic", *Christian Apologetics Journal* 4 (Spring 2005): 1–2.

[7] "History of Southern Evangelical Seminary", Southern Evangelical Seminary website, accessed August 6, 2014, http://ses.edu/about-us/history-of-ses.

studied at Catholic universities. The works of Aquinas and his (mostly Catholic) commentators are assigned as readings far more frequently than those of Augustine, Luther, Calvin, or any number of modern Evangelical Protestant writers.

These latter considerations have led some to be suspicious of SES' Evangelical commitments—a suspicion that may appear vindicated by the growing number of SES' previous associates who no longer hold to the seminary's distinctive teachings. In the decade spanning 2004 through 2014 alone, over two dozen of SES' faculty, students, or alumni have entered the Catholic Church.[8] The question many Evangelicals ask is: How can a school cofounded by an Evangelical theologian-apologist who has written two books and several articles critical of Roman Catholics produce so many of them?[9] And what can be done about it?[10]

Conversion Considerations

The issue of Evangelicals converting to Roman Catholicism is currently a hot topic that has recently been addressed in books and online lectures. Most of the authors of this book have friends with Evangelical backgrounds who have converted (or are considering converting) to Roman Catholicism, Anglicanism, Eastern Orthodoxy, and even Armenian Orthodoxy.

Secondhand explanations for these conversions range from the realistic to the ridiculous, and it is partly because of the latter that this book was written. We were taught at SES that we did not have

[8] This book thus represents a small sample and should not be taken to be representative of others associated with the seminary. It should also be noted that several students became Eastern or Oriental Orthodox in this period. These conversions were rarely made public due to fears of losing academic recommendations and to other predictable issues commonly associated with such moves.

[9] Two dozen might not sound like very many over a decade, but when one considers that SES typically graduated only a few dozen students per year, the numbers (which may be higher than this, given that over half of SES' students do not attend the school in person) become more relevant.

[10] In the summer of 2014, after years of requests, SES began offering a class in Roman Catholicism, taught by Geisler. One might wonder what the effect of this will be, given that Geisler's coauthor of his second book on Catholicism (*Is Rome the True Church?*) became Catholic within months of its publication (see Joshua Betancourt's chapter in this book).

the right to criticize someone's view until we could state that criticism to his satisfaction, and we have provided these stories to help those who really want to know the truth.

One important facet of these stories is that the questions one asks often determine the sorts of answers he will receive (or accept), and the questions converts ask during their journeys are often not the same as those of an Evangelical who is simply looking for a new church to attend. It is important, therefore, that when trying to understand a convert's reasoning, one must begin with the questions the convert is asking (or has asked and had answered). Once these questions are clarified, the answers provided should make sense whether one agrees with them or not.

A second important consideration is that the move from being an Evangelical to a Catholic is a much larger one than that of going from Evangelical to Baptist or one of the more traditional Protestant denominations. Such a move is the result of much more than a mere change of mind (or heart). In fact, whether one is a Christian or not, becoming Catholic is more properly likened to a paradigm shift.[11]

This terminology is borrowed from Thomas Kuhn, who popularized the phrase *paradigm shift* in his book *The Structure of Scientific Revolutions*.[12] Kuhn argued that scientific theories do not arise from a slow, linear development but rather in a series of violent revolutions that overthrow entire worldviews all at once. These paradigm shifts are preceded by a time of peace, when one sits comfortably in his given worldview despite some minor difficulties ("anomalies") for which it does not seem to account adequately. Over time, if these anomalies grow in number or importance, they can cause a crisis for the current paradigm. Eventually one will have to look outside his paradigm for another that has the elements of his current paradigm and can also deal with its anomalies. When this new paradigm is discovered, the only consistent reaction is to adopt it.

When it comes to religious paradigm shifts, several difficulties arise. First, comparing paradigms is often fraught with misunderstandings. We have only so many words in our language, so different paradigms

---

[11] See Christian Smith, *How to Go from Being a Good Evangelical to a Committed Catholic in Ninety-Five Difficult Steps* (Eugene, Ore.: Wipf and Stock, 2011).

[12] Thomas S. Kuhn, *The Structure of Scientific Revolutions* (Chicago: University of Chicago Press, 1962).

often use the same words in different ways. Until both paradigms' "lexicons" are understood, miscommunication is inevitable. It takes great effort (more than many are willing to exert) to get to a place of common understanding to overcome this difficulty.

Second, moving from one paradigm to another can cause severe personal stress. In many cases one faces the loss of, or serious strain in, many relationships. Often family, friends, coworkers, colleagues, and other acquaintances simply will not understand the motives of a paradigm shift because they either do not see, or do not appreciate, the role the anomalies have played in pushing the convert to look outside their previously shared paradigm. Many religious converts face rejection from their current ministries, ministry partners, places of employment, and even family and friends. Every author in this book has faced at least some of these difficulties—and some have experienced them all.

Third, once the paradigm shift has occurred, the reverse of the first problem can occur. As one embraces and begins living in the new paradigm, its influences become simultaneously stronger and less noticeable. New vocabulary, cultural references, group activities, and many other experiences contribute to potential alienation, and it becomes easy to forget what life was like in the previous paradigm. And this all results in an amplification of the second problem.

Thus, in the end, although becoming Catholic might not seem to be much more than joining any Christian denomination, the authors of this book can agree with Flannery O'Connor, who said, "I am a Catholic not like someone else would be a Baptist or a Methodist, but like someone else would be an atheist."[13]

As stated above, in the past decade, dozens of students, alumni, and professors from Southern Evangelical Seminary have converted to Catholicism. Each time, speculation arose, and often the phenomenon was simply written off as a quirk of the convert's psychology. At times, though, even the convert's basic Christian commitment was questioned. Sometimes his salvation was doubted. The true stories behind the conversion of these seminary-trained Evangelicals will thus be a beneficial corrective to both sides, as well as those watching from the sidelines.

---

[13] Flannery O'Connor, *Collected Works* (New York: Library of America, 1988), 930.

Closing Remarks

In closing, all of us contributors would like to affirm our love for our SES colleagues and associates. Although, of necessity, SES' theology will often be the subject of discussion in these pages, criticism is not to be construed as personal disparagement or mockery.[14] Moving from other Christian communions to Catholicism might feel as dramatic as accepting the gospel in the first place, but it has a very different effect. People converting from atheism or paganism to Christianity might wish to denounce completely their former anti-Christian paradigm, but, for an Evangelical, becoming Catholic does not engender such negativity. The Catholic sees his conversion as a reception of the fullness of the faith rather than a rejection of what brought him to it.

Further, it will be useful to answer a common question up front: What do we think of the faith of our Evangelical friends now—in particular, are they saved? The answer requires a nuance not found in the Evangelical paradigm and so is difficult to communicate simply. While in Evangelicalism, salvation is strictly binary (one is saved or one is not, and that is all there is to the story), in Catholicism salvation is seen as more of a process. In both, however, the answer can never be given as more than a hypothetical (You are saved if ...; you are damned if ...), for only God knows all. Thus, the best answer is that we cannot know for sure, because we do not know either their hearts or the future.[15]

On the other hand, we have a clear answer as to whether our Evangelical bothers are part of Christ's Church. So long as one is validly baptized, he is part of this one Church (Eph 4:5), even if he is not in perfect communion with her, because the Church is Christ's

---

[14] Interaction with SES' theology will—of necessity—largely involve the writings of Norman Geisler, the professor who taught (or whose material was used to teach) most of the subjects relevant to this book. He is also one of the only SES professors who has published relevant materials that can be cited in support of SES' teachings.

[15] Many Evangelicals will point to 1 Jn 5:13 ("I write this to you who believe in the name of the Son of God, that you may know that you have eternal life") as indicating that we can indeed know whether we are saved. First, this is a subjective assessment ("so that *you* may know that *you* have eternal life") and thus does not help when assessing others' salvation. Second, the "things" John writes of are not limited to belief alone—there are also commands to walk with God, love God, obey God's commandments, abide in God, love our brothers and not the world, keep from being deceived, practice righteousness, and cease sinning. Very few of these are open to easy assessment, whether subjective or objective.

body (1 Cor 12:27)—not a bunch of body *parts*—and Christ cannot be divided (1 Cor 1:13). This unity, however, does not stop Christians from making licit in-house distinctions (Rom 14:2–3). Unfortunately, it also does not keep them from causing illicit divisions (1 Cor 1:12). The latter occur when one departs from the faith (*apostasy*—1 Jn 2:19), knowingly commits to serious doctrinal error (*heresy*—2 Pet 2:1), refuses to submit to the authority of the Church (*schism*—1 Cor 1:10), or breaks unity over secondary issues (*disputes*—Tit 3:10). Depending on which of these wounds to unity are at work, the resultant communion relationship is altered. For the Catholic, only total apostasy breaks one off from the Church completely.

These distinctions also help explain the Catholic Church's view of salvation. Because the Catholic Church distinguishes between full and partial communion, non-Catholics are not automatically "outside the Church". Thus, the fearsome statement that "outside the Church there is no salvation" does not simply apply across the board to all non-Catholics. Salvation is not limited to members of the Catholic Church, nor even to those in communion with her, because God is not limited in his abilities to reach people, even when they lie outside his normative means.[16]

Thus, the authors, along with the Catholic Church, embrace our Evangelical professors, mentors, students, colleagues, and friends "as brothers, with respect and affection. For men who believe in Christ and have been truly baptized are in communion with the Catholic Church even though this communion is imperfect.... All who have been justified by faith in Baptism are members of Christ's body, and have a right to be called Christian, and so are correctly accepted as brothers by the children of the Catholic Church."[17]

We hope that the stories in this book will be of benefit to anyone considering Catholicism (whether he wishes to discern it from the outside as a friend or an enemy) as well as those who are Catholic and simply like to know why others are drawn to the faith.

---

[16] The anathemas pronounced at the Council of Trent against Protestants must also be understood according to the above distinctions. Trent was dealing with Catholics who were protesting Catholic doctrine (as heretics or schismatics)—not people who were simply raised Protestant. The anathemas pronounced declared that *Catholics* who rejected Catholic dogma were no longer Catholic. This obviously would not apply to a Protestant today unless he was a Catholic who had become Protestant by knowingly rejecting the Catholic Church. In other words, it requires an informed will, not just circumstances.

[17] Second Vatican Council, *Decree on Ecumenism*, November 21, 1964, no. 3.

Tiber Treading No More

By Douglas Beaumont

The more shame I felt that, having been so long deluded and deceived
by the promise of certainties, I had, with puerile error and petulance,
prated of so many uncertainties as if they were certainties.
For that they were falsehoods became apparent to me afterwards.
However, I was certain that they were uncertain, and that I had formerly
    held them as certain when with a blind contentiousness I accused Your
    Catholic Church,
which though I had not yet discovered to teach truly,
yet not to teach that of which I had so vehemently accused her.

—Saint Augustine, *Confessions* 6:4

Dry and Dusty Paths

Converts to Catholicism are often described as having "swum the Tiber"—an allusion to the river in Italy that has been used metonymically to refer to Rome and, by extension, to Roman Catholicism. This is the story of how I found myself eyeing the Tiber's far shores, occasionally splashing around in it, and then furiously treading neck-deep in the middle before I truly started swimming.

Although I was not raised to be "religious", I was never a full-blown atheist, and I happily said my prayers at night with my folks. I also spent time at vacation Bible school during some summers, and on one of these occasions, I was given the chance to "accept Jesus into my heart". I raised my hand and was led in the Sinner's Prayer. I still remember the moment I said it—and I meant it. Unfortunately, with no follow-up or discipleship, the moment rather quickly faded into the background of my life. I basically was left to make up my own beliefs.

Although I was something of a "theist" throughout elementary and middle school, in high school I was more of a considered agnostic. It did not seem to me that people who thought the world was flat a few centuries earlier could legitimately claim to have a lock on ultimate reality. I also knew that there were thousands of religions out there and that I would never have the time to learn each one to be sure any of them was the right one. Finally, and most importantly, I liked my life just fine without religion.

I have heard people quote Pascal as saying that there is a God-shaped hole inside all people, but I can honestly say I did not feel that way.[1] I was in honors classes and had good friends and a loving family; everything was good as far as I was concerned. Further, whenever a Christian would attempt to "witness" to me, he could never answer my agnostic criticisms. So not only did I not see a need for religion, but those who did could not seem to justify it. All of this occurred in the context of typical teenage arrogance—not good conversion material!

That all began to change rapidly toward the end of my senior year. After experiencing a healing that would be difficult to explain without divine intervention, my implicit theism came more to the fore. Within a couple of months, two Christian evangelists (one a coworker, one a chimney sweep) discussed the gospel with me. I gave my usual responses, but these two evangelists actually knew their faith and easily demolished my pretentious arguments. I was left with the realization that if I continued in my disbelief, it was now intentional and not based on any legitimate doubts.

Not wishing to go to hell, I said the Sinner's Prayer again. But again, I had no idea what to do next. Each time my faith flared up, it

---

[1] Pascal actually thought the hole was "happiness shaped". The common misquotation is derived from *Pensées* 425: "What is it then that this desire and this inability proclaim to us, but that there was once in man a true happiness of which there now remain to him only the mark and empty trace, which he in vain tries to fill from all his surroundings, seeking from things absent the help he does not obtain in things present? But these are all inadequate, because the infinite abyss can only be filled by an infinite and immutable object, that is to say, only by God Himself."

seemed to die out just as quickly in the arid landscape through which I moved. A thirst had arisen, though—I just needed to find something to quench it.

On Evangelical Shores

The summer after high school graduation I got a job as a counselor at (of all things) a Christian summer camp. I can only assume God had his hand in it, because there is no way I should have gotten that job! In any case, we spent the first week learning how to teach the gospel to children. It was just what I needed, and by the time the campers arrived, I was all in. That summer proved to be transformative, and I spent the next couple of years trying to sort out this new life. I was not in the habit of going to church, and without a lot of Christian friends back home, I found it was difficult to force myself to go. This lack of fellowship threatened to shipwreck my faith once again, but when I left home for college, I joined a great Christian college group in which I learned quite a bit. I became active at local churches (first a Baptist church, then Calvary Chapel), and I eventually started teaching.

I discovered that teaching was something I was good at and loved to do. I started studying like crazy, and within a couple of years I became the go-to guy for theological questions within my small circle of friends. In the early days of the Internet, I created an apologetics website (with an entire section dedicated to what I saw as the errors of Catholicism!). After graduating from college, I began looking to further my theological education in a formal setting. I visited a few seminaries, but it seemed as if all of them were preparing people to be either pastors or missionaries, and I was not interested in either of those roles. Then I discovered Southern Evangelical Seminary (SES).

I was at work listening to the *Bible Answer Man* radio show at lunch, and the host (Hank Hanegraaff) had Norman Geisler on as a guest. I loved Geisler's books (two of them had been graduation gifts), and when I heard that he had started a seminary that had degrees in apologetics, my decision was made. I told my girlfriend, Elaine, that I planned to move to North Carolina, so if we stayed together, she would be moving too. Three years later we were married and driving across the country in an overloaded pickup truck, heading for a seminary that consisted of two trailers in a gravel parking lot. The adventure had begun.

Surveying the Tiber

Catholicism began working its way into my life in the early days of seminary. Another student had briefly sat in on a couple of classes, and one night he and I spent over an hour discussing problems of biblical interpretation. He could not seem to get past the fact that otherwise good Christians could not seem to agree on what the Bible teaches. I assured him that with proper hermeneutics and good philosophy, correct results were attainable. He asked how we could know what counted as proper hermeneutics and good philosophy apart from the Bible itself. Each time I suggested some other safeguard to accurate biblical interpretation, I was met with the same basic problems: How can we know which of the numerous competing claims to accurate biblical interpretation were correct? Eventually this exhausting conversation simply petered out, but it stayed in the back of my mind for some time. I assumed that after completing seminary I would have a better response.[2]

I later discovered that this student's questions had also influenced my friend Jeremiah Cowart, a previous SES employee. The year after I replaced him as director of distance education at SES, the faculty and staff got a letter from him stating that he had become Catholic! This led to a couple of months of e-mail dialogue between us. I have to admit that Jeremiah had the upper hand in a distressing number of cases. Our debate finally fizzled out when I decided that we were both using our reason up to a certain point, but that when it came to our theological disagreements, he had simply given his over to the Pope. That argument kept Catholicism's waves at bay for some time, but the Evangelical shores I walked upon continued eroding nonetheless.

[2] Not long after this conversation (which was repeated with others), this student became Catholic and now teaches at a Catholic university.

I did well in seminary, received a presidential scholarship, and was honored to be asked to serve as Geisler's grader and research assistant. After graduating, I was hired full-time at SES in various roles (director of distance education, recruitment, webmaster, and assistant professor). I was ordained by my Southern Baptist church, which I later left to help SES start a new church (the aptly titled Southern Evangelical Church—SEC).

In the following years I spoke at dozens of Evangelical churches, conferences, and ministries across the nation. I continued teaching at various Evangelical schools and had my first book published by an Evangelical publisher (Moody) in 2009. This in turn led to even more speaking engagements and interviews on a multitude of Evangelical TV and radio programs. I do not say any of this to brag but rather to stress the fact that, as far as the word *Evangelical* came to a serious agreed-upon definition, I pretty much met it. I felt I had pretty much arrived. But the winds of change were starting to blow.

After a decade of experiencing what I thought was the best that Evangelical life had to offer, a series of crises both personal and professional developed at SES and SEC. They not only removed from me any remaining traces of hero worship (a condition I am embarrassed to admit I had suffered most of my life) but also revealed several foundational problems with Evangelicalism itself. Evangelicalism's inability to settle problems of faith and morals authoritatively became glaring as I watched what should have been the best church imaginable crumble to pieces in just a few short years. If the faculty, students, and board of SES could not hold its own church together, what chance did any other have?

About that time, a colleague brought in his former college leader (now an Anglican priest) to speak to his class, and I sat in. I found myself taken by the priest's concern for Church history (a subject that was not offered in the graduate programs at SES) and excited by the possibilities revealed in his responses to several ministry-related problems brought up in class. It was really the first time I thought that some form of Christianity outside of Evangelicalism was worth considering. I decided to spend a bit of time tentatively putting my toes into some non-Evangelical waters and found them quite welcoming. What followed was a five-year journey of faith reevaluation that took me further than I ever imagined it could.

Diving In

My journey away from Evangelicalism did not begin with losing long-held beliefs. Instead, it began as I tried to make better sense of them.

After entering the doctoral program at SES, I spent time researching some of the more important teachings I had imbibed at the seminary.[3] As I did, I became more and more dissatisfied with the answers I had been given to fundamental questions such as "How was the biblical canon decided?" and "What makes one doctrine essential to Christianity but not another?" Although other factors would eventually enter in, it was primarily these issues that motivated my research.

I had been taught, for example, that the Church only "discovered" the canon but did not "determine" it. That was a fine theological distinction, but it did not answer the question of what this process of "discovery" was or why it should be trusted to have produced an infallible table of contents.[4] The "reverse engineered" canonization process I was taught depended heavily on ahistorical speculations that made it sound simple. The reality was much messier, with books coming in and out of fashion and centuries passing before the dust began to settle. I was surprised to learn that the first canon list to match the current New Testament was made by Athanasius in A.D. 367 in a (nonauthoritative) letter. The first Church council to produce such a list was that of Rome in A.D. 382, and no ecumenical council ruled definitively on the canon until the sixteenth-century Council of Trent (1545–1563).

As to settling orthodoxy, the "logical" and "hermeneutical" methods I had been taught simply failed.[5] How could we Evangelicals claim to have unity if we disagreed on so much (even when we supposedly used the same methods)?[6] Morals and theology (even the Protestant überessential doctrine of salvation by faith alone) were hotly debated

---

[3] Although I do not wish to disparage SES with my criticism of its teachings, much of my journey makes sense only against the backdrop of my experience there.

[4] Norman L. Geisler and William E. Nix, *A General Introduction to the Bible*, rev. ed. (Chicago: Moody Press, 1996), 133.

[5] See appendix 2.

[6] Such disagreement is evidenced by the proliferation of "debate style" publications pitting scholars against one another—often including those espousing adherence to the grammatical-historical method of hermeneutics as well as sola scriptura. See, for example, IVP Academic's Spectrum Multiview Books or Zondervan's Counterpoints series.

among Evangelicals, who all claimed the Bible as their source.[7] There were so many in-house disagreements that it was practically impossible even to define *Evangelicalism*. My long-held assumptions were being challenged not only by skeptics such as Bart Ehrman and Sam Harris but by Evangelical scholars such as D. H. Williams, Craig Allert, Mark Noll, and Os Guinness.[8]

During my time at SES I had been told that we were learning to define and defend the historic Christian faith. But as I enlarged my studies, I began to realize that many of SES' distinctive teachings could not be counted as historic in the implied sense. Much of SES' doctrinal statement (to which students and faculty were held) contained a mix of Reformation theology, Anabaptist doctrines, and even late nineteenth-century beliefs.[9] True or false, these did not seem legitimately to constitute the historic Christian faith. This issue was really brought home to me while I was doing research for Geisler's *Systematic Theology*.[10] My job was to find quotations from the early, medieval, and Reformed writers that supported his views. This was easy for volume 2 (which concerned the nature of God), but it was very difficult for volume 4 (dealing with the nature of the Church and the Last Things). It became clear that the theology I had been taught was very different from the majority position of the Church of history. In the end, I simply used a word search and listed any quotations that sounded as if they *could* support his view and hoped that they would not be cited out of context.[11]

---

[7] See James K. Beilby, *Justification: Five Views* (Downers Grove, Ill.: IVP Academic, 2011).

[8] Actually it was *mostly* Evangelical scholars who brought these issues to my attention. See, for example, Craig D. Allert, *A High View of Scripture?: The Authority of the Bible and the Formation of the New Testament Canon* (Grand Rapids: Baker Academic, 2007); Os Guinness, *Fit Bodies, Fat Minds: Why Evangelicals Don't Think and What to Do about It* (Grand Rapids: Baker, 1994). Mark Noll, *The Scandal of the Evangelical Mind* (Grand Rapids: Eerdmans, 1994); D. H. Williams, *Evangelicals and Tradition: The Formative Influence of the Early Church* (Grand Rapids: Baker Academic, 2005).

[9] E.g., total depravity, sola fide, sola scriptura, the Protestant canon, eternal security, Free Grace theology, the premillennial and imminent return of Jesus, memorial-only baptism and communion. See "Doctrinal Statement", Southern Evangelical Seminary website, http://ses .edu/about-us/doctrinal-statement.

[10] Specifically, Norman L. Geisler, *Systematic Theology*, vols. 2 and 4 (Minneapolis: Bethany House Publishers, 2003 and 2005).

[11] Such a massive job left no time to do this research on my own, and it was not my job anyway.

The more I learned about the great thinkers of the past, the more I saw that what I was being taught at SES simply did not match up. For example, I discovered that what Geisler taught about Thomas Aquinas (his philosophical hero) concerning God's sovereignty was not only incorrect, but was used by Aquinas as an example of an error when he explained his own view.[12] Likewise, his explanation of Aquinas' view on God's impassibility was clearly not what Aquinas believed.[13] I found this rather upsetting because while Geisler was certainly free to believe whatever he wished, if he misunderstood the early Church Fathers and his favorite theologian, I was not sure how trustworthy his other positions were.[14]

I found the same spirit reflected in a conversation I had with a colleague at SES.[15] I was assured that the Nicene Creed could be

---

[12] Geisler writes, "God gives us the power of free choice, but we are responsible for exercising it.... He gave the fact of freedom, but we are responsible for the acts of freedom." Geisler, *Systematic Theology*, 2:548. As Aquinas points out, however, this is actually *Origen's* view: "God causes willing and accomplishing within us in the sense that he causes in us the power of willing, but not in such a way that he makes us will this or that." Origen, *Peri Archon* III, 1: PG 11, 293. Aquinas specifically notes this error in *Summa Contra Gentiles* 89: "Some people, as a matter of fact, not understanding how God could cause a movement of the will in us without prejudice to freedom of will ... say that God causes willing and accomplishing within us in the sense that he causes in us the power of willing, but not in such a way that he makes us will this or that." (See also Saint Thomas Aquinas, *On the Power of God* 72.)

[13] In his *Systematic Theology*, 2:112, Geisler teaches that God has feelings and emotions, and although he does not cite any classical sources for his definition, it seems clear from the context that he considers this to be tantamount to the classical formulation of the doctrine. In chapter 2 of *Creating God in the Image of Man?* (Minneapolis: Bethany House Publishers, 1997) Geisler labels the attributes of God as he understands them as belonging to "classical Christian theism", which he seems to equate with the theology of Thomas Aquinas (who is cited 43/46 times). No citations of any kind are given in the impassibility section, however (see also Normal L. Geisler and H. Wayne House, *The Battle for God: Responding to the Challenge of Neotheism* [Grand Rapids: Kregel, 2001], 170). In an online article, Geisler asserts that "classical theists, including Thomas Aquinas, do not believe that God is without feeling but only that He has no *changing* passions (feelings)." Norman L. Geisler, "Is God an Android?", Dr. Norman L. Geisler, June 29, 2011, http://www.normangeisler.com/; emphasis in the original. Aquinas, however, actually gives several reasons why God cannot have passions, emotions, or feelings—and only one of them is that God does not undergo change. Aquinas' contention is that God cannot have passions, emotions, or feelings (changing or not), because God would require a body for that (see, e.g., *De Veritate* 26, 2, or *Summa Contra Gentiles* 1, 89, 3).

[14] Similar complaints have been levied against Geisler's understanding of Calvinism, as evidenced by the substantial endorsement section of James White's *The Potter's Freedom* (Amityville, N.Y.: Calvary Press, 2004).

[15] In the interest of remaining "above reproach", I will not name anyone who has not published the statements or views in question in some form.

affirmed by Baptists because when it says, "one baptism for the for-giveness of sins", that means *spirit* baptism, and when it says, "one, holy, catholic, and apostolic church", that means there was one uni-versal, *invisible* church that *taught what the apostles taught*.[16] This did not sound right, and a quick glance through the writings of Nicene-era theologians confirmed that these things were certainly not what was meant.[17] Again, SES' professors were free to teach whatever they believed to be true, but it seemed that the actual teachings of the ancient Church were being misrepresented.

Moreover, I was finding that the Bible-alone approach I had been taught generated more disunity than I realized. Although rarely a concern in my insulated Evangelical experience, Christian disunity is clearly sinful according to Scripture. Although there are only a few biblical examples or principles concerning "proper" division, there are numerous exhortations to maintain unity from several authors (e.g., Lk 11:17; Jn 17:20–23; Rom 15:6; 16:17–18; 1 Cor; Eph 4:3–7; Phil 2:2; Col 3:14; 1 Pet 3:8; Tit 3:10–11). The issue of division bothered Jesus so much that he specifically prayed for unity in his last major prayer—even relating it to those who would come to faith in Christ. The apostle Paul detested division so much that he dedicated one of his longest letters (1 Corinthians) to addressing it and several other passages to fighting it (e.g., Rom 15:6; Eph 4:3–7; Phil 2:2; Col 3:14; Tit 3:10–11; see also Lk 11:17; Jn 17:20–23; 1 Pet 3:8). Even if the canon problem could be sorted out, it did little good to agree on the Bible's contents if Christians could legitimately disagree about practically everything it taught.[18]

---

[16] I was later told by another SES administrator that SES' doctrine was what the apostles taught!

[17] Any good history of theology will confirm this, but an especially helpful one is *Ancient Christian Doctrine*, ed. Thomas C. Oden, vol. 5, *We Believe in One Holy Catholic and Apostolic Church* (Downers Grove, Ill.: InterVarsity Press, 2009).

[18] Without making claims as to their cause or solution, I offer this list of the continu-ing theological debates within Evangelical / Protestant Christianity that are significant due to their theological or ethical importance (e.g., salvation or morality), pedigree (e.g., academic or popular), or position variance (quantitative or qualitative). An asterisk indicates that the topic has generated its own multiview debate book(s): abortion, Adam's historicity,* alcohol con-sumption, apologetic methodology,* applicability of biblical practices, baptism's meaning and procedure,* biblical authorship / origins, biblical higher criticism, biblical inerrancy,* Christ's atonement,* Christian education, Christian spirituality, Church definition, Church govern-ment, Church growth,* Communion (Eucharist / Lord's Supper),* contraception, Covenant

Finally, it seemed to me that the cultural problems evident in Evangelicalism were not accidental but rather a natural outcome of how it operated. I knew many Evangelicals who were upset with what various Evangelical churches, ministries, and leaders were doing, but they lacked principled, authoritative responses. In a movement in which everyone could do what was right in his own eyes, how could anyone complain in an authoritative way? I eventually discovered that, to be successful in Evangelicalism, one simply had to be popular. With its leadership grounded in self-proclamation, and one's authority based on the collective opinion of the masses, Evangelicals could attain success only by gaining and maintaining a fan base. As in the secular world, this often required either compromise (to keep fans) or controversy (to expel those who were not fans), and whatever fame resulted regularly engendered the same problems it did in the secular world. Lacking an objective, authoritative standard for leadership, narcissism became a virtual prerequisite—and despotism was often the norm.

So I waded away from my comfortable Evangelical shore and explored some of the older ports at its edges.

Wading Past Protestant Ports

Evangelicals are often accused of being ignorant of history. Although there are obviously exceptions to this, I was not one of them, nor,

---

theology,* creationism,* the meaning and authority of the Church's creeds and councils, the destiny of the unevangelized,* Dispensationalism,* divine foreknowledge,* Eastern Orthodoxy's compatibility with Evangelicalism,* election / predestination, entertainment involvement (e.g., music listening or TV or movie watching), essentials of the faith, eternal security,* Evangelicalism's nature, evolution,* faith's definition, faith's relation to reason, family ministry, Free Grace salvation, free will, God's will,* God and time,* God's providence,* God's attributes,* Gospel conditions, hell,* hermeneutics, Judaism and Christianity, justification,* law and gospel relationship,* marriage / divorce / remarriage,* the Millennial Kingdom,* the mind-body problem,* miracles / miraculous gifts,* natural law, the New Testament use of the Old Testament,* Old Testament genocide,* the Old Testament canon, Pauline soteriology,* Paul's status in Romans 7, Peter's role and importance, the prosperity gospel, psychology, purgatory, Rapture timing,* Revelation's interpretation,* Sabbath observance, salvific pluralism,* sanctification,* the relationship between science and religion,* social activities (e.g., dating, dancing, playing cards, celebrating holidays), spiritual gifts, spiritual warfare, tithing, war,* warning passages in Hebrews,* women's role in ministry,* works' role in the Final Judgment,* worship styles,* youth ministry.*

it seemed, were many of the Evangelicals I interacted with regularly (for example, I was sometimes attacked for "teaching Catholicism" when I was simply affirming *Protestant* teachings such as infant baptism!). According to some Protestant scholars such as James R. Payton, the Reformation is misunderstood by many Protestants as well. So I dug in to see what I might discover.

After studying more about Church history, I saw on the horizon no better answers to my questions. The biblical canon was basically accepted from the early Church—but why? Skeptics argued that the biblical canon was just the "books that won out" in history, and Protestants such as R. C. Sproul said that the Bible was just a "fallible collection of infallible books".[19] That explained Protestant exclusion of the Old Testament Apocrypha as well as Luther's low opinions of some New Testament books, but it did little to inspire confidence in the canon I had simply taken for granted all these years.[20] Many modern Protestant scholars accepted this paradigm and embraced the idea that the canon was something fluid and nonauthoritative.[21]

As to the question of orthodoxy, Protestant denominations generally understood the Bible through some official confessions that were written when their particular group was founded, but in the end they could grant these no more binding authority than Evangelical "doctrinal statements". It seemed to me that if one were going to trust some official statement, why choose these latecomers as authoritative? Further, even on the most important Reformation teaching (sola fide) there was still disagreement after five hundred years![22]

---

[19] R. C. Sproul, *Grace Unknown: The Heart of Reformed Theology* (Grand Rapids: Baker Books, 1997), 58.

[20] For more on the so-called Apocrypha, see Douglas Beaumont, "Defending the Deuterocanonicals", Douglas Beaumont, September 11, 2014, accessed May 28, 2105, http://douglasbeaumont.com/2014/09/11/defending-the-deuterocanonicals/.

[21] See, e.g., Michael J. Kruger, *Canon Revisited: Establishing the Origins and Authority of the New Testament Books* (Wheaton, Ill.: Crossway, 2012), pt. 1.

[22] Ironically, Luther wrote the following during his Reformation: "Therefore come forward, you and all the Sophists together, and produce any one mystery which is still abstruse in the Scriptures. But, if many things still remain abstruse to many, this does not arise from obscurity in the Scriptures, but from their own blindness or want of understanding, who do not go the way to see the all-perfect clearness of the truth." Martin Luther, *Bondage of the Will* IV.

The final difficulty I had was choosing between Protestant denominations. Other Protestants seemed to choose based on which denomination agreed most nearly with their own interpretations of the Bible. In other words, one read the Bible, decided between a myriad of Protestant doctrinal disagreements, and then looked for the denomination that "got it right". The real authority, then, was not so much the Bible as the individual's interpretation of the Bible. Protestant denominations, then, seemed to be just one step removed from Evangelical churches—each could have "authority" (such as it was) over a group of churches instead of just one congregation. If the individual Protestant felt that his pastor or church was in serious error, he could take it to the denomination for judgment, but if the denomination leadership was thought to be in error, one could simply leave for another one (or start his own). This, I saw, was the history behind Protestant denominations. Division has been (and remains) the causal factor behind Protestant denominations (each one convinced that it has Christianity right).

It did not take long for me to realize that I could not drop anchor at any of these ports. I was convinced that the Church that Jesus founded had to be both authoritative and objectively identifiable. That meant it was unified, universal, and visible (Mt 16:18–19; Eph 2:20; 1 Cor 12:30; Jn 17:20–21). If this Church was not identifiable by the subjective comparison of private interpretations, it would have to be discovered based on historical matters. The Bible clearly taught that the Church was built on authoritative apostolic teaching—both written and verbal (2 Thess 2:25; 3:6; 2 Tim 2:2). Further, this Church was said to be unable to be overcome (Mt 16:18). (So much for the apostasy narratives of the cults and many Christian groups!) It only made sense that this Church was guided by God to determine orthodoxy accurately (e.g., Acts 15; 1 Tim 3:15) and that if the Church had lost this ability, even the biblical canon could be called into question.

Because Protestant groups denied some or all of these important points (and many simply accepted the dire consequences of those denials), I decided I needed to look elsewhere to find terra firma. The apostolic Church was the determining historical factor, but I held out hope that some form of Protestantism could lay claim to being that Church. I found one making the claim, but it required leaving the continent behind.

Crossing the Channel

I turned next to the communion spawned by the English Reformation: the Church of England (a.k.a. Anglicanism or, in America, Episcopalianism). It was obvious to me by this time that the Episcopal Church in America was drowning in liberal apostasy, so I wasted no time in its murky bog. Instead my family and I attended two great Anglican churches for about three years. Both churches were formed by conservative Anglican groups that had broken away from the Episcopalians. Due to their appreciation of history, liturgy, creeds, et cetera, these faithful Anglicans were very helpful in my exploration. The liturgical trappings all felt very odd at first, but I found that my appreciation of them easily outdistanced my discomfort.

My first Anglican priest gave me my first icon for my birthday and was very helpful in explaining a major component of the faith that I had been missing. The issue, as he saw it, was that Protestantism often embraced a sort of "functional Gnosticism". Gnosticism was a Christian heresy that arose in the early days of the Church and made a strict distinction between the physical and spiritual worlds, to the point of seeing material creation as evil. Following a similar principle, Protestantism's history shows a steady decline in the appreciation for the role of material creation in Christian faith and practice. What began in iconoclasm reached its logical conclusion in Evangelicalism, where churches mirror meeting halls and preachers dress in street clothes. This also explained the lack of incense, holy water, candles, pictures, statues, bells, chants, and even physical movements. These things were designed to engage the whole person, while Evangelicalism, I saw, limited faith expressions to between-the-ears activity.

I also saw this tendency revealed in Evangelical services, such as when communion was served (in the rare instances when it was practiced).[23] Wine and bread were regularly exchanged for juice and crackers that were passed around on a big platter for everyone to feed himself. As a friend pointed out to me, if water matters in baptism, why do bread and wine not matter in communion?[24] Even the layout of Evangelical churches pointed to this "functional Gnosticism"—with

---

[23] Most Evangelical churches practice communion only a few times per year.
[24] Thanks to Matt Barclay for calling that out.

Jesus absent from the "altar", the preacher's lectern was moved to the front and center of a stage. Evangelical "liturgy" typically consisted of a few songs, a long-winded sermon, and nothing else.[25] In a group that considers all sacramental reality to be merely memorial or symbolic of the spiritual, though, this sort of thing was not surprising. For my part, I quickly learned to appreciate the act of communion "as often as ye gather", as well as the tactual worship services that respected our nature as embodied beings.[26]

I was soon disappointed to find that the Anglican waters were not as smooth as I had hoped. The problem was that the very existence of these conservative Anglican breakaway groups was made possible by the same principle that led to the existence of tens of thousands of other Protestant denominations—namely, some group would take issue with the denomination's decisions that did not comport with their own understanding of Scripture. This was seen as justification for creating a new movement. Although I agreed that the Anglican Communion as a whole made some bad calls, the decision to divide led to the same problematic situation as in other Protestant denominations (if on a smaller scale).

Further, although Anglicanism at first seemed better able to offer answers to my foundational questions, its responses basically fell on a continuum between the same insufficient Protestant replies and more robust attempts that sounded too Catholic. Much Anglican doctrine was the same: an attempt to please both sides of the Catholic-Protestant divide. And this practice led to dogma that was ambiguous or vague—embracing only statements that could easily be massaged to mean whatever the individual wished them to mean. In trying to please everyone, Anglicanism excluded nothing (hence its fall into theological and moral liberalism).

Finally, I knew I would have difficulty defending not only the *effects* of Anglican compromises (e.g., divorce, contraception, homosexual marriage and ordination, heretical bishops) but the very *cause*

---

[25] It is not uncommon for Evangelical preachers to sermonize for forty-five minutes to an hour. While this is often referred to as "bringing the Word", the reality is that the vast majority of most sermons consist of the preacher's own thoughts—not Bible readings. The average Catholic liturgy often has far more Bible readings than the average Evangelical church service.

[26] For a helpful discussion of this subject, see David P. Lang, *Why Matter Matters: Philosophical and Scriptural Reflections on the Sacraments* (Huntington, Ind.: Our Sunday Visitor, 2002).

of the founding of the Anglican church (i.e., Henry VIII's desire to divorce his wife). No amount of respect for the early Church or liturgical uniformity could rectify these problems, for neither could amend Anglicanism's foundational doctrinal and moral pluralism. Thus, although the particular Anglicans I worshipped with were solid believers, I could not ultimately commit to Anglicanism.

I hoped I could find the foundation I was looking for even further back in history—and that meant looking to the pre-Protestant Church. So I recrossed the channel, skirted the continent into the Mediterranean, and explored its ancient shores.

The Seas of the Ancient Church

I had found in the New Testament a Church that was not always what it should have been (e.g., Paul's accusations in his letter to the Galatians, or Jesus' criticisms and warnings levied against the churches of Revelation 2–3). But rather than proving that the Church could not be trusted, this merely showed that her leaders were not always trustworthy (just like the authors of the Bible!). More importantly, I found that this Church had authoritative means of correcting herself—that, at times, she acted with God's supervision and oversight (e.g., Acts 15) and so *could* be trusted (again, just like the authors of the Bible!). This ability was never considered to have been lost by the Church: authoritative councils continued to be enacted, and authoritative creeds continued to be written even after the deaths of the apostles. Much of this occurred well before the New Testament canon was even settled—much less readily available.[27]

Now, I had been taught that relying on the Church to resolve doctrinal issues was not trustworthy, for her tradition simply reflected the opinions of fallible men. But it was these very traditions that, historically speaking, grounded the orthodox creeds, councils, and even the canon of Scripture itself. Without an authoritative and infallible tradition, Christianity's foundation seemed doomed to relativism—however, if the biblical canon and Christian orthodoxy were trustworthy, then so was the Church that produced them.

[27] See appendix 1.

The ancient Church offered answers to these questions that comported with (and helped explain) Church history. Yes, the Church *did* decide which books would be included in the Bible and what counted as orthodoxy. We can trust the fallible men who made these decisions, for the same reason we can trust the writings of the fallible men who authored the Bible: God kept them safe from error. The product of Jesus' ministry was a Church that he entrusted to *produce* a Bible. And although the Bible that the Church produced is not *deficient,* it is often *difficult*—undetermined in its meaning and lacking a complete blueprint for the faith. This is why Christianity is found in a Church (which Paul calls "the pillar and bulwark of truth"— 1 Tim 3:15) *with* a Bible.

Given this outlook, many Evangelical conundrums began to evaporate, and the skeptical attacks of critical scholars became less and less threatening to me. Although the true history of the biblical canon and Christian orthodoxy were perhaps a stumbling block to those who did not trust the tradition of the Church, they were relatively uninteresting to those who did.

The problem was that the Church that produced the creeds of orthodoxy and the canon of Scripture was neither Evangelical nor Protestant! These later traditions, therefore, had serious difficulty grounding the faith without inconsistently trusting the Church whose other teachings they rejected. Much of what set Evangelical and Protestant groups apart from the ancient Church were late doctrinal innovations, and both groups began in—and have since fostered— unparalleled division in the Body of Christ. These realizations called both their roots and fruits into question (cf. Ps 11:3 and Mt 12:33).

It was about this time that I ran across the website Called to Communion while researching for a paper on the biblical canon. I was shocked at the website's erudite posts—many read like graduate-level research papers! As I surfed through its postings, I came across Bryan Cross' article on the *tu quoque* argument.[28] In it, Cross responded to the objection that someone who becomes Catholic does so for the same reason Protestants choose a denomination—namely, because it most closely conforms to his own interpretation of Scripture—and

---

[28] Bryan Cross, "The *Tu Quoque*", Called to Communion, May 24, 2010, accessed May 28, 2015, http://www.calledtocommunion.com/2010/05/the-tu-quoque/.

that therefore the Catholic cannot complain about Protestants doing so. I immediately recognized this as the "bailout" argument I had been relying on since my debate with Jeremiah years earlier. As I finished reading Cross' successful refutation of the argument, I realized I was in serious trouble.

I finally saw that, rather than arriving at my own theological opinions through personal study and then looking for a tradition that affirmed them, I should identify the Church objectively—by looking at whom the original apostles ordained to continue the Church's authoritative functions (and whom they, in turn, ordained and so forth). Since this Church had to be the one that settled the biblical canon and creedal orthodoxy, it should be rather easy to identify. I soon discovered, however, that the problem with this historic Church was that she seemed to be a thing of the past. Just after the turn of the first millennium, a great schism broke the ancient Church into Eastern Orthodoxy and Roman Catholicism, and these two great branches of the Church continued to the present day.[29]

My time in the great sea was over—its currents were drawing me inexorably toward the headwaters of two great rivers. My Evangelical background made the initial choice easy. Following what I call the ABC (*Anything but Catholic!*) rule, I swam eastward.

The Orthodox Branch

Once I was convinced that the ancient Church was the Christian Church, new questions had to be asked. Catholics and Orthodox both had a legitimate historical claim to this identity, so the same procedure for discerning between them would not work as it had for the Protestant question.

I definitely had a taste for the East's tradition, which is at once beautiful, ancient, apostolic, and orthodox. It was also attractive because it did not come with much of the baggage that Catholicism did (e.g., the Pope, the Crusades, Galileo, the Inquisition, or even

---

[29] Although they are an important part of Church history (and a good friend of mine—another SES alumnus—is now studying to be a priest in one of them), I am not going to worry over the Oriental church issue here. Many have since returned to communion with Orthodox churches anyway.

the Reformation). So I started meeting with some great Orthodox priests, whom I pummeled with questions, and often visited an amazing Orthodox church. I eventually took a class in Orthodoxy there with some friends from SES (three of whom converted to Orthodoxy that year).

Although my experiences were good, I found Eastern Orthodoxy very culturally divided, both internally and externally. Its external divisions were obvious from the titles of its churches (e.g., Greek Orthodox, Russian Orthodox). Although these were not nearly as divisive as those between many Evangelical / Protestant groups, they were serious enough to make the various communities disagree on which of the others could be considered Orthodox![30] Because of this, and the fact that they remain in schism with the Western Church, the Orthodox Church had ceased to call authoritative, universally binding councils—which seemed an important part of the Church's function.

Internally, there often seemed to be a cultural clique mentality that excluded those outside the community.[31] I feared what would happen if I ever moved away from my great local Orthodox church and had to take my family to one that did not accept us Westerners (if I could even find another Orthodox church). Finally, much of what attracted me to Eastern Orthodoxy could be found in the Eastern rites of the Catholic Church.[32] In the end, I had to admit that my theology had been formed by the great thinkers of the Western world—and I was not going to give them up. I found myself agreeing with Thomas Howard's assessment of the situation: I did not start the schism, I probably cannot resolve it, and, for better or worse, I am a Western thinker.[33] That left only one viable option—one I never thought I would even consider. I had to break the ABC rule and look Romeward. It seemed that the only Christian body that

[30] For example, consider the controversy over the Orthodox Church in America. See "Recognition of the OCA", Orthodox Church in America website, accessed May 15, 2015, http://oca.org/questions/oca/recognition-of-the-oca.

[31] This was not so much my experience as it was reported to me by many Orthodox believers themselves. In fact, the church I attended was specifically tasked with trying to overcome this problem.

[32] See Andrew Preslar's chapter in this book.

[33] Thomas Howard, *Evangelical Is Not Enough: Worship of God in Liturgy and Sacrament* (Nashville, Tenn.: Thomas Nelson, 1984), postscript.

retained apostolic succession, dogmatic unity, and universal authority and appeal was the Catholic Church.

So I swam to the sandy bar that distinguished the two branches of this ancient river, climbed out, and walked to the shore of the Tiber.

Toes in the Tiber

One might think that narrowing the choices down to only one would be enough for me to make the final swim easily. It probably would have been easy, but the Tiber seemed strewn with doctrinal and moral obstacles. What about Catholicism's idolatry, legalism, and licentiousness? How could I ever accept the papacy, the Apocrypha, or purgatory? Why would I want to align myself with those responsible for the Crusades, the Inquisition, or martyrdom? Sure, the Catholic Church had Augustine, Anselm, and Aquinas—but it also had to answer for Huss, Luther, and Galileo. How could I turn my back on twenty-five years of dismissive criticism?

Space does not permit even cursory answers to these issues (and I have written about them elsewhere). It will have to suffice here to say that what I discovered as I investigated each of these questions (and many more besides) was that most of the background information that fueled them was simply wrong. When Catholicism was not a big issue for me, I had uncritically relied on secondhand (non-Catholic) literature for my data. As I found myself sinking deeper into the Tiber's waters, I started reading primary sources—and when I did, I found Catholicism to be quite different from what I had envisioned.

I found that I was, in fact, already in agreement with much more of Catholicism than I would have guessed. Many "problematic" Catholic teachings actually made quite a bit more sense when I learned what they actually were, and I saw that many of the things I initially found objectionable were easily justified on principles that I already held as an Evangelical (but had never extrapolated). Transubstantiation, for example, made sense from a philosophical explanation of change (e.g., why a cow can become hamburger, which can then become my body while seemingly remaining the same material), as well as a biblical explanation of Jesus' literalism concerning the

Eucharist (cf. Lk 22:19–20; Jn 6:48–68; 1 Cor 11:23–32). Purgatory made sense of biblical principles of both mercy and justice that a bare-bones Evangelical gospel did not—namely, it made sense of the intuition shared by all Christians that what we do really matters and has effects beyond this life. The Rosary prayers turned out to be quite conservative—some of the most "Catholic" prayers being mere Scripture quotations or affirmations of doctrine that followed from them. Mary and the saints were a welcome addition to the Christian family I already had—if they were not dead (Lk 20:38; cf. Heb 12:1), why not include them in my prayer requests, just like those living on Earth? The "merit" involved in salvation turned out to be not legalistic at all—rather, it referred to God's promised preparation of our souls for heaven (not earning entrance based on the law).

Once these and other misconceptions were cleared away, I began to suspect that perhaps Catholicism wasn't a cult after all!

Wading In

A major difficulty that I faced during this time of investigation was that I was still firmly enmeshed in Evangelical life. As more converts kept coming out of the SES pool, a witch hunt against Catholics began to develop.[34] It pained me not to be able to discuss my thoughts with the people with whom I had been having theological discussions for years—but my job and ministry were threatened by friends and foes alike, and I did not want to be fired just for considering alternate views.[35] I had discovered that simply presenting Catholicism's views accurately engendered suspicion. Few people could hold down a reasonable conversation on the topic of Catholicism for more than a few minutes once I demanded accuracy. In the end, these kinds of reactions served to convince me that perhaps I was on

---

[34] I nearly called it the "Evangelical Inquisition", but I chose this description for its irony—as Catholics are often blamed for the witch hunts of Europe even though they were the first to condemn them.

[35] If this sounds overdramatic, consider the ostracism that Michael Licona faced from the SES faculty over his allowance for the mere possibility of a nonliteral view of Matthew 27:51–54 in a footnote in his 700-page book defending the historicity of Jesus' Resurrection.

to something—for if simply stating a view correctly sounds like an argument for that view, it might be worth looking into!

The overall response to my "new" thinking, though, was surprisingly positive (unless someone smelled Catholicism!), and critical responses usually offered little in the way of deterrent. Many times objections to the Catholic view consisted of uncharitable or shallow criticisms that traded on misrepresentation or unsupported assertions, and many retorts boiled down to "But . . . that's Catholic!" (the ABC rule again).

With all the time I spent dealing with the standard anti-Catholic arguments (both good and bad), I eventually came to think that arguing against Catholicism from a Protestant standpoint was practically doomed to failure. Catholicism did not seem disprovable *logically*, because unresolvable contradictions in any system are rare, and Catholic philosophy is top-notch (as even many Protestants admit). Further, Catholicism did not seem disprovable *scripturally*, because disagreement alone is insufficient (especially given that the disagreements between sola scriptura Protestants cover nearly every facet of the faith and have resulted in tens of thousands of distinct Protestant groups), and if the Protestant notion of justification by faith alone (sola fide) could be reconciled with James 2:24, I did not see how they could ever catch Catholics in a biblical contradiction! Finally, Catholicism did not seem disprovable *historically*, because specifically Catholic teachings (such as apostolic succession) existed very early on in the Church's history, and many existed for 1,500 years before Protestantism came along.

Tiber Treading

So I kept up the investigation, and the more I studied, the more I found myself thinking like a Catholic. I already believed that what we do in this life matters to our afterlife, that faith and good works went together—that these were no more opposed to salvation than vows and sacrifice were to marriage. I already believed that what we do in worship really mattered, that our faith needs to be more than just correct thoughts—they had to be lived out. Further, I already believed the Church was to be unified, that division was not a point of spiritual pride, and that Christianity was not to be treated like a cafeteria—rather, true Christian faith is a package deal (as opposed to the "faith" of heretics).[36]

I dove into everything I could read on Evangelical-Catholic conversion. I blogged, debated, taught, and discussed these issues as much as possible. In the process, I made many Catholic friends and, unfortunately, lost some Evangelical friends. Some I lost naturally, as our mutual interests began to lessen; others I lost due to unfortunately uncharitable debate (on both sides, I am sure we would agree). I lost some Evangelical friends, though, because they *became* Catholic friends (usually over the same issues I was looking into)!

After five years of study and discussion, I found it difficult to keep my head above water. I felt I had reached a point of culpability for my continued indecision, personal and professional relationships were getting strained, and it was time to start swimming for one shore or the other. I realized that becoming Catholic would entail a life change on a scale I had never faced before—but I did not want to hide from whatever truth I found. I had a strong sense that the investigation's end had to come soon.

I could not tread forever.

In the spring of 2013, I found myself looking for a good reason *not* to convert. I gave up my teaching position at SES, and that Fall I began attending the Rite of Christian Initiation for Adults (RCIA), classes for those interested in joining, or just learning more about, the Catholic Church. Although I had heard stories of how bad RCIA was at many parishes, the one offered at the parish that most of my local Catholic friends attended was excellent. My issues began to be settled, my questions were answered, and my mistaken notions were clarified.

The more I experienced what true Catholicism was, the less I could see myself ever returning to any other Christian "tradition". Catholicism filled in so many of the holes I always had to step around in Evangelicalism and offered *more* of everything I already had and appreciated as an Evangelical. From its robust biblical interpretation to its respect for human nature and its consistent moral teachings, it just made more sense out of what I already believed (and often more besides).

---

[36] See Saint Thomas Aquinas, *Summa Theologiae* II-II, 5, 3.

Muscle Cramps

Lest this journey sound like an idyllic romp of theological reflection, candles, and stained glass, I want to add that there was considerable suffering involved as well—and not just for me.

For my part, although I had been critical of Evangelicalism for some time, twenty years of intense involvement made it difficult to shake it off emotionally, even if it was (relatively) easy to do so intellectually. Evangelicalism is so *simple*—and so *accommodating*. Virtually everything beyond a quick salvation prayer was optional for Evangelical spirituality, and there was enough theological and moral variation to suit virtually any taste. Due to Evangelicalism's radically personalized nature, its churches were often very alluring and gratifying. There was also opportunity for practically anyone to reach whatever ministry position he wished. Finally, Evangelicalism's customizable nature meant that in-house conflicts were much easier to "resolve" by either compromising or dividing.

Moreover, I experienced difficulty that was both practical and emotional. Many of my Evangelical relationships were becoming uncomfortable, and it became easier just to keep my distance in many cases. This strategy was neither possible nor desirable for close friends and family, though, and some were upset over my changing views.

The most important of these was my dear wife, whom I had been dragging from one church to another since we married. Her promise to "go where I go" was already being strained by these regular moves, but Catholicism stretched it nearly to the breaking point. Looking back, I realized that I had been doing much of my thinking privately—not wishing to upset her with my musings unless they were really going to lead somewhere. Now that they had pretty much reached their conclusion, I discovered that we were in more serious disagreement than I had realized. The possibility of raising our children in a "divided house" sickened me, and she is to be commended for allowing me to continue to lead the family even when she was not in agreement.

Finally, as if all this were not difficult enough, I had to give up my teaching position at SES (along with half my income) as well as the doctoral degree I had been working on for three years there. Just to keep things interesting, all this occurred within weeks of discovering that my wife and I had another baby on the way! So while it was all very exciting, it was also tearful and sometimes terrifying.

Dog Paddling to Shore

I eventually asked myself, "If every Christian who had ever lived came back to life next Sunday and went to his respective church, where would I want to attend?" The Church of Ignatius, Ambrose, Jerome, Augustine, Anselm, Aquinas, Dante, J. R. R. Tolkien, G. K. Chesterton, John Henry Newman, Étienne Gilson, Mother Teresa, Flannery O'Connor, Francis Beckwith, Ed Feser, and Peter Kreeft sounded pretty good! How could all these great Christians throughout history—many who formed, expounded, lived, and defended so much of the Christian faith as we know it today—have gotten it as horribly wrong as Protestants believe they have? How could Catholicism have produced such a wealth of intellectually bright, morally upstanding, and spiritually illuminated Christians yet have gotten Christianity itself wrong?

Somewhere along the line I came across this quotation from Thomas Aquinas that really convicted me of my theological autonomy:

> Now the formal object of faith is the First Truth, as manifested in Holy Writ and the teaching of the Church, which proceeds from the First Truth. Consequently whoever does not adhere, as to an infallible and Divine rule, to the teaching of the Church, which proceeds from the First Truth manifested in Holy Writ, has not the habit of faith, but holds that which is of faith otherwise than by faith.... Now it is manifest that he who adheres to the teaching of the Church, as to an infallible rule, assents to whatever the Church teaches; otherwise, if, of the things taught by the Church, he holds what he chooses to hold, and rejects what he chooses to reject, he no longer adheres to the teaching of the Church as to an infallible rule, but to his own will. (*Summa Theologiae* II-II, 5, 3)

This description of how heretics treated theology was dangerously close to my own. It seemed I had really been trusting in my own thinking and experience all along (and indirectly teaching others to do the same). While I rejected this practice in principle, it was difficult to transition out of it. Becoming Catholic would mean choosing to trust the Church instead of myself, and sometimes the two did not sync well.

To be honest, I never really reached a point of total comfort with the idea of becoming Catholic, but I came to think that perhaps God wanted me to make a true *faith* decision—not just one more move from one form of Christianity to another according to my personal preference. God had made it *possible* for me to make this choice—but not *necessary*. I resonated with Peter's words recorded in John's Gospel: "To whom shall I go?" (cf. Jn 6:68).

And so it was that during the Easter Vigil of 2014, I dragged myself, exhausted, onto the Tiber's far bank and was received into full communion with the Catholic Church. Although I was not "the most dejected and reluctant Catholic in all America", I cannot say I was completely euphoric.[37]

But I was finally on solid ground.

Conclusion

In closing, let me say that I do not think that Evangelicals or any other non-Catholics are necessarily hell-bound or false Christians (and neither does the Catholic Church). One thing I noticed during this whole inquiry was that ex-Catholic Evangelicals tended to hate (and misunderstand) Catholicism, while ex-Evangelical Catholics generally appreciated (and correctly understood) much in Evangelicalism.

At first I had a difficult time understanding how this could be. Why weren't Catholics angry about their previous experience when they converted? What I discovered was that for many, like me, Catholicism is not so much a repudiation of past belief as its development (dare I say "maturing"?). Becoming Catholic is much more about *receiving* than *relinquishing*.

Although I have settled on a different shore from many of my fellow Christians, I appreciate, respect, and love them still. If you are eyeing the Tiber's far shore as I once was, know that I am working to

---

[37] To riff off C. S. Lewis' description of his conversion to Christianity.

build bridges to aid you in your journey.[38] As Richard John Neuhaus beautifully put it:

> To those of you with whom I have traveled in the past, know that we travel together still. In the mystery of Christ and his Church nothing is lost, and the broken will be mended. If, as I am persuaded, my communion with Christ's Church is now the fuller, then it follows that my unity with all who are in Christ is now the stronger. We travel together still.[39]

---

[38] An abbreviated version of this chapter is available at the author's website: http://douglasbeaumont.com/2014/04/22/tiber-treading-no-more.

[39] Richard John Neuhaus, "How I Became the Catholic I Was", *First Things* (April 2002), accessed May 28, 2015, http://www.firstthings.com/article/2002/04/001-how-i-became-the-catholic-i-was.

2

Rome: The True Church and Refuge for Sinners

By Joshua Betancourt

Cradle Baptist

There I was, in front of a life-size statue of Jesus at a rural parish in Northern California—my eyes fixed on his, and his seemingly on mine. I remember feeling ambivalent about what I saw, intrigued yet fearful. I was intrigued because I had never seen an image—let alone a statue—of Jesus in my Evangelical church back home in Southern California. I felt fearful because the statue was staring right at me; his eyes followed me as I moved slowly to the left or to the right. This encounter felt real: this Jesus whom I had read and sung about in Sunday school was standing before me. Once my fear dissipated and intrigue took over, I slowly began to trace the statue's cold, pierced acrylic hand with my index finger and to recall what my parents had taught me: "For God so loved the world that he gave his only Son . . ." This was my first experience visiting a Catholic parish. I was nine years old and on a routine summer vacation to visit my uncle John Phillip Vallejo (an ordained deacon from the Diocese of Stockton) and his family in Modesto, California.[1]

---

[1] I also remember being in awe of the vaulted ceilings, the flickering candles, and the beautiful lifelike statues of Mary and Joseph. I remember going home and asking my mother about my uncle's "brand" of Christianity and why my uncle wore a "dress" (clergy vestments). My mother graciously juxtaposed the Catholic faith with Evangelicalism with respect and candor.

I was born into an Evangelical family. My father, who is from Mexico, was born and raised in a Baptist home. My grandmother, who had been baptized a Catholic, converted to Evangelicalism in the Baptist tradition and thus raised my father and his siblings as such. My mother, who was born and raised in the Eastside of Los Angeles, was baptized and raised Catholic; she received her sacraments at the local barrio parish. However, she stopped practicing her faith in her young-adult years and came to faith in Jesus Christ within the context of Evangelicalism in a Calvary Chapel church. Both my parents were committed to raising their children within a Christian home, teaching us about Jesus and his sacrificial love. It was in the context of these two great Evangelical traditions (Baptist and nondenominational) that I learned to memorize Scripture and experienced God's love for me.

My parents alternated taking us to their respective faith communities; on one Sunday, we would attended my mother's Calvary Chapel community, called Harvest Christian Fellowship, and on the following Sunday, we would attend my father's much smaller independent Baptist church. My sister and I enjoyed them both and came to know Jesus as our personal Lord and Savior in these two faith communities. And for this I am forever grateful.

Interestingly, I experienced a somewhat "second great (spiritual) awakening" in my early twenties one fall evening while walking my Boxer puppy. For the most part, the voices of truth and virtue had gone silent as I entered high school and moved on to college and entered the workforce, but that all changed when an older gentleman named "Art" befriended me. We both had Boxers, which made for a great common ground. In addition to being a lover of dogs, Art was an even greater lover of God. After a number of walks and talks, he eventually offered me an invitation to recommit my life to Christ, which I accepted.

From that point forward, I experienced a profound change of heart, which resulted in a major shift in lifestyle, friends, language, and entertainment choices. I suddenly developed a deep desire to read the Bible, to attend church and fellowship with other believers, and to share the gospel with everyone. My sense of call to ministry soon followed. Reading and teaching Scripture became my passion, and evangelizing others—even reaching out to those "unsaved" Catholics—became for me a common practice.

Faith Seeking Clarity

Maria von Trapp of *The Sound of Music* fame once said that Cath-olics are often "oversacramentalized", and many observers have noted that they are "underevangelized" in the process. Conversely, Evangelicals are plenty evangelized but are devoid of the sacraments (save baptism and communion). I was saturated with Scripture but had not received baptism or communion until I was about ten years old. To be sure, Evangelicals and Baptists are extremely serious about the Bible and use it as the basis for teaching, preaching, and evangelizing. It was this threefold approach to ministry—teaching, preaching, and evangelizing—that inspired me to become a student of the Bible and pursue full-time ministry. As I matured in my walk with the Lord, I began to lean more toward the Calvary Chapel side of the Evangelical spectrum and enjoyed the contemporary flavor of the megachurch scene, where there was a greater emphasis on wor-ship and evangelizing. I was therefore inspired to learn the Word of God under the great Calvary Chapel pastor-teachers and evan-gelists, such as Chuck Smith and Brian Brodersen, at the popular Calvary Chapel Bible College (CCBC).

During my studies there, I enrolled in an apologetics course. Prior to this, I had never really considered the historicity of Christianity and the importance of Jesus' bodily Resurrection and his claim to be the Son of God. In one class, we built a case for the veracity of Chris-tianity, beginning with the "knowability of truth", based on the first principles of thought, and concluded with the reliability of the New Testament. We studied 1 Corinthians 15:3 and following, where the apostle Paul argues for the importance of Christ's physical Resur-rection in establishing the faith and our salvation, saying, "If Christ has not been raised, your faith is futile and you are still in your sins" (1 Cor 15:17). This course sparked my interest in other apologetic-type courses, such as the Kingdom of the Cults and Logic / Critical Thinking. The instructors who taught these courses had received their seminary training from the same institution: Southern Evangel-ical Seminary (SES). These select Calvary Chapel instructors had sat under the tutelage of some of Evangelicalism's finest minds, and they were eager to pass their knowledge on to those students who demon-strated a propensity for learning and defending the Christian faith. After I had graduated from CCBC, I packed my bags and moved across the country to Charlotte, North Carolina, to attend SES in my quest to deepen my knowledge of Christianity.

Meeting the "A-Team": Aquinas, Anselm, and Augustine

My first semester at SES was invigorating and eye-opening. The Introduction to Apologetics course at SES was more robust than the one I had taken at CCBC. At SES, we spent more time considering the classical apologetic method of Saint Thomas Aquinas. We studied his arguments for God's existence, especially from causality and design.[2] We also considered arguments from other classical apologists, such as Saint Anselm of Canterbury, who is famous for his ontological argument for God's existence, especially from God's "necessity" and "perfection". In another course on soteriology (the study of salvation), we studied Saint Augustine's doctrine of sin and grace. We were taught that it featured two distinct phases: (1) his early years—in which he focuses more on man's freedom and his cooperation with God's grace; and (2) his later years—in which he focuses on man's depravity and fallen nature and God's predestination of man for salvation.

Our seminary was famous for taking a "moderate Calvinistic" stance on predestination: we understood that man, morally depraved as he is, is still capable of responding to God's grace by virtue of being made in the image of God—thus the image of God is "effaced but not erased". Our more "extreme Calvinistic" brothers (those of the Reformed tradition) followed Martin Luther's and John Calvin's doctrines of sin and salvation, teaching that man is totally depraved and thus is incapable of responding to God's grace without being regenerated first.[3] Thus, in response to Saint Augustine, our professors would often state, "The way you refute Saint Augustine's later

---

[2] Saint Thomas' "five ways" (or arguments) for defending the existence of God are from motion, causality, necessity, perfection, and design. While we studied all of these, primacy was given to the arguments from causality and design.

[3] Luther taught that Original Sin has obliterated the *Imago Dei* of man. The *Imago Dei* is restored in the justification of the believer, received by "faith alone". Calvin, on the other hand, taught that although man is "totally depraved", he still maintains the *Imago Dei*, which is maintained before, during, and after justification. The order of salvation within Reformed theology (also called in Latin the *ordo salutis*) is as follows: (1) regeneration, (2) justification, (3) sanctification, and (4) glorification.

doctrine of predestination is to use Saint Augustine's earlier doctrine of grace." According to our professors, alluding to the earlier Augustine, God predestined man to salvation but always *in accordance* with man's free will. In short, we were taught that God's grace is cooperative, not merely operative (synergism versus monergism). As one professor crassly put, "God is not a divine rapist."

The seminary taught a more mitigated version of Saint Thomas Aquinas' view of election, which follows from his principle of causality. To be sure, Saint Thomas taught the doctrine of predestination and argues that election has its primary cause in God's will, but man's free will is the secondary cause flowing from God's decree; this seems to be compatible with the Catholic Church's teaching on *cooperative* grace in man's justification.[4] The *Catechism of the Catholic Church* says, "Justification establishes *cooperation between God's grace and man's freedom*. On man's part it is expressed by the assent of faith to the Word of God, which invites him to conversation, and in the *cooperation* [emphasis added] of charity with the prompting of the Holy Spirit who precedes and preserves his assent."[5] Thus, the Church permits Catholics to hold to a stronger Augustinian-Thomistic view of election so long as it does not include double predestination (the election of the reprobate to damnation).

For all intents and purposes, Saint Thomas Aquinas was the seminary's "patron saint", but no one would ever dare frame it in such terms. In fact, one of the seminary's cofounders, Norman Geisler, penned a book on the life and works of Aquinas, titled *Thomas Aquinas: An Evangelical Appraisal*, with the intriguing subtitle *Should Old Aquinas Be Forgot? Many Say Yes, but the Author Says No!*[6] To his credit, in the book's epilogue he points out areas of disagreement he has with the Angelic Doctor; for instance, he disagrees with Saint Thomas' views on infant baptism, baptismal regeneration, and transubstantiation. In a more recent article, Geisler argues that there is no logical connection between embracing Thomism and converting to Catholicism.[7] Although this might be true, it does not eliminate the

---

[4] See Saint Thomas Aquinas, *Summa Theologiae* I, 22, 3.

[5] *CCC* 1993.

[6] See Norman L. Geisler, *Thomas Aquinas: An Evangelical Appraisal* (Eugene, Ore.: Wipf and Stock, 2003).

[7] Norman L. Geisler, "Does Thomism Lead to Catholicism?" (unpublished article, 2014).

fact that Saint Thomas was, well, Catholic, and many Thomists are now Catholic!

Thomism is so important to Catholic teaching that Pope Leo XIII stated that it was the definitive exposition of Church doctrine. This was troubling to me as an Evangelical. Why did we as an Evangelical institution place so much stock in this Catholic man's theology and philosophy? Well, because it was "good philosophy". It was good philosophy because it was sound philosophy! I then began to wonder whether Saint Thomas' views on Catholic doctrine could also be true. If he was so insightful when it came to natural theology, why couldn't he be when it came to divine revelation and what the Church teaches regarding the sacraments?

Although Saint Thomas often left our hearts yearning for more learning, he also often left pebbles in our shoes and our stomachs turning. I found myself in a love-hate relationship with him. Saint Thomas was as much a formidable foe as he was a close friend. But he wasn't the only problem that I faced. There were others upon whose shoulders he stood—namely, the early Church Fathers. I was introduced to them shortly after I was introduced to their younger brother in the faith.

Facing the Giants: The Early Church Fathers

During my second semester at SES, I had to choose a topic for my master's thesis. Having caught wind of former Evangelicals who had converted to the Catholic faith, such as Scott Hahn and Peter Kreeft, I wanted to know why they chose to leave biblical Christianity for a faith that seemed so riddled with medieval superstition. I consulted with my academic adviser, Geisler, who happened to be the seminary's president at the time, and presented the thesis topic of why Evangelicals convert to Catholicism. He shot the idea down, however, and said that such a topic would be much too subjective and that it needed to be more apologetic in nature. So he suggested that I research the topic of "papal infallibility" instead. I obliged. My thesis was titled "An Examination of the Infallibility of the Bishop of Rome".[8]

---

[8] This became the basis for the book I coauthored with Norman Geisler, *Is Rome the True Church: An Examination of the Roman Catholic Claim* (Wheaton, Ill.: Crossway, 2008).

Geisler assigned readings in Catholic primary sources, such as Ludwig Ott's *Fundamentals of Catholic Dogma* and Henry Denzinger's *Sources of Catholic Dogma*, and also recommended that I consult the early Church Fathers. He assured me that the dogmas concerning the papacy would be absent among their writings, since the papacy was a well-developed dogma that took centuries to crystallize.

I first turned my attention to Saint Clement's letter to the Corinthians. I knew that the Church regarded Saint Clement to be the third successor to Saint Peter, but what I did not know was that the concept of apostolic succession would be present as early as the late first and early second centuries. In chapter 42 of his epistle, Saint Clement mentions the threefold office of bishop, priest, and deacon. Clement then writes, "Our apostles also knew, through our Lord Jesus Christ, that there would be strife on account of the office of the episcopate. For this reason, therefore, inasmuch as they had obtained a perfect foreknowledge of this, they appointed those [ministers] already mentioned, and afterward gave instructions, that when these should fall asleep, other approved men should *succeed* them in their ministry."[9]

I also found Saint Ignatius of Antioch's *Letter to the Trallians* to be as jarring as Clement's regarding the presence of the threefold office of bishop, priest, and deacon. Writing on the Church's order, Ignatius states, "He that is within the sanctuary is pure; but he that is outside the sanctuary is not pure. In other words, anyone who acts *without* the bishop and the presbytery and the deacons does not have a clear conscience."[10] Here was another second-century counterexample of what I thought was a late development in the Church's ecclesiology.

If this were not troubling enough for this young Evangelical, I was very surprised when I read Saint Irenaeus of Lyons, the disciple of Polycarp (who was mentored by the apostle John). Not only does Irenaeus explicitly mention the papacy, but he uses the office and authority of the papacy (as well as papal successors) to defend the catholicity of the Church against the Gnostics, who allegedly held to a form of esotericism (secret knowledge) that was not compatible

---

[9] Saint Clement of Rome, *First Epistle of Clement to the Corinthians* 44; emphasis added.

[10] Saint Ignatius of Antioch, *Letter to the Trallians* 7, 2; emphasis added. Ignatius also stated, "Let everyone revere the deacons as Jesus Christ, the bishop as the image of the Father, and the presbyters as the senate of God and the assembly of the apostles. For without them one cannot speak of the Church." *Letter to the Trallians* 3, 1.

with the universal nature of the Church's teachings. Irenaeus wrote (ca. A.D. 175–185):

> Since, however, it would be very tedious, in such a volume as this, to reckon up the successions of all the churches, we do put to confusion all those who, in whatever manner, whether by an evil self-pleasing, by vainglory, or by blindness and perverse opinion, assemble in unauthorized meetings; [we do this, I say,] by indicating that tradition derived from the apostles, of the very great, the very ancient, and universally known Church founded and organized at Rome by the two most glorious apostles, Peter and Paul; as also [by pointing out] the faith preached to men, which comes down to our time by means of the successions of the bishops. For it is a matter of necessity that every Church should agree [Latin: *convenireis*] with this Church, on account of her preeminent authority, that is, the faithful everywhere, inasmuch as the tradition has been preserved continuously by those [faithful men] who exist everywhere.[11]

I brought this troubling passage to Geisler's attention, and he pointed me to a commentary by a respected Protestant scholar, J. N. D. Kelly, who dealt with this very passage in his classic book on early Christian doctrines. Kelly argued that "the normal meaning of *convenireis*, 'resort to,' 'foregather at,' and *necesse est* does not easily bear the sense of 'ought.'"[12] Kelly and Geisler argued that Irenaeus' comment was merely *reflective* of the political status of the Roman Empire at the time, and this no doubt had an effect on its capital and the Church that resided there (for better and for worse). The passage, therefore, could be understood descriptively and not necessarily prescriptively.

I initially accepted Kelly's commentary and my adviser's direction in dealing with this troubling passage. But the more I read and reread Saint Irenaeus' defense, the more it became clear to me that he was using the authority of the Church, i.e., the papacy, to defend the catholicity of the Church. I soon learned that it was this same authority that first defined the canon of Scripture in the councils of Carthage (A.D. 387) and Hippo (A.D. 397).

---

[11] Saint Irenaeus, *Against Heresies* 3, 3; emphasis added.
[12] J. N. D. Kelly, *Early Christian Doctrines*, rev. ed. (New York: Harper, 1960), 193.

Called to Commune with Him

By this time I was becoming more and more convinced that apostolic succession and the authority of the Church (especially the papacy) was indeed present in the second and third centuries. And although there certainly was an element of development to the Church's teaching regarding the papacy, the basic forms of these doctrines were embedded in the writings of the earliest Christians. If the Church possesses Christ's authority (as the early Church Fathers claimed), then it follows that whatever she teaches is true as well as binding on all the faithful. This led me to consider the Church's teaching on one of her most central—and most controversial—doctrines, namely, Christ's true presence in the Eucharist.

Growing up as an Evangelical, I knew very well that the climax of the worship service was the sermon. The worship music that opened the service prepared one to receive the Word of God as delivered by the preacher. Communion was not something done regularly at my home church. In fact, it was our practice to receive communion only on a quarterly basis. To Catholics this is unthinkable! The Catholic Church teaches that the Mass, not the sermon, is central in worship, calling the Eucharist "the source and summit of the Christian life". So, I asked the question: If the Catholic doctrine of the papacy is present in the earliest centuries of the Church, then could the Eucharist also be present?

Indeed, the Church's teaching regarding the Eucharist was clearly articulated in the writings of the early Church Fathers. Ignatius of Antioch, writing in the second century, says in his *Letter to the Smyrnaeans*, "They [the Docetists] abstain from the Eucharist and prayer because they do not admit that the Eucharist is the flesh of our Savior Jesus Christ, which suffered for our sins, which the Father in his goodness raised up."[13] This same Ignatius, in his letter to the Ephesians, describes the Eucharist as "breaking one bread, which is the medicine of immortality, the antidote against death, which gives eternal life in Jesus Christ".[14]

In a similar fashion, Irenaeus of Lyons, writing shortly after Ignatius, says this about Jesus as Priest and Victim in the Eucharist: "Inasmuch

---

[13] Saint Ignatius of Antioch, *Epistle to the Smyrnaeans* 6.
[14] Saint Ignatius of Antioch, *Epistle to the Ephesians* 20.

therefore as the Church offers simplicity of heart, her gift is rightly considered a pure sacrifice with God.... For we are bound to make oblation to God.... And this oblation the Church offers pure to the Creator, presenting to him with thanksgiving from his creation.... For as the bread of the earth, receiving the invocation of God, is no longer common bread but Eucharist, consisting of two things, an earthly and a heavenly; so also our bodies, partaking of the Eucharist, are no longer corruptible, having the hope of eternal resurrection."[15]

I soon began to realize that the Eucharist was essential to the spiritual life, since Jesus said, "Truly, truly, I say to you, unless you eat the flesh of the Son of Man and drink his blood, you have no life in you.... For my flesh is food indeed, and my blood is drink indeed. He who eats my flesh and drinks my blood abides in me, and I in him" (Jn 6:53, 55–66). Yet, I didn't have the assurance that any Protestant tradition, much less my own, had truly maintained the apostolic tradition faithfully.

I thought perhaps the Anglican tradition had retained it, since the Anglican church claimed apostolic succession for their bishops as well. Some Evangelicals who had become aware of the early Church Fathers' views on the Eucharist chose to embrace Anglicanism (Episcopalianism), since it was the closest but safest thing outside Catholicism (and considered by some the "halfway house"—the *via media*—between Protestantism and Catholicism). This suited me best out of all Protestant denominational choices, since it featured prima facie the "best of both worlds". However, the Anglican church defected from Rome under King Henry VIII, and this meant that the church's orders were severely compromised and thus illicit (remaining valid but not authorized by the Catholic Church) at best, or invalid altogether at worst, which would invalidate their Eucharistic celebrations.

This led me to read up on the Catholic position on Anglican ordinations. In 1896 Pope Leo XIII, in his letter *Apostolic Curae*, under no uncertain terms declared "that ordinations carried out according to the Anglican rite have been, and are, absolutely null and utterly void" (no. 36) as a result of the introduction of the Edwardine Ordinal (1562), since it lacked the proper *form* (that which is essential) to the

[15] Saint Irenaeus, *Against Heresies* IV, 18, 4–6.

sacrificial nature of the priesthood, "which is chiefly the power 'of consecrating and of offering the true Body and Blood of the Lord'" (see no. 29); the Anglican retention and practice of the "imposition of hands" (the matter) was not enough to guarantee valid ordinations, argued Pope Leo XIII (see no. 24). My hope that the Anglican tradition safeguarded this apostolic succession was dashed by Rome, and my safe ecclesial halfway house suddenly crumbled.

In short, I was convinced that early Christianity was indeed sacramental and that the center of the worship service was primarily the Eucharist and not necessarily the sermon. The Roman Catholic Church had faithfully practiced this, and, for me, this unquestionably demonstrated her authenticity and historical pedigree. It seemed, therefore, that in the Catholic Church was the *guarantee* that I could receive what God had intended for his children to receive all along—the most Holy Eucharist as provided by validly ordained men.

Faith Seeking Charity

Catholics and Protestants affirm together that a person is justified by faith through grace, especially that "God forgives sin by grace and at the same time frees human beings from sin's enslaving power and imparts the gift of new life in Christ." So, "when persons come by faith to share in Christ, God no longer imputes to them their sin and through the Holy Spirit effects in them an active love. These two aspects of God's gracious action are not to be separated, for persons are by faith united with Christ, who in his person is our righteousness (1 Cor. 1:30): both the forgiveness of sin and the saving presence of God himself."[16] Catholics and Protestants are in agreement here.

Protestants, however, emphasize that the righteousness of Christ is our righteousness—the sinner thus at once is granted righteousness before God in Christ through the *declaration* of forgiveness in justification—and that only in union with Christ is one's life renewed (through a lifelong process of sanctification, which prepares us for final glorification). The condition for justification is faith alone (sola

---

[16]Lutheran World Federation and the Catholic Church, *Joint Declaration on the Doctrine of Justification*, no. 22.

fide); justification is not dependent (as in Catholicism) on the life-renewing effects of grace in men—that is, the change in status from "sinner" to "righteous" is a "celestial transaction" in which Christ's righteousness is credited to the sinner; nothing happens intrinsically to the believer at this point. It is forensic in nature. That is, justification is a *legal exchange* in which we get Christ's righteousness while he gets our sins (which he bore on the Cross).

Catholic teaching on justification emphasizes the renewal of the *interior person* through the reception of sanctifying grace imparted, or infused into our soul, as a gift; God's forgiving grace always brings with it a gift of *new life*, especially in baptism, in which the Holy Spirit becomes effective in active love (charity). Whereas Protestants separate justification and sanctification, for Catholics, "justification entails the *sanctification* of [one's] whole being."[17] When one is justified, he is simultaneously sanctified; he becomes a child of God and a partaker of the divine nature and of eternal life.[18] The emphasis in the Catholic teaching on justification is *becoming* righteous and not simply being *declared* righteous, as is taught within Protestant Evangelicalism. In Catholicism, justification is an ongoing process, and in Protestantism, it is a one-time event. The Church teaches that the purpose of our justification is our beatitude—so that we become partakers of God's beatitude and inheritors of his Kingdom.[19]

Understanding these two positions on justification also clarified for me why Protestants always emphasize God as a Judge who views us as sinners unable to pay the penalty for our transgressions, while Catholics understand God as a Father who views us as his adopted children through our faith in Christ, and he disciplines us (throughout our maturation process) when we do wrong (Heb 12:6, Prov 3:11; 13:24) and rewards us when we do right (Mt 6:4–6, 16, 18; cf. 2 Jn 8; Rev 22:12), until we are welcomed into his heavenly Kingdom. This also juxtaposes two views of the covenant: the Protestant view sees a

---

[17] *CCC* 1995

[18] *CCC* 1996.

[19] *CCC* 1719. "The New Testament uses several expressions to characterize the beatitude to which God calls man: (1) the coming of the Kingdom of God [cf. Mt 4:17]; (2) the vision of God: 'Blessed are the pure in heart, for they shall see God' [Mt 5:8; cf. 1 Jn 2; 1 Cor 13:12]; (3) entering into the joy of the Lord [Mt 25:21–23]; (4) entering into God's rest [cf. Heb. 4:7–11]"; ibid., 1720.

covenant as a contract, an exchange of goods, whereas the Catholic sees covenant as a "kinship bond", an exchange of persons.[20]

As an Evangelical, I initially took comfort in the Protestant understanding of justification. I believed that even the faith that I possessed was entirely a gift from God and that my holiness was signed, sealed, and delivered by Christ. I needed only to focus on the practical aspects of my salvation (not on attaining it, as that took place during justification); that is, I needed to grow in holiness and work "to attain a reward in heaven", which were not synonymous with salvation. The reward had more to do with degrees of "happiness" in heaven. As one professor put it, "While everyone in heaven is happy, not everyone in heaven is *equally* happy."

Faith Seeking Virtue[21]

The *Catechism* says that "the way of perfection passes by way of the Cross. There is no holiness without *renunciation* and *spiritual battle* [cf. 2 Tim 4]."[22] And that was the problem for me. As an Evangelical, I found myself sometimes defeated, deflated, and discouraged. When I asked my professors and pastors how to grow in holiness, I was told just to pray, read my Bible, memorize Scripture, and seek fellowship.[23] Although all of these are vitally important, and did help me attain a high level of Christian maturity and satisfaction, I

---

[20] See Scott Hahn, *A Father Who Keeps His Promises*, for a popular treatment on the Catholic view of the covenant; see O. Palmer Robertson, *Christ of the Covenants*, for a classical Reformed treatment on covenant theology.

[21] This section and those that follow are written in honor of my sponsor in the faith, John W. Garcia, who inspired me to the study of Catholic moral theology and spiritual warfare (see his excellent work, *Tracing Our Sins to Adam and Eve: Healing Our Emotions Through Jesus Christ* [Covina, Calif.: Saint Joseph Communications, 2011]).

[22] *CCC* 2015; emphasis added.

[23] Of course many Evangelicals believe that there is more to the spiritual life than what was mentioned above. For example, charismatic Evangelicals often pursue what is called the "the baptism of the Holy Spirit" (a phenomenon of spiritual empowerment that can happen at the moment of salvation or sometime thereafter, or both), which can be accompanied and manifested by "sign gifts" such as tongues. Conversely, many conservative and mainline Protestants are typically "cessationists" and thus deny that there is such a thing as a spiritual phenomenon called "baptism of the Holy Spirit" apart from salvation. The sign gifts (such as tongues), then, are no longer in use and were exclusive to the time of the apostles during the establishment of the Church.

still felt empty at times. I would ask myself, "Is this the sum of the Christian life?"

Dread would sometimes consume me. I did not understand suffering and what I was supposed to do with it. When I would experience trials of varying degrees, it certainly did not always feel assuring to be told that "in everything God works for good with those who love him, who are called according to his purpose" (Rom 8:28). I often liken my preparation for spiritual battle as an Evangelical to a boxer preparing for a prize fight and being coached only to use jabs—no uppercuts, no power or counterpunches, no combination shots to the body, et cetera.

The Fall of Man and Concupiscence

An SES course on sin and salvation covered the Fall of man and how his original state of uprightness was lost because of his disobedience and lack of confidence (trust) in God.[24] The consequences included our inheritance of Original Sin and death from our first parents. We were taught that once we place our faith in Christ, we are no longer guilty of any sin (personal or otherwise). I believed this. But there was no emphasis on the reality of the prevailing bent toward sin (as Saint Paul explicitly mentions in Romans 7:14–24).

I came to the conclusion that Protestant Evangelicalism is devoid of the spiritual resources that God intended to help regulate our concupiscence (or disordered passions). The truth is that we have a human nature that is wounded by sin, and God has provided us with the means to receive healing: the sacraments. Evangelicals are known for encouraging other believers "to be more like Jesus", but the only way to do this is to partake of the divine nature (becoming more like God) through the sacraments, by which we receive the very life of God into our souls (2 Pet 1:8).

Our Vocation to Beatitude and Desire for Happiness

In one of my philosophy courses, I was introduced to Aristotle's concept of *eudaimonia*, which loosely means happiness or the highest

---

[24] The Church teaches that Adam originally lived in total harmony with God—in a state of holiness and justice, possessing preternatural gifts and supernatural life. See *CCC* 374ff.

human good. I began to wonder what this might be in the Christian life. I didn't bother to pay attention to this idea again until I began to consider the Catholic faith. Within Catholic circles, conversations would often revolve around one's vocation in life. The options were primarily the call to religious life or to married life. I soon discovered that these were just the means—the pathways—by which we fulfilled our greater vocation: *our call to God's beatitude*. The *Catechism* says it best: "God put us in the world to know, to love, and to serve him, and so to come to paradise. Beatitude makes us 'partakers of the divine nature' and of eternal life [2 Pet 1:4; cf. Jn 17:3]. With beatitude, man enters into the glory of Christ [cf. Rom 8:18] and into the joy of the Trinitarian life."[25]

Terry Barber and Jesse Romero, Catholic radio cohosts and mentors of mine in the work of evangelization, often say, "Holiness equals happiness!" They often reiterate during their program that the happiest people who ever lived were the saints—namely, those whose lives were marked by heroic virtue. The saints are often depicted as having lived lives completely dedicated to the service of God. Saints were confronted with decisive moral decisions to renounce this world and to live, and be ready to die, for God. The *Catechism* says that "true happiness is not found in riches or well-being, in human fame or power, or in any human achievement—however beneficial it may be—such as science, technology, and art, or indeed in any creature, but in God alone, the source of every good and of all love."[26] What this means is that, like the saints before us, we are called not to count the cost but to deny ourselves and pick up our cross daily and follow our Lord. In doing so we find true happiness and the fulfillment that our hearts long for. In the words of Saint Augustine, "You have made us for yourself, and our hearts are restless until they rest in you."[27] On a similar note, I once heard someone say, "He is no fool who gives what he cannot keep to gain that which he cannot lose."[28] This resonates with what our Lord taught: "Do not lay up for yourselves treasures on earth, where

---

[25] *CCC* 1721.

[26] *CCC* 1723.

[27] Saint Augustine, *Confessions of St. Augustine* (Totowa, N.J.: Catholic Book Publishing, 1997), 19.

[28] Elisabeth Elliot, *Shadow of the Almighty: The Life and Testament of Jim Elliot* (New York: Harper, 1958), 108.

moth and rust consume and where thieves break in and steal, but lay up for yourselves treasures in heaven.... For where your treasure is, there will your heart be also" (Mt 6:19–20, 21).

Freedom and Virtue

Saint Pope John Paul II once said, "Freedom consists not in doing what we like, but in having the right to do what we ought."[29] So, "the more one does what is good, the freer one becomes. There is no true freedom except in the service of what is good and just. The choice to disobey and do evil is an abuse of freedom and leads to 'the slavery of sin' [cf. Rom 6:17]"[30] I remember having a conversation about sanctification with one of my dorm mates in Bible college, and he opined that when we come to faith in Christ, we become naturally inclined to doing and choosing "the good" freely all the time. Although my heart was willing to accept this, my flesh knew better. The reality is that "doing and choosing the good" does not always come easily or naturally—whether one is saved or not. What is needed is the cultivation of good habits.

It did not take long for me to notice that the Catholic Church constantly produced saints. The saints possessed a habitual and firm disposition to do the good. There were certainly many inspiring and virtuous Evangelicals whose lives were marked by obedience and perseverance—many of whom were my friends and peers at CCBC and SES. But there was no Evangelical theological framework or prototype that provided me with the meaning or motivation to pursue or choose the good. The Church, in nuancing the doctrine of grace, also teaches the concept of *habitual* grace, which can be described as the *firm* disposition to live and act in keeping with God's call.[31] This assists the faithful to become more inclined to choose the good as

---

[29] Saint Pope John Paul II, Homily during a Eucharistic celebration at Oriole Park, Baltimore, Maryland, October 8, 1995, no. 7, http://w2.vatican.va/content/john-paul-ii/en/homilies/1995.

[30] CCC 1733.

[31] CCC 2000. The *Catechism* uses the phrase "*permanent* disposition" in describing habitual grace, but for the sake of clarity and continuity with this writing, the phrase "*firm* disposition" is preferred here, since this grace can be lost by mortal sin.

well as to grow in beatitude and be more "like God".[32] That is, it is a constant supernatural quality of the soul that sanctifies a person inherently and makes him just and pleasing to God.

How then did the saints attain this? They loved God above all else and loved their neighbor secondly. They chose simply to will the good of others as others. They repeatedly chose acts that cultivated the (cardinal) virtues of prudence, justice, fortitude, and temperance. They frequented the sacraments and thus increased in the theological virtues of faith, hope, and charity. They constantly regulated their disordered passions and allowed their emotions and feelings to be taken up into the virtues rather than be perverted by vices. In short, the saints' lives were marked by self-denial, self-mastery, and, above all, charity. They had what I had—namely, Jesus—but they clearly walked in the mystery of Christ and habitually chose the good in accordance with a conscience properly formed by reason and divine law. The *Catechism* sums it up well, stating, "Progress in virtue, knowledge of the good, and ascesis [i.e., self-discipline] enhance the mastery of the will over its acts."[33] To be sure, the saints exemplified these well.

The Role of the Blessed Mother and the Saints

I had a candid conversation with my uncle (the Catholic deacon) one evening concerning the nature of the family. He struck a chord with me when he mentioned that the Church is our family. He then mentioned the Holy Family: Jesus, Mary, and Joseph. He patiently explained that Christ's Mother was *our Mother* (see Jn 19:26) and that we were called to honor her just as Jesus did (in keeping with the Fourth Commandment). My relationship with Jesus was intact, but I had not made Jesus' family my own. What role did they have in the lives of the faithful? The Church is our family, my uncle shared: God is our Father, Mary our Mother, Jesus and the angels and saints

---

[32] In Eastern Orthodox soteriology, following Saint Athanasius, the emphasis on salvation is not justification but divinization (Greek: *theosis*), becoming like God at the moment we participate in God's *energies*, whereas the Catholic Church uses the language "participation in the life of God" (i.e., sanctifying grace).

[33] *CCC* 1734.

our brethren. These were the great cloud of witnesses mentioned in
Hebrews 12:1. I was told that the saints in heaven are interceding for
us—literally cheering us on and praying for our spiritual well-being
on our journey. I knew that if they were in fact praying for me, their
prayers would be efficacious, since in the epistle of Saint James we
hear, "The prayer of a righteous man has great power in its effects"
(Jas 5:16). If Mary and the saints are alive in heaven interceding for
the faithful, there is reason to believe that their prayers are beneficial
to those who invoke their names.[34]

As an Evangelical, I and many other believers often defaulted to
a "me and Jesus" mentality and practiced a form of Christian individualism. The Catholic Church articulates the exact opposite—the
remedy for individualism. The purpose of coming together is as follows: "It is in the Church, in communion with the baptized, that the
Christian *fulfills his vocation*."[35] The *Catechism* provides the reasons for
maintaining solidarity with the Church:

> From the Church he receives [1] the Word of God containing the
> teachings of the "law of Christ" [Gal 6:2]. From the Church he
> receives [2] the grace of the sacraments that sustains him on the "way."
> From the Church he learns [3] the *example of holiness* and recognizes
> its model and source in the all-holy Virgin Mary; he discerns it in the
> authentic witness of those who live it; he discovers it in the spiritual
> direction and long history of the saints who have gone before him and
> whom the liturgy celebrates in the rhythms of the sanctoral cycle [that
> is, the feast days, or propers, of the saints].[36]

With this rationale, I saw my need to be in full communion with
Holy Mother Church for my spiritual well-being. It wasn't a matter
of *if*, but only a matter of *when*.

Redemptive Suffering

There are many Bible verses that confound Protestants. One that
I found extremely troubling was Colossians 1:24: "Now I rejoice

---

[34] These are the *continued bonds* that God established to aid the faithful in their journey
toward heaven.

[35] *CCC* 2030; emphasis added.

[36] Ibid.

in my sufferings for your sake, and in my flesh I complete what is lacking in Christ's afflictions for the sake of his body, that is, the Church."[37] I had no idea what to do with this verse. I could not find adequate answers from professors, peers, or commentators. The vexing question was: What could possibly be lacking in the suffering of Christ? This verse made sense only within the Catholic teaching of *redemptive suffering.*

The Church teaches that as death and suffering entered the world (by the sin of our first parents), Christ's obedience to the will of his Father made it possible for our afflictions and sufferings to be endowed with redemptive power in a *participatory* way. As one Catholic writer explained, "By virtue of our being made one with Christ in Baptism, we can *join* our suffering to that of Our Savior on the Cross at Calvary and thereby *assist* in His work of salvation for the entire world. The suffering of illness and dying brings the Catholic a grace-filled opportunity to offer prayer for oneself, for loved ones, and for the whole human race. *Christ is with us during our illness and shares in our suffering as we share in His.*"[38] In view of this, Saint Paul's words are really a positive statement on the participatory nature of our sufferings with Christ's sufferings and its redemptive value for us and for others.[39] For the apostle Paul, then, nothing is lacking in the Cross of Christ (since our Lord's merits are infinite) except Paul's afflictions and those of the entire Church (as Christ and the Church are one mystical person).[40]

The question every believer must face then is: What shall I *do with* my suffering? God chose to permit each one of us to participate in

---

[37] Saint Paul in his epistle to the Philippians states, "For [Christ's] sake I have *suffered* the loss of all things, and count them as refuse, in order that I may gain Christ.... [And] that I may know him and the power of his resurrection, and may share his *sufferings*, becoming like him in his death, that if possible I may attain the resurrection from the dead" (Phil 3:8, 10; emphasis added).

[38] National Catholic Bioethics Center, "A Catholic Guide to End-of-Life Decisions: An Explanation of Church Teaching on Advance Directives, Euthanasia, and Physician Assisted Suicide" (Philadelphia: National Catholic Bioethics Center, 2011), 1; emphasis added.

[39] As well as the Church Suffering, i.e., the souls in purgatory.

[40] Scott Hahn and Curtis Mitch, eds., *Ignatius Catholic Study Bible: New Testament* (San Francisco: Ignatius Press, 2010), 366. Hahn and Mitch note that Saint Paul's words "could be misunderstood to mean that the suffering of Christ was not sufficient for redemption and that the suffering of the saints must be added to complete it. This, however, would be heretical. Christ and the Church are one mystical person, and while the merits of Christ, the head, are infinite, the saints acquire merit in a *limited* degree." Hahn and Mitch, *Ignatius Catholic Study Bible*, 366; emphasis added.

Christ's work for our salvation. For the merits of Christ's Passion to be applied to us, we need to *cooperate* by bearing the sufferings that come to us, i.e., by taking up our cross and following Christ ("He who does not take his cross and follow me is not worthy of me" [Mt 10:38]). Ultimately, salvation requires that we accept what Christ has merited for us, and that means accepting the suffering that comes to us in our daily lives as Christians in the world, both the minor things (such as the annoyance of delayed gratification) and the heavier things (such as crises relating to grief and loss); therein lies the reason why our suffering is rightly called "redemptive".[41] Evangelical apologists often do a fine job of answering the problem of evil (i.e., If God exists, why does suffering exist?), but very little attention is ever given to the *practicality* of suffering. Only in the Catholic Church does suffering become something of value. It is not something to be feared or avoided; on the contrary, it is something to draw you closer to Christ and his Passion. And for me, this mysterious, troubling verse finally made sense in light of Catholic teaching on redemptive suffering.[42]

The Rosary and Sacramentals

A friend of mine, Charlie Aeschliman, who is a popular Catholic speaker and former Navy SEAL, once told me that trying to find success in the spiritual life and fare well in the spiritual battle without the Church is the equivalent of trying to put out a forest fire with a squirt gun. The Catholic is equipped with a variety of prayers and spiritual exercises, such as sacramentals,[43] meditation, and contemplative

[41] See Saint Pope John Paul II's apostolic letter "On the Christian Meaning of Human Suffering", *Salvifici Doloris*, February 11, 1984.

[42] Saint Clare of Assisi (1194–1255) echoes Saint Paul the apostle: "If you suffer with him [Christ], *you will reign with him*. [If you] weep [with him], you shall rejoice with him; [if you] die with him on the cross of tribulation, you shall possess heavenly mansions *in the splendor of the saints* and, in the *Book of Life*, your *name* shall be called glorious among men." Cited in *Magnificat* 16.16 (August 2014): 152; emphasis in the original.

[43] *The New Saint Joseph Baltimore Catechism* defines *sacramentals* as "holy things or actions of which the Church makes use to obtain for us from God spiritual and temporal favors". According to this classic catechism, "the sacramentals most used by Catholics are: holy water, blessed candles, ashes, palms, crucifixes, medals, rosaries, scapulars, and images of Our Lord, the Blessed Virgin, and the saints." *The New Saint Joseph Baltimore Catechism*, rev. ed. (New York: Catholic Book Publishing, 1966), 171.

prayers.[44] I was accustomed to praying only extemporaneously as an Evangelical. I deepened my prayer life with the Rosary and the Divine Mercy Chaplet, which encourage the faithful to meditate on the lives of Jesus and Mary (in the Rosary) and on the mercy of Jesus (in the Divine Mercy Chaplet). These devotions have brought me a great deal of comfort during crises as well as during the course of my ordinary day.

The words of Saint Peter in his second epistle came to life when I considered the treasure trove of spiritual resources found in the Catholic Church. It is written that God "has granted to us all things that pertain to life and godliness" (2 Pet 1:3). It is God's desire that all should come into full communion with the Church, so that we can be best equipped to live a life of virtue and happiness and thus become the "best version of ourselves", as Matthew Kelly says, and reach our ultimate end: the Kingdom of heaven.

Conclusion

I never thought in my wildest dreams that I would be a Catholic, especially in the light of the fact that I had dedicated my master's thesis to undermining the truth claims of the Church. By God's grace, after six years of inquiring and studying the faith, seeking the spiritual resources to become what God had intended for me as his child, I was received into full communion in 2011 at the Easter Vigil at Saint Paul the Apostle Church in Chino Hills, California. The transition for my family to become Catholic was relatively seamless (for which I'm grateful, since that was not the case for some of my peers, as demonstrated in their chapters in this book), although they followed me into the Church a year later. For my wife, Carolina, having been raised Catholic and having become an Evangelical later in life, the return to the Church was rather smooth, and our decision to raise our children Catholic was almost natural.

Rome is the true Church, and God desires everyone to come home to it. My journey home to the Catholic Church was not only an intellectual one (especially theologically, philosophically, and

---

[44] See *CCC* 2700–24.

historically) but also one of healing and reconciliation (morally), and I will be forever grateful to God for giving us the Church and the sacraments. I am grateful for my Evangelical roots, as they gave me a love for Christ and his Word. This has not changed since I have become Catholic. Now I possess a love for Christ in the Eucharist and his Church too. My Catholic faith and convictions are all the more grounded as a result of my Protestant beginnings. I am also grateful that whatever suffering I experience in this life isn't for naught. The truth is that when an Evangelical becomes Catholic, he loses nothing and gains everything.

3

Crawl, Walk, Run: My Progression toward Mother Church

By Jeremiah Cowart

Unimpressed with Religion

First, let me say that at this moment in my life, I am quite impressed with various religions as a whole. Of course, I am most impressed with Catholicism, but that was certainly not always the case (more on that in a minute). During my undergraduate education, I assimilated a certain intellectual value, and this value would guide and define much of my intellectual development in the ensuing years. One of my favorite philosophers, Aristotle, apparently said (though I have never found where he wrote it), "It is the mark of an educated mind to be able to entertain a thought without accepting it."[1] And in a similar vein, my Evangelical mentor, Norman Geisler, said that before you ever have the right to criticize another point of view, you must do two things: understand that point of view and learn something from it. These are indeed wise words, and I believe I will take these Aristotelian and "Geislerian" philosophies of intellectual engagement with me to the grave. I believe these underlying principles helped ease my transition into Catholicism in 2004, though I really never saw that "conversion" coming.[2]

When I was an Evangelical Christian, I noticed that many of my fellow Evangelicals looked for a "defining moment" in their

---

[1] This quotation is often attributed to Aristotle. It most likely is a discombobulated quotation from *Nichomachean Ethics*, book I, 1094.b24.

[2] Of all my extended family that I have known, none have been Catholic.

respective spiritual journeys toward God. There is a widespread belief among Evangelicals that there is a specific moment when they know they have committed themselves to Christ (have been "saved"). For many Evangelicals, this moment comes in the form of making a public profession of faith in Christ in the presence of witnesses (think Billy Graham crusades). In strong contrast to this, I have noticed in my religious experience that there were *many* defining moments spread out over several years that, when taken together, amounted to a full acceptance that Catholicism is the best path to God that this world has to offer. What follows below is an attempt to retrace some of the more significant defining moments in my religious journey. I hope it will be a useful story to some readers, if not slightly interesting as well.

I once heard Peter Kreeft give a lecture with the not-so-modest title "Why Should Everybody in the World Be a Roman Catholic?"[3] In that lecture, Professor Kreeft said that most people who begin to believe anything about religion do so in the most natural way possible—they pay attention to their parents. If their parents are living a good life, children tend to grow up adhering to very similar religious beliefs. I suppose that was more or less my experience. I was raised in a home that was not unfriendly to religion, yet not overly encouraging of it either. My parents never openly disparaged religion or religious folks, yet we could hardly be called a churchgoing family either. My folks were very much children of the 1960s, fairly typical baby boomers who were influenced by the New Age hippie spirituality that defined much of that era. (The religious reading material in my childhood home consisted of random Carlos Castaneda works, for example.) So even though I grew up in the Bible Belt, we weren't the type of family who attended church (not even the type who attended on Christmas and Easter just in case it all turned out to be true).

And yet, at certain times throughout my earlier childhood, I did occasionally attend Vacation Bible School with friends. Sometimes I went to a religious service when I stayed with my aunt Susan, who

---

[3] Peter Kreeft, "Why I Am a Catholic", *7 Reasons with Peter Kreeft*, five-part lecture series, Lighthouse Media, November 12, 2011. This lecture can be found on YouTube under the title "Why I Am a Catholic—(7 Reasons with Peter Kreeft)". Kreeft proceeds to provide the audience with seven reasons.

had given me two Bibles while I was in elementary school: a Gideon pocket New Testament (which I have to this day) and a King James Bible (which fell apart long ago, though not because of frequent use). The deepest philosophy I was exposed to as a young adolescent was probably in the Marvel comic books that I consumed. What I am getting at is that I had little exposure to Christianity as a child. And if I were to guess the impact of this upbringing on my attitude, I would say that my lack of exposure just left me unimpressed with religion as a whole.

The "Church of God"

But in 1992, when I was a sophomore in high school, my older brother and my mom simultaneously became very interested in Christianity. They may have even had their own defining moments; I've never asked. My mother got so excited in her newfound zeal that she bought me a humongous study Bible (New International Version). It was a much easier translation to follow than the King James Bible, which meant that I might have read a little of it. But nearly every night, my brother would ask me if he could borrow my NIV Bible to read from. I always said yes because, although I did not want to disappoint my mother, I was not using it. But by the time I was sixteen, my mother and my brother had developed an ardent desire to follow Christ and learn more about his teachings. My brother did this in a mostly private way, through Bible study. But my mother had found a home in the nearby Mount Paran Church of God in Marietta, Georgia.

So there I was, doing nothing of particular interest in my teenage years, but my family was becoming passionate about religion. I didn't really want the train to leave the station without me on it! (I think my father felt the same way too.) I figured that my mom and my brother might have been on to something, so I took Pascal's Wager without realizing I was doing so. I began to do a little Bible reading (and church attending too). My mother had always been a singer and even managed to get me involved in the youth choir at church. This series of events culminated with my family firmly in the grasp of one Evangelical denomination: the Church of God (Cleveland,

Tennessee). We all made public commitments to Christ in the early '90s. I think I was baptized too (though I do not remember much besides the teenage awkwardness of the moment and getting fully immersed in water).

But what was important about all of this was that my family was plugged into a vibrant Christian community for the first time. This community was not without its fair share of oddities (e.g., speaking in tongues, laying on of hands to heal bodily sickness, lots of folks crying with hands raised to heaven), but it was active and engaging to me as a young teen. I joined the youth group and became acquainted with some of the most passionate people I had ever met in my young life. These teens would challenge me about my personal "walk with God" and ask me whether I had been "saved" or had received the "gift of the Spirit", which referred to speaking in tongues, I think. And they would do so in a quasi-confrontational manner. To be honest, although I appreciated their passion for God, they often made me uncomfortable. I do not think their passion made me uncomfortable, but their in-your-face expression of that passion made me not want to be around them much. But again, I did not want to miss the boat to heaven, so I continued on with the youth-group stuff until high school extracurricular activities got in the way.

In my junior year of high school, I befriended a classmate who had been a part of the Mount Paran Church of Atlanta from his early childhood. I had no real plans for college, so this friend persuaded me to attend college with him in Cleveland, Tennessee, which was the hub for the division of the Church of God of which Mount Paran was a member. (I had been surprised to learn that there were other Church of God denominations within the United States, besides the one based in Cleveland. Perhaps this was my first glimpse into one of Protestantism's main oddities—the plague of denominationalism.) So, in 1994, my friend and I headed off for our freshman year at Lee College,[4] a Church of God institution of higher learning. That college was vibrant and welcoming in the same way that my church had been. It was an active, loving community, full of in-your-face Christians who did not mind continuing to make me uncomfortable.

[4] Now Lee University.

During my freshman year at Lee, two remarkable things happened. First, I met two fellow freshmen who were avid Bible readers and very passionate about their Christian faith. They befriended me right away, and their friendship felt significant. I guess they both seemed somewhat "holy" to me, in a way that I had not experienced in other people. They challenged me to read the Bible more and to pray spontaneously more often. It was largely because of their influence that I read all of the apostle Paul's epistles that year (1995). And as I read, I noticed a recurring theme that Saint Paul simply hammered into his audience, and this theme would stick with me for years to come. Saint Paul repeated that the Church is the "Body of Christ". I do not know if I ever counted precisely how many times Saint Paul said this, but it was often enough to strike me as an overt repetition in his writings. He wanted the reader to bring this idea home and grasp it firmly: the Church is Christ's Body. I was not exactly sure what that expression meant, but I was reasonably sure that it meant that the Church was one, as in unified. It was one thing as a body is one thing. Apparently it was alive too.

Something else important happened to me while at Lee, and this experience would set the groundwork for the rest of my religious life. A friend of mine at Lee challenged me to read the entire (Protestant) Bible. I eventually read the Protestant Bible through in one year, following a chronological plan to cover three to four chapters every day. It was a painstaking task, but in 1997 I finished it. And I have to say that was easily one of the most profoundly religious experiences of my life. It completely revolutionized my Christian thinking, especially regarding the Old Testament. I began to recognize continuity that I never knew existed between the two Testaments of the Bible.

Being at Lee was an overall positive experience, but I stayed only one year. I ran out of the requisite money to attend an out-of-state private college, so I went back home to Georgia. For the next decade or so, I attended many mainstream Protestant churches, both progressive and conservative Evangelical churches. I tried out Presbyterian, Baptist, various Pentecostal, Lutheran, Methodist, and so on. I was always looking for "the real Church" (this Body of Christ that Paul spoke of). I never seemed to find it, although I am not even sure what that meant to me at the time. I was not very sure what I was looking for. Part of me just thought I would recognize it when I experienced it.

One of the strategies I used to find the true Church was to apply various tests during my searching. For example, I would ask myself whether the doctrinal statements of this or that denomination lined up with what I understood "biblical truth" to be. If it did, I would attend services for a few months and see how the worship experience was, whether there was an inclusive and strong sense of community, et cetera. And above all that, I was looking for something grand, a church that was much larger than me and my small world. I had a sneaking suspicion that the Body of Christ was global in extent. So I would ask myself why the true Body of Christ would be exemplified by the Southern Baptists. If it were, that would imply that Christ's Body on Earth is more or less confined to the Bible Belt. What kind of sense would that make? Or why would it be embodied by the Presbyterian church *in America*, as if the United States had a hold on proper religion? None of that made any sense to me. Besides all this, I never felt at home anywhere I went to worship. I guess this feeling was my most subjective test. But since I had recently read through the whole Bible, I wondered why the worship experience of the Jewish people, as recounted in the Old Testament, had little or no convergence with the worship found at Protestant churches.

Continuity

The Old Testament Hebrews worshipped via a heavy liturgy, one that was articulated to the very last detail within the pages of Sacred Scripture. Community prayers and community worship were routine for the Jewish people, and family was everything to them. In the Old Testament, I read about devout women and men giving the highest praise to God for giving them children. Children were, in the Hebrew mind, among the greatest blessings to come from above.[5] God was also described as being intensely immanent in the world and

---

[5] When I read this and discussed this fact with my wife, we decided to stop using birth control. This was one incremental step leading us down a path toward the Catholic Church (unbeknownst to us, of course).

deeply concerned with the affairs of his people. The Jewish people had a priestly class to handle worship and the sacrifices for sin. God spoke to his people largely through the priests and prophets. And there was no shortage of interesting-sounding statues, fabrics, candles, et cetera, all within the worship area itself. It sounded like a truly aesthetic and powerful experience to enter either the Jewish Tabernacle or the Temple.

I absorbed this picture of Old Testament life into my mind and heart and naturally asked why Protestant churches bore so little resemblance to that Old Testament experience. I wondered why the same God would make his worship experiences today be so vastly different from those of three thousand years ago. This was just another thing that made no sense to me. Where did the priests go? Where did the liturgy go? Where did the beauty go?

Reading the Bible laid all the groundwork I needed to become Catholic. It is difficult to retrace all the particular steps that eventuated in the road that led to Rome. But it was mostly a series of baby steps, I think, which all culminated in my realization that I was quite Catholic in my heart and mind, even years before the actual conversion took place.[6]

John Henry Cardinal Newman once quipped, "To be deep in history is to cease to be Protestant." I do not know that I can honestly say that I was ever deep in history. But majoring in philosophy at the University of Georgia did expose me to the grand history of philosophical thought. It also helped to make me a lifelong fan of the virtue ethics of Aristotle. Then I attended graduate school at Southern Evangelical Seminary, which praised and promoted the teachings of some of the largest minds of the Church prior to the Reformation. The more I was exposed to the writings of Saints Augustine, Anselm, and Aquinas (not to mention Blessed John Duns Scotus), the more keenly aware I became of how different "church" was for those folks than for me. There was the strongest contrast imaginable between modern-day American Evangelical churches on the one hand and the ancient faith on the other. And when I say "ancient faith", I mean both the ancient Jewish faith and the ancient Church. I saw then,

---

[6] The word *conversion* is a bit of an overstatement, of course, since I was already a baptized Christian many years before I was confirmed Catholic.

and have seen more clearly every year since, the continuity that exists between ancient Judaism, early Christianity, medieval Catholicism, and the modern Catholic Church. In fact, continuity in an important way defines the Church. Or, perhaps more accurately, continuity defines how God interacts with his people over time. There is an underlying identity to the Church that has existed over these last two thousand years. You can find this identity by paying close attention to the continuity—the sameness of the Church over time.

Catholics recite the Nicene Creed during every Sunday Mass and confess together, "I believe in one, holy, catholic, and apostolic Church." The true church is everywhere, meaning it is catholic (universal). And of course it would be, would it not? It would not be largely confined to a certain country or region. It would be global in extent and influence, just as the Catholic Church is. Holiness (being set apart) would define the true Church. One would expect to see lives entirely devoted to God (monks, nuns, and clergy). One would also expect the Church to be somewhat holy herself from the wider culture around her. The true Church on Earth would certainly speak the truth about God and with the authority of the apostles. It would be apostolic, in other words. Even from my earliest teenage years, when I was just flirting with Christianity, I believed that the Church would speak the truth about God. Of all things the Church must possess, truth is a big one. Finally, just as Saint Paul used the analogy of the body to describe the Church, I knew that the true Church had to be one thing, not many separate and divided things. Specifically, the Church must be one organic thing, alive, just as Christ (who is her head) is alive.

In my heart and mind, I always believed the true Church on Earth would be unified, apostolic, universal, and exhibiting holiness. I do not think I would have expressed it this way. But thankfully that work of finding the right expression to describe the true Church was not a responsibility left to me. It resided with the bishops of Nicene and Constantinople in A.D. 381 and has been handed down to posterity. During my search for the true Church, I did not always clearly know what I was looking for, but when I found that the ancient Christians believed that their Church was one, holy, catholic, and apostolic, I had an "aha" moment. *That* is what I had been looking for all along, the Church with those four marks. I cannot say with all candor that that is all I have found within Catholicism, but I can say that Catholicism has the right formula for producing these four marks. At any rate, I see no other real contenders for the job, besides Eastern Orthodoxy perhaps.[7]

Discontinuity

So what about all the many non-Catholic churches in the world? Sadly, I would have to say that *discontinuity* is the word that best describes Protestantism and the faiths to which it has given rise. Protestantism has enormous problems with incoherency too. The problem of canonicity is enormous and likely insurmountable for my Protestant brothers and sisters. The oft-repeated Protestant quip about the Bible being a "fallible list of infallible books" never made any sense to me. If the list itself is fallible, then of course you have no idea which books should or should not be in it. It is an incoherent explanation of the biblical canon.

I have also never understood the Evangelical Protestant emphasis on the doctrine of sola fide because the "saved" inevitably do good works anyway. Being saved and doing good works are inexorably linked, according to most Protestant expressions of sola fide that I have come across. Now, I do not mean to belittle these doctrinal distinctions of Protestantism. They were and are important means of division, which is really just another way of pointing out Protestantism's discontinuity with what came before it (Catholicism and Orthodoxy). And the discontinuity of Protestantism really made me see it as a remote chain of islands, all on their own, surrounded by water as far as the eye can see, and not well stocked. It reminds me of the film *Cast Away*. Spiritually, you can survive within Protestantism, but how well you will thrive depends on what is on the island of your brand of Protestantism.

Protestantism has (rightly or wrongly) been described as a "religion of the book"; that is to say, the Bible is considered the nucleus of Protestantism, and very little else is considered relevant or part and parcel of Christianity. In the average American Evangelical Sunday

---

[7]But with all due respect to our Orthodox brothers and sisters in Christ, where is the catholicity of Orthodoxy? How does Orthodoxy exhibit universality throughout the globe? And what about apostolicity? Did God stop communicating with his people through the bishops when the Great Schism happened a millennium ago? I must give it to the Orthodox, though: they do extremely well at exemplifying unity and holiness.

service, there is a little singing (either of hymns or modern praise songs) to begin with, generally followed by a short Bible reading, followed by forty-five minutes of biblical teaching, which we all hope is somehow related to the Scripture we just heard. And that pretty much sums it up! Anyone acquainted with ancient Judaism, early Christianity, or the Church of the High Middle Ages would be left desiring much more. Where is the liturgy? Where is the real presence of Christ with his people? Why are the ancient prayers and creeds not recited, as they had been for centuries before? Why does the God of the Old Testament so little resemble the Protestant understanding of the God of the New Testament? Why are we not publicly and privately confessing our sins? Why are we not doing an enormous amount of reading from the Bible, instead of reading a line or two and having someone explain it to us for an hour? Where are the aesthetics? Does a plain cross have aesthetic value? How do I know that the pastor up there is teaching what the Church has taught throughout the ages? Maybe that teacher up there is just teaching some fad that is popular today. How do I know that he is any more of an expert in the Bible than I am? Again, think *Cast Away*—Protestantism is paltry, and this paltriness just kept me searching for something more.

Now, do not get me wrong. There are beautiful Protestant churches around (e.g., Episcopalian). There are churches that hold to some liturgical traditions too (e.g., Lutheran, Missouri Synod). But for the most part, discontinuity with history is what defines Protestantism, and more especially American Evangelicalism. This was my opinion anyway, as I attended various churches in the Charlotte, North Carolina, area during my years at Southern Evangelical Seminary. Each church seemed like its own island doing its own thing, with very little to connect it to the other islands (other churches), let alone to the mainland (the historic Church through the ages). And each time I visited a new Protestant church, I had the inescapable belief that there just had to be more. Something was missing. Maybe many things were missing.

To Be Shallow in History Is at Least Something!

I do not know how deep in history one has to be before he ceases to be Protestant. But for me that happened sometime in 2002, toward the end of my seminary experience. There was a friend who helped nudge me toward the Catholic Church. (Well, he gently pushed me, really, but I am forever grateful that he did.) I do not know whether I would have gotten there so quickly without his help. (When I met him I was beginning to lean toward Eastern Orthodoxy because I was so fed up with the insufficiency that was Evangelicalism!) In the summer of 2004, just after the birth of my youngest boy, my children and I entered the Catholic Church. All four of my young boys were baptized into the Church at that time. I had my first confession, received my first Communion, and was confirmed in the Catholic faith. It was the highlight of my spiritual journey, a journey that seemed to take an eternity. But, hey, better late than never, right?

And since then I have never looked back. Peter Kreeft wryly noted that Walker Percy once explained that whenever he was asked why he was a Catholic, at least one answer was, "What else is there?"[8] That is how I came to view the whole matter too. If a person willingly goes through the difficult and wonderful, burdensome and glorious, task of being a Christian at all, really what other way is there to do it besides the Catholic way? I found that the Catholic Church is the one place you will find those four marks contained within our ancient and universal creed. All the many denominations I had tried over a span of ten years left me feeling high and dry. I came to see that there is no other way that will not leave you feeling deeply unsatisfied. I once heard Scott Hahn say that being a Protestant is like having the menu without getting the meal. Catholics have the menu and the meal. The Catholic Church is not perfect, as we all know (nothing with human intervention, short of inspired Scripture, ever could be), but by the grace of God, I became convinced that Catholicism is the fullness of the Christian faith. Walker Percy was right. God's grace saves us, but also, what else is there?[9]

[8] Walker Percy quoted by Peter Kreeft in "Why I Am a Catholic", *7 Reasons with Peter Kreeft*, five-part lecture series, Lighthouse Media, November 12, 2011, https://www.youtube.com/watch?v=qAu5VL6mImA.

[9] See Walker Percy, interview by Zoltán Abádi-Nagy, conducted by mail from May to October 1986, *Paris Review*, http://www.theparisreview.org/interviews/2643/the-art-of-fiction-no-97-walker-percy.

4

That Great Revolution of Mind

By Brandon Dahm

And now that I am about to trace, as far as I can, the course of that great revolution of mind, which led me to leave my own home, to which I was bound by so many strong and tender ties, I feel overcome with the difficulty of satisfying myself in my account of it, and have recoiled from doing so, till the near approach of the day, on which these lines must be given to the world, forces me to set about the task. For who can know himself, and the multitude of subtle influences which act upon him?

—John Henry Newman, *Apologia pro Vita Sua*

In her poem "The Light of Interiors"[1] Kay Ryan describes the transformation of light as it enters a home through windows, doors, and cracks and is altered by every surface as it makes its way to the home's interior. Finally, the light coalesces into a glow that is the result of being "baffled equally by the scatter and order of love and failure". This interior light, which has "an ideal and now sourceless texture", cannot simply be traced to the picture window in the den or the skylight in the kitchen. Instead, every way that the home is exposed to the outside world and every surface in the home conspire to produce this seemingly preternatural light. I think Ryan's beautiful description of interior light—and I apologize for the pun—illuminates conversion.

Reflecting upon his own conversion to Catholicism, Blessed John Henry Newman tried to provide an account of faith and persuasion that avoided the errors of a rationalism that reduces faith to inference and

[1] Kay Ryan, "The Light of Interiors", in *The Best of It* (New York: Grove Press, 2010), 242–43.

a fideism that denies the need for evidence and argument. Although Newman was clear that faith is a gift from God, he focused his analysis in *An Essay in Aid of a Grammar of Assent* on the human side of conversion. Newman cogently argues at length that conversion is not the result of a series of abstract, formalized arguments.[2] Instead, through a process of what he calls "natural reasoning" we come to believe as "the result of an assemblage of concurring and converging probabilities".[3] The convert has taken any manner of information from any number of sources, e.g., the historical argument for the Resurrection, a sense of purpose in life, the sacrificial love of his grandmother, guilt and the desire for forgiveness, the seemingly miraculous nature of the Church, the overwhelming beauty in nature, awe at the strangeness of existence, et cetera. Each of these experiences plays some role in our new believer's conversion, yet he did not develop for each one a formal argument to judge the likelihood of the truth of Christianity.[4] Instead, the streams of evidence converge and coalesce in such a way that each step cannot be made explicit, so that one cannot easily point out exactly why one now holds his new beliefs—which are like the interior light—with the conviction he does.

An unlikely team, Newman and Ryan complement each other well here. After conversion, a person can point out some important sources of light—the windows in the kitchen in the afternoon—but he cannot identify each source, for there are many small cracks, "loose fits, leaks, and other breaches of surface".[5] After conversion, a person can identify points of intersection between some rays of light, but he cannot trace every convergence, reflection, and diffusion. Upon entering the inner chambers of the home, one can recognize the interior light without being able to explain exactly how it came to be.

When talking about my conversion, then, I can walk you into the kitchen and show you the casement window over the sink, or the picture window in the den, or even where some light gets in underneath

---

[2] See John Henry Newman, *An Essay in Aid of a Grammar of Assent*, chaps. 8 and 9.

[3] John Henry Newman, *Apologia pro Vita Sua*, pt. 3: "History of My Religious Opinions up to 1833", 49–50.

[4] Newman argues further that attempting to do so would actually skew the evidence by removing the force of things in their concreteness. *An Essay in Aid of a Grammar of Assent*, chap. 8, sect. 1.

[5] Ryan, "The Light of Interiors", 242.

the side door. We can then follow the light, and I can show you the hall mirror that reflects the light, the heavy carpet in the living room that dampens the light, and the point on the stairway where two sources of light converge. We can even talk about the light and what it is. Yet, even after identifying each of these lines of evidence and modes of convergence and appropriation, even after having an idea of what light is, I have not provided a complete account of how the interior light came to be. So please read this as a friendly tour of the light of a home instead of an exhaustive demonstration of what I now believe.

The Catholic Question

In college, when we would share testimonies, I remember being a little disappointed with mine. I do not remember a time when I was not a Christian, and I never had a conversion moment. Of course, there were many moments when things would take on new significance for me—the depth of Christ's love, that I could love God with my mind, that only God could really satisfy my deepest desires—but I never had a dramatic moment when I repented and said the sinner's prayer. Instead, being a Christian was always just part of my identity: we went to church, believed what was taught, and prayed. As I got older, I was encouraged to do Christian things independently of family activities and to make Christianity my own. This initially involved going to youth group and my school's chapter of the Fellowship of Christian Athletes, which provided opportunities to explore my faith.

One of the ways I began to appropriate Christianity further was to try to understand what I believed. Although I grew up Christian, I had little awareness of the deep theological divisions separating the types of churches I went to regularly with my family— Reformed, Methodist, and Baptist. In high school, the father of a friend and pastor of other friends introduced me to Reformed theology, and thereby theology in general. The prospect of giving a more precise and reasoned account of my faith was enticing, and I began to read things that I did not understand. I remember long conversations with my friends about end times and reading the *Left Behind* series with excitement. But this was just a taste of the Christian intellectual life that I would discover in college.

Although I had a natural and nurtured tendency to question and pursue answers, it was enhanced and focused during my first years at Iowa State. I was invited to a Bible study during my freshman year by an acquaintance from near my hometown. We had worked at a restaurant together and, despite being from rival towns, had hit it off talking hard-core rock bands we both liked. Someone else in the Bible study, who would also go to SES, Cambridge, and convert to Catholicism, had the apologetics bug and infected the rest of us. I realized that one of the things I loved about apologetics was the philosophy involved, so I switched my major to philosophy.

Because conversions involve uncountable slight adjustments in belief, desire, and understanding, it can be hard to find a clear and fixed reference point for my conversion. One decisive moment for me was when I realized I had to give the Catholic question—"Is Catholicism true?"—careful consideration. It happened during my sophomore year of college. A small group of friends and I had started a campus organization called—wait for it—Truth Bucket, in which we discussed Christian apologetics. Beginning with the law of non-contradiction, then arguing for God's existence, and considering the historical evidence for the Resurrection of Jesus of Nazareth, we concluded that Christianity is true. Using some of J. Budziszewski's work on natural law, I gave a talk on the moral argument for God's existence during that first semester of Truth Bucket.

The comedian Jim Gaffigan does a bit in which he asks, "Who here has read a book that changed your life?" After a moment of silence, he says, "Yeah, me neither." I love Jim, but this joke makes me a little sad. Since I began college, my life has consisted of reading one life-changing book after another. One of the first books in this category was Professor Budziszewski's *What We Can't Not Know*. It transformed the way I understood morality, psychology, and myself. My respect for Budzi (as we affectionately called him) only increased when he was generous enough to respond to the questions we e-mailed him. So, when I heard the news that he had become Catholic, I was concerned.

At the time, Catholicism was not even on my radar as an option. I grew up in a small Dutch town and wasn't aware that I knew any Catholics. I didn't have any animosity toward Catholics; they were just "other" (we visited a Catholic church on a school field trip to unfamiliar places of worship). And reading Norman Geisler, the cofounder of Southern Evangelical Seminary, had reinforced that Catholicism wasn't an option. Although he affirmed that Catholics got a lot right, Geisler gave the impression that Catholicism was obviously wrong on the key disagreements between Catholics and Protestants. But, because I respected Budziszewski, I went straight to the source instead of just wondering why such an exemplar of intelligence and wisdom would convert. I e-mailed him with brashness that is painful to recollect and said something like, "I always thought it was more reasonable not to be Catholic than to be Catholic. So why did you convert?" Budziszewski answered my e-mail. He explained that the issues were many and complex, better suited to discussion than e-mail; so I called him, and he told me some of his story, answered some of my questions, and responded to objections I hadn't even thought of. After that conversation, the Catholic question became something I had to take seriously.

We had started Truth Bucket, and we were in over our heads. Through the ministry we attended, we got to know an Iowa State and SES alum who was working on his PhD in philosophy. We had met him at a philosophy conference in our freshmen year, and our friendship and mentorship were solidified over the next couple of years as he guided us. He helped instill in us an ideal: to follow the truth wherever it leads (he thought Truth Bucket should have been called Truth Seekers). So, although we were not always charitable toward other points of view during those early years, we did have a noble goal. When the Catholic question arose, then, my habitual desire to pursue the truth wherever it led kept me from completely tossing the question aside.

It was not just philosophy in general that we were studying either. The apologist we read most was Norman Geisler, who was deeply influenced by the thirteenth-century Catholic theologian Saint Thomas Aquinas. Through Geisler, we became Thomists; that is, we took Aquinas as a philosophical guide. This meant that I had to respect Aquinas as a thinker, which required me at least to try to give his theology a fair hearing.

The light coming in was not exclusively intellectual light, though; I also made my first Catholic friends as an undergrad. One—Jeff— was someone I had known in high school. Jeff also made his faith his own in college, and I was lucky enough to be alongside him as he did; so my first experience with a Catholic was someone living his faith. About a decade later, I got to see Jeff ordained and celebrate his first Mass. The other Catholic I got to know was a Dominican sister who wrote a textbook on Aristotelian logic. I had written to her for help, and she wrote back explaining that I did not understand logic, which was true, and told me to stay close to Jesus. Sister Mary Michael Spangler and I continued writing, and she helped me a great deal in learning about logic and Aquinas. More importantly, her devotion was apparent, if implicit. I actually visited her convent, Saint Mary of the Springs in Columbus, Ohio, on the way to an SES apologetics conference during the year I took off after college.

During this time, one of the four Bucketeers (which we never called ourselves) moved away and started reading a lot of Catholic theology and spirituality. Whenever he visited us, we would have long discussions about what he had been reading, and the Catholic question would always get a little more serious. This culminated in an infamous conversation with my girlfriend—now my wife— Andrea. It was clear that our relationship was heading for marriage, so I thought she deserved to be warned that there was a real chance I would become Catholic. She cried. But she stuck around.

I took a year off after college to wait for Andrea to graduate but continued studying philosophy and theology. I also led a Bible study for some high schoolers, read Alasdair MacIntyre's *After Virtue* (which I will return to later), and worked full-time doing social work and then customer service. The drift toward Catholicism continued without any major developments. One major life event did occur, though: marriage. Two weeks after our wedding, Andrea and I were on our way to Charlotte, North Carolina, for me to start at SES and for Andrea to start work as a graphic designer.

Southern Evangelical Seminary

The transition into life in Charlotte was smooth. We had good friends at the seminary, my best friend's parents lived in town, and Andrea worked with great people. We attended Southern Evangelical Church, the church attached to the seminary. Norman Geisler was the head pastor of the church, as well president of the seminary. We had a great social life, and I enjoyed school.

Through my coursework at SES, I changed my mind on issues centrally related to the Catholic question. First, I wrote a paper on the Catholic view of justification and grace for a systematic theology class on sin and salvation. Although I focused on Aquinas' account, I saw that it was clearly of a piece with the Council of Trent and the *Catechism of the Catholic Church*. I learned a lot. I learned that Aquinas clearly teaches that every step of salvation—justification, sanctification, and glorification in my Protestant division—is accomplished by grace. I learned that apart from grace—and the entire Catholic tradition is very clear on this doctrine—man can do nothing pleasing to God.[6] Justification is by grace, but I was convinced that it involves a real change in the person justified. Aquinas argues that justice involves a kind of equality between persons. Yet, we have sinned. So, through the infusion of grace that is justification, we are reborn friends of God. Justification changes a core part of our identity—from enemies of God to friends of God—and thus a core part of our being. Studying Aquinas' theological and philosophical account suddenly illuminated scriptural passages about being reborn and being a new creation. Because he loves us, God, by grace—Aquinas and the Catholic Church argue—does not just declare us righteous but *makes* us righteous.

I concluded the paper with the following:

> Roman Catholicism is one of the major traditions within Christianity, and many aspects of their views concerning grace and justification trace back at least to Augustine. Understanding this view has at least three practical benefits. First, it helps me understand what our brothers and sisters in the Catholic tradition think, which helps me better understand and relate to them. Second, it gives me another historical Christian interpretation of Scripture to consider as I read and try to understand God's Word. Third, the Catholic claim is an important truth claim that must be seriously considered by every Christian. It cannot be considered without being understood. To reject or refute it before understanding it is to decide the truth instead of attempting to discover it. This paper has been my first step in understanding the Catholic claims regarding justification.

[6] Louis Bouyer shows this in *The Spirit and Forms of Protestantism*, chap. 2.

In fact, through my research for the paper, I had been convinced of an important Catholic position.

During my second semester at SES I took Systematic Theology 1: Prolegomena and Bible with Geisler. The canon of Scripture was one of the class topics, so we spent time examining why the Bible contains the books it does. Geisler critiqued the Catholic canon, which includes a somewhat different set of books, and argued for why the Protestant canon is exactly right. Although I took the arguments against Catholicism on Geisler's authority at the time, his positive case left me unsatisfied. I thought the arguments for the general reliability of the New Testament and the Resurrection of Jesus were good but realized I would need to examine the issue of the canon further.

Also during this time—I have no distinct memory of when or how this came about—I became convinced that Christ was really present at communion. I had not yet done a deep study of the history of the disagreement over Christ's real presence (only a survey of views in one of my systematic theology courses) or seen any of the texts from Church Fathers talking about the Eucharist.[7] Instead, I was convinced by John 6. Of course, there is debate about the meaning of this passage, but what else would Jesus need to say if he wanted to tell us something like the Catholic view of the real presence? I was convinced, but I was unaware of the historical connection of the Eucharistic celebration and apostolic authority,[8] its continuity with the Old Testament practices,[9] and the consequences of such a view (e.g., what do we do with the leftover bread and juice if it is truly Christ's Body and Blood, and can just anyone say the words and transform the elements into Christ?). So I thought the juice and bread at my Presbyterian church were really becoming the Blood and Body of Christ during communion.

At this point, we had left Southern Evangelical Church (which devastatingly imploded due to an internal power struggle and never recovered) and were attending Lake Forest Church, north of

---

[7] Tim A. Troutman, "The Church Fathers on Transubstantiation", Called to Communion, December 13, 2010, http://www.calledtocommunion.com/2010/12/church-fathers-on-transubstantiation/.

[8] John D. Zizioulas, *Eucharist, Bishop, Church: The Unity of the Church in the Divine Eucharist and the Bishop during the First Three Centuries*, translated by Elizabeth Theokritoff (Brookline, Mass.: Holy Cross Orthodox Press, 2001).

[9] Brant Pitre, *Jesus and the Jewish Roots of the Eucharist* (New York: Doubleday, 2011).

Charlotte. The pastor at our new church was unapologetically orthodox but also incorporated the best parts of the emerging church
movement. So the church started observing Lent and even prayed
the Stations of the Cross. We participated in these ancient practices
because we trusted our pastor. But since they, like so many Catholic spiritual practices, are embodied—incarnational—practices that
incorporate one's whole being, they began influencing my understanding of sanctification. Catholic spirituality continued to draw me
in as my pursuit of sanctification became more tangible.

During my first year at SES, I found out about a summer seminar
at Princeton on Aquinas' view of natural law. I had been interested
in natural law ever since reading J. Budziszewski's *What We Can't
Not Know* as an undergraduate. Natural law theory is an account of
morality that explains what is good for man in terms of his nature
and how man "naturally" knows the basics about good and evil.[10]
C. S. Lewis talks about a kind of natural law theory when he discusses
the Tao in *The Abolition of Man*. Although I was intimidated by the
prospect of doing it on my own, I applied to the seminar and was
accepted. So, in the summer of 2008, I spent two wonderful weeks
studying natural law at Princeton. It was there that I made the con-
nections that became my gateway to Cambridge University, where
Andrea and I spent a year. But more on that later.

In addition to making some great friends and learning about natural law, I read Aquinas' treatise on happiness for the first time. I may
have skimmed through it before, but reading it for the seminar was
a life-changing experience. Morality, virtue, love, faith, emotions,
and happiness were all integrated into a cohesive view of life. God
made us to enjoy perfect happiness—that is, a state in which all of our
desires are fulfilled—through friendship with him. By God's grace,
we attain some measure of this happiness in this life through faith,
hope, love, and other virtues, such as temperance, courage, justice,
and prudence; through disciplines such as prayer and fasting; through
concrete means of grace in the sacraments; and through friendships
and contemplation. Yet, all of this is but a taste of what we will enjoy
when we see God face-to-face in the next life.

---

[10] For a good introduction to the history of natural law theory, see J. Budziszewski, *Written
on the Heart* (Downers Grove, Ill.: InterVarsity Press, 1997).

At least this is Aquinas' account, and I was taken with it. It offered a unity and intelligibility to my experience and beliefs that were satisfying, as things of great beauty and explanatory power are satisfying. And Aquinas' view is an articulation that was then deeply integrated into Catholic theology. Consider the first sentences of the *Catechism of the Catholic Church*:

> God, infinitely perfect and blessed in himself, in a plan of sheer goodness freely created man to make him share in his own blessed life. For this reason, at every time and in every place, God draws close to man. He calls man to seek him, to know him, to love him with all his strength. He calls together all men, scattered and divided by sin, into the unity of his family, the Church. (*CCC* 1)

Whether or not you are Catholic, that is a beautiful picture of reality.

The following year, I studied two thinkers who deeply affected my thinking: Gotthold Lessing and Alasdair MacIntyre. I heard about Lessing's "ugly ditch" for the first time while hanging out after a student event. Lessing concludes a brief essay arguing for a chasm between apologetic arguments and Christian faith, "That, then, is the ugly, broad ditch which I cannot get across, however often and however earnestly I have tried to make the leap."[11] Although Lessing conflates at least three ditches, he identifies one problem that hit home for me.[12] Even if arguments for the existence of God and Jesus' Resurrection succeed, probable arguments that Christianity is true are not sufficient to ground Christian faith. I had been trained to think that faith was bound up with inferences in such a way that the arguments were what secured the faith. Lessing's arguments showed me that faith requires more than just probable inference. Faith, unlike probabilistic inference, is an all-in kind of commitment—intellectual and volitional—that does more than track likelihoods.

At the same time, I was reading a book that surveyed the thought of Alasdair MacIntyre, one of the most important philosophers of the

---

[11] Gotthold Lessing, *Lessing's Theological Writings*, trans. Henry Chadwick (Stanford: Stanford University Press, 1956), 55.

[12] For an extensive treatment of the ditches, see Gordon E. Michalson Jr., *Lessing's "Ugly Ditch": A Study of Theology and History* (University Park, Pa.: Pennsylvania State University Press, 1985), and Matthew A. Benton, "The Modal Gap: The Objective Problem of Lessing's Ditch(es) and Kierkegaard's Subjective Reply", *Religious Studies* 42 (2006): 27–44.

last century. I had read his *After Virtue* during my year off, but the force of his project did not hit me until I read *Tradition, Rationality, and Virtue* by Thomas D'Andrea, my Cambridge professor. The relevant insight is that we are embodied, historical thinkers who come to problems with questions, concepts, and things we take for granted—all framed by where and when we live. We are not ahistorical angelic intellects that approach a question from the standpoint of pure reason. MacIntyre explains:

> A person is confronted by the claims of each of the traditions which we have considered as well as by those of other traditions. How is it rational to respond to them? The initial answer is: that will depend upon who you are and how you understand yourself. This is not the kind of answer we have been educated to expect in philosophy, but that is because our education in and about philosophy has presupposed what is not in fact true, that there are standards of rationality, adequate for the evaluation of rival answers to such questions, equally available, at least in principle, to all persons, whatever tradition they happen to find themselves in and whether or not they happen to inhabit any tradition.[13]

The upshot here is *not* any kind of relativism but a recognition of the fact that we are knowers and desirers partially formed by our setting. In other words, we bring ourselves to the table when we think about a question, and we need to reflect on what this means. MacIntyre forced me to confront my assumptions and consider whether I was justified in taking them for granted.

I began to examine what my Protestant tradition took for granted. One thing that helped me examine this question was the debate over the nature of justification that N. T. Wright's work was causing at the time. Wright offered a powerful biblical argument for a view of justification that was generally Protestant but incompatible with Luther's and Calvin's views.[14] The nature of the debate and its appeals to the authority of Luther and Calvin made me realize

---

[13] Alasdair MacIntyre, *Whose Justice? Which Rationality?* (Notre Dame, Ind.: Notre Dame Press, 1980), 393.

[14] N. T. Wright, *Justification: God's Plan and Paul's Vision* (Downers Grove, Ill.: IVP Academic, 2009).

how difficult it was to support adequately some of the doctrines I took for granted from Scripture alone. Even central doctrines such as the creedal accounts of the Trinity and the Incarnation are under-determined by Scripture.[15] So I realized that a certain Evangelical-Protestant tradition had informed my reading of the Bible; I was often reading my theology into Scripture as much as getting it out of Scripture. Once I returned from Cambridge, this realization turned into a serious problem.

Cambridge

Through a series of very fortunate events, I was able to study at the University of Cambridge as a visiting scholar during the academic year of 2009 to 2010. I was part of a small group studying Aqui-nas' *Summa Theologiae*. The *Summa* is a massive work, and people rarely have the luxury of reading it from cover to cover, so we were very lucky to have the opportunity. Following the brilliant student of Aquinas, Étienne Gilson, we began with the treatise on faith, which is over halfway into the *Summa*. Here our professor, Thomas D'Andrea, stressed that, for Aquinas, faith is not an inference. On the human side, faith is assent, through an act of trust, to what God reveals. On the divine side, faith is an infused light by which we see the truth of what God reveals. Faith is not just a belief proportioned to the evidence, like so many of our other beliefs, but an acceptance of certain truths because God has told them to us. It is a participa-tion in God's knowledge. Pope Francis' recent encyclical *Lumen Fidei* (The Light of Faith) captures some of the aspects of faith that reading Aquinas opened up to us:

> In faith, Christ is not simply the one in whom we believe, the supreme manifestation of God's love; he is also the one with whom we are united precisely in order to believe. Faith does not merely gaze at

---

[15] We see evidence for this when Bible-believing Evangelical scholars reject aspects of the creed. For example, William Lane Craig rejects aspects of the Nicene Creed. William Lane Craig, "Is God the Father Causally Prior to the Son?", Reasonable Faith with Wil-liam Lane Craig, October 22, 2007, accessed May 28, 2015, http://www.reasonablefaith.org /is-god-the-father-causally-prior-to-the-son.

Jesus, but sees things as Jesus himself sees them, with his own eyes: it is a participation in his way of seeing. In many areas in our lives we trust others who know more than we do. We trust the architect who builds our home, the pharmacist who gives us medicine for healing, the lawyer who defends us in court. We also need someone trustworthy and knowledgeable where God is concerned. Jesus, the Son of God, is the one who makes God known to us (cf. Jn 1:18). Christ's life, his way of knowing the Father and living in complete and constant relationship with him, opens up new and inviting vistas for human experience. Saint John brings out the importance of a personal relationship with Jesus for our faith by using various forms of the verb "to believe". In addition to "believing that" what Jesus tells us is true, John also speaks of "believing" Jesus and "believing in" Jesus. We "believe" Jesus when we accept his word, his testimony, because he is truthful. We "believe in" Jesus when we personally welcome him into our lives and journey towards him, clinging to him in love and following in his footsteps along the way. (chap. 1, no. 18)

This understanding of faith spoke directly to the problems MacIntyre and Lessing had introduced. Although I still needed Newman's account of natural reasoning (which I briefly explained in my opening lines) to understand this process better, things were starting to make sense.

The *Summa* Group was about evenly divided between Catholics and Protestants. So the first few months involved a lot of Catholic-Protestant dialogue, discussion, and debate. Through this debate, some objections were answered and some questions were clarified. One argument our professor gave especially resonated with me. After noting the passages in Paul and the Gospels that stress the unity of the church, he explained that it only made sense that God would institute some mechanism to provide the desired unity. The argument can be spelled out—What kind of unity? Why is there no unity? What counts as a mechanism?—but the point is that Catholicism provides a mechanism for the kind of unity the Church needs: at the very least, doctrinal unity regarding the essentials of faith and a canon of Scripture. I had read Protestant accounts of the canon and knew they were not promising. Now I began to realize that the prospects for a good Protestant account of a standard of orthodoxy were not good either. But this problem did not become acute until we returned to SES.

We attended a High Church Anglican parish that year at Cambridge. Although we were originally drawn in by the beauty of the liturgy, the liturgical rhythm of life and the Eucharistic heart of the Mass changed us. It became clearer and clearer that we were participating in something bigger, something we did not make. It is hard to overestimate the effect that year had on me. I have given examples of a couple of the larger rays of light and how they moved inward, but we had hundreds of conversations about things Catholic, directly or indirectly. Regarding some objections and questions, I can remember where I was standing when a shift occurred; regarding others, I only realized that something had changed. In any case, we returned to Charlotte with the intention of attending a Catholic church while I finished at SES and applied for PhD programs. We had no concrete plans to convert, but it was clear that we were moving in that direction.

Back at SES

When I returned to SES, a dilemma crystallized for me. There is some standard for orthodoxy—right belief—in Christianity; i.e., there are some doctrines that are heresies. Yet, I had been convinced that creedal doctrines of the Trinity and the Incarnation, which are the standard examples of orthodox doctrines, ruled out certain other doctrines about the Godhead and the Incarnation, e.g., modalism and Arianism. But what was the standard by which we divided orthodox from heretical? There were only two plausible answers: sola scriptura (only Scripture) and Tradition.

The first is the Protestant answer: heresies are those doctrines that are not consistent with the essence of biblical teaching, or, in a word, sola scriptura. The problem, I realized, is that sola scriptura does not get us creedal Christianity. Although the creedal accounts of the Trinity and the Incarnation have a strong claim to be the best interpretation of Scripture, they are still probabilistic interpretations. In other words, if we want creedal orthodoxy as a normative rule for what Christianity is, then the Protestant answer doesn't work. So, to retain creedal Christianity requires adopting an extrabiblical authority. Moreover, what determines whether a doctrine is essential to Christianity?

The same dilemma presents itself in relation to the canon. Evangelical Craig Allert concludes the following after his discussion of the canon in *A High View of Scripture?*:

> I am not claiming that we should have no confidence in the canon we have, but rather that we should be aware of how we received the canon we acknowledge as authoritative. My point here is that a knowledge of the formation of the New Testament canon has implications for the way Evangelicals have understood the nature and function of the Bible in our own traditions. No matter how one looks at the history, it is difficult to maintain that the church had a closed New Testament canon for the first four hundred years of its existence. This means that an appeal to the "Bible" as the early church's sole rule for faith and life is anachronistic.
>
> Further, we need to recognize the manner in which the various documents found their way into the New Testament canon. The assertion that these documents forced their way into the canon by virtue of their unique inspiration has little historical support. In our desire to avoid the corrupting influence of tradition, we have often missed the fact that the very Bible we claim to accept as our only guide is itself a product of the very tradition we avoid. I will not mince words here because no serious study of the formation of the New Testament canon can avoid the fact that the church had a great deal to do with this formation. The Bible is the church's book, and as many of the fathers show, the church has the responsibility to properly interpret the Bible because this same church has formed it....
>
> The Christian faith did not grow in response to a book but as a response to God's interaction with the community of faith. The Bible must be viewed as a product of the community because traditions of the community provide the context in which Scripture was produced.[16]

So, we are stuck trusting the church. And if we already trust the early Church to formulate the canon we take as normative, by what principled reason do we distrust the Church on so much else: her nature as an authoritative teacher, that grace is sacramental, that justification is intrinsic, et cetera? My inconsistent trust in the Church

---

[16] Craig Allert, *A High View of Scripture? The Authority of the Bible and the Formation of the New Testament Canon* (Grand Rapids: Baker Academic, 2007), 145.

became apparent to me. Newman makes this point regarding the balancing act the Church performed by clarifying the basic doctrines of trinitarian and incarnational orthodoxy:

> The series of ecclesiastical decisions, in which its progress was ever and anon signified, alternate between the one and the other side of the theological dogma especially in question, as if fashioning it into shape by opposite strokes. The controversy began in Apollinaris, who confused or denied the Two Natures in Christ, and was condemned by Pope Damasus. A reaction followed, and Theodore of Mopsuestia suggested by his teaching the doctrine of Two Persons. After Nestorius had brought that heresy into public view, and had incurred in consequence the anathema of the Third Ecumenical Council, the current of controversy again shifted its direction; for Eutyches appeared, maintained the One Nature, and was condemned at Chalcedon. Something however was still wanting to the overthrow of the Nestorian doctrine of Two Persons, and the Fifth Council was formally directed against the writings of Theodore and his party. Then followed the Monothelite heresy, which was a revival of the Eutychian or Monophysite, and was condemned in the Sixth. Lastly, Nestorianism once more showed itself in the Adoptionists of Spain, and gave occasion to the great Council of Frankfort. Any one false step would have thrown the whole theory of the doctrine into irretrievable confusion; but it was as if some one individual and perspicacious intellect, to speak humanly, ruled the theological discussion from first to last. That in the long course of centuries, and in spite of the failure, in points of detail, of the most gifted Fathers and Saints, the Church thus wrought out the one and only consistent theory which can be taken on the great doctrine in dispute, proves how clear, simple, and exact her vision of that doctrine was. But it proves more than this. Is it not utterly incredible, that with this thorough comprehension of so great a mystery, as far as the human mind can know it, she should be at that very time in the commission of the grossest errors in religious worship, and should be hiding the God and Mediator, whose Incarnation she contemplated with so clear an intellect, behind a crowd of idols?[17]

I had never considered Newman's point because I had never *really* studied Church history. I thought the creeds were just clear summaries

---

[17]John Henry Newman, *An Essay on the Development of Doctrine*, 2, 12, 4; emphasis added.

of the biblical teaching. Newman here shows that there was a lot going on in the early Church and, especially since there wasn't a normative canon yet, the Church was doing much more than just summarizing.

During this time, one of my friends requested that I explain why I thought something more than the Bible was needed. I wrote the following short essay (with some minor edits) to him as an explanation, which was deeply influenced by my recent reading of Newman's *Essay on the Development of Doctrine*—one of the books that helped the above dilemma coalesce for me.

The Need for a Regula Fidei

Over the past year I have become increasingly convinced that a *regula fidei* (rule or standard of faith) other than the Bible is needed in Christianity. It has not been because of one argument or a distinct fact, but the intersection and confluence of many lines of thought. I will briefly explain six different, albeit related, lines of thought that manifest the need for a rule.

A note on what this is not trying to accomplish: I am not trying to *demonstrate* that there *must* be an extrabiblical regula fidei. Although I think the reasons I offer are supportive and persuasive, they are partial and not finally conclusive. I am also not concluding that Catholicism is true. Catholicism is, in my opinion, the most likely candidate for providing the needed standard.

Beginning with something that has been part of my experience of faith is the fact that I already accept an extrabiblical standard for what Christianity is. I have, and do, implicitly trust that the early creedal definitions of the Trinity and the Incarnation are normative. They tell us what Christianity is, and departures from three Persons in one essence and two natures in one Person are departures, in some way, from Christianity. Although I hold this, my Protestant principles cannot account for it. Granting that these formulations are the most reasonable account of what is taught in Scripture regarding Christ and God, there is undoubtedly room for other explanations. And this is why it took centuries to clarify the teaching. The topics are some of the most difficult possible, and putting together the scriptural claims into creedal formulations required great intelligence, patience, and conceptual ingenuity.

These are qualities possessed by few, with even fewer having the circumstances to use these gifts. If Scripture is all we have, then each person must study the contents of Scripture according to his own lights, determining what it is to be a Christian both theoretically and practically. Viewed historically, when the extent of the canon was not clearly defined (and was definitely not identical with the Protestant canon), many people were illiterate, and even if literate, access to the needed helps (lexicons, historical information, commentaries, et cetera) was minimal; this becomes an enormous hurdle that each Christian must face. Even today conservative Protestant scholars are reinterpreting fundamental doctrines like justification in light of recent historical discoveries (e.g., N.T. Wright). Without an extrabiblical standard, this flux will be interminable, leaving much fundamental doctrine tenuous. And we see this played out in the history of Protestant theology, where the motion is not toward agreement.

With this in mind, it begins to seem strange that we would be left without an extrabiblical regula fidei. Christ came and founded a Church, a communal life. We know from analogy with nature that when God creates something, he sustains it, especially something as important as his body. When we plant a vine, commonly used as a metaphor for the Church in Scripture, it is irresponsible not to provide the conditions for it to flourish. And to flourish, a vine needs to be both nurtured and protected.

A regula fidei protects the Church by pruning away the diseased parts and keeping the healthy parts away from disease. We are warned of wolves, false teachers, because they corrupt our minds and thereby our faith. Heresy can destroy and prevent faith, but heresy is often difficult to discern. Not every Christian, in fact very few Christians, are capable of avoiding heresy on their own through careful study of Scripture. Imagine reading the New Testament as a first-century Jew or pagan. Which of us would realize the creeds? We would end in error, which would hinder our relationship with the Truth. A rule prevents this. It protects us from dangerous falsehoods, from division from Truth itself.

The Church is nurtured by this extrabiblical standard because it allows us to progress to solid food. After rebuking Christians for being immature, only ready for spiritual milk instead of the solid food they should be eating, Paul says, "Therefore, let us leave behind the basic teaching about Christ and advance to maturity, without laying the foundation all over again: repentance from dead works and faith in God, instruction about baptisms and laying on of hands, resurrection of the dead and eternal judgment" (Heb 6:1–2). But some of these are what each Protestant must figure out. Without a rule beyond Scripture, we are stuck with spiritual milk. The regula fidei nurtures us, allowing us to move on to solid food.

Vines, like people, stories, and ideas, grow in a direction, toward something. As historical, each of these is forced to develop, make explicit what is implicit in itself, respond to criticism and attack, and define itself against others. Christianity is similarly historical. Its seed was planted by Christ, grown by the apostles, and, by necessity, continued to grow. What Christianity is has not changed, but its meaning needed to expand. Thus, creeds were authored at the councils, defining what Christianity must mean in response to the myriad of heresies it was facing. Without a standard outside of Scripture, this growth is stifled. Instead of a communal life, it is left in a kind of stasis. Growth is prevented because we cannot get beyond the seed.

Let us make one last approach to the issue before concluding. The unity of believers is clearly a priority of Christ and the apostles. As I have argued above, Protestantism does not provide the means for Christians to be united. We see this borne out in history, and it is not surprising from the emphasis on individual opinion and the lack of an extrabiblical guide. If there is not a regula fidei, we are left with the incongruity that God, who desires the unity of his Church, left that Church without a mechanism to make this unity possible. Scripture alone is insufficient, and most of us know this by experience.[18]

In short, the problem is that there is nothing outside of Scripture to tell us what Christianity is. What is essential to our faith? Something must be, but this most important question is left without a clear answer if we are without an extrabiblical regula fidei. So I was faced with a dilemma: either I give up the normativity of the creeds for faith, or I give up sola scriptura. I never really considered abandoning the creeds a live option—I did not want a choose-your-own-adventure

---

[18] Brandon Dahm, "The Need for a Regula Fidei" (2010).

theology. Sticking with the creeds showed me that I already trusted the Church.

Although I have talked about how my coursework related to some of these changes, I have said very little about how SES fits into this story. This is because it had very little to do with my conversion directly. Of course, the proclaimed ethos of defending the historical faith, taking opposing views seriously, and looking to Aquinas for answers pushed me to take the questions seriously, but SES was not a safe place to explore these questions. People who had challenged the status quo had had problems, and taking the Catholic question seriously was definitely a challenge to the status quo. It was also clear to us who were considering Orthodoxy or Catholicism that most of the faculty did not understand either tradition well enough to answer our questions.

Although we knew we were going to go to a Catholic church when we returned to Charlotte, we visited our old church a couple of times. Only then did we realize how much we had changed while away. The music was still very high quality, the preaching was excellent, and the people were friendly, but it just was not church to us anymore. Sunday worship was now embodied in a certain kind of liturgy and centered on the celebration of the Eucharist. Participating in the historical liturgy had transformed us, and we knew the liturgical rhythm of life was something we would need from then on.

We primarily attended the Catholic parish near our house during that year but also attended a Greek Orthodox church with some friends who had recently converted to Orthodoxy. Eastern Orthodoxy was on my radar as the other Christian tradition that could ground the canon and the rule of faith. We really enjoyed getting to know Greek Orthodox liturgy and are happy for our friends who did become Greek Orthodox, but we decided that Catholicism had the stronger historical and theological claim for reasons I will not go into here.[19] So we returned to the Catholic parish for the rest of the year.

[19] For a fair-minded history of Catholic-Orthodox relations that follows one issue from biblical times to the present, see A. Edward Siecienski, *The Filioque—History of a Doctrinal Controversy* (New York: Oxford University Press, 2010). A reliable entry point for understanding Eastern Orthodoxy is Timothy Ware's *The Orthodox Church* (New York: Penguin Books, 1993).

On the spiritual-practice side, something really important happened to me that year as well. Our Catholic friends invited us to go to adoration with them. Eucharistic adoration is a time when the host is exposed—is visible—so that people can come pray in its presence. Remember, the Eucharist is not just a symbol but is Christ himself. So think of adoration as going to spend time with Jesus. My first adoration was a powerful experience. I read a little from Thomas Merton's *No Man Is an Island* and spent some time in silence with Jesus. The following text from Saint John Paul II captures my experience of adoration:

> It is pleasant to spend time with him, to lie close to his breast like the Beloved Disciple (cf. Jn 13:25) and to feel the infinite love present in his heart. If in our time Christians must be distinguished above all by the "art of prayer," how can we not feel a renewed need to spend time in spiritual converse, in silent adoration, in heartfelt love before Christ present in the Most Holy Sacrament? How often, dear brother and sisters, have I experienced this, and drawn from it strength, consolation and support![20]

Again, actually participating in Catholic spirituality gave existential confirmation of Church teaching.

Between finishing up at SES, applying for PhD programs in philosophy, and the uncertainty of waiting to see whether and where I would get accepted, it was a stressful year. Despite all that, we had great times discussing with friends the nature of faith and conversion. Baylor was one of my top choices, and I was very happy to be accepted. Although our years in Charlotte had been happy ones and we were sad to say good-bye to so many good friends, we were ready to move on from SES to the next phase.

Baylor

We love Baylor and have been very happy here. A big part of that is the philosophy program. It is full of brilliant and supportive people

[20] Saint Pope John Paul II, encyclical letter *Ecclesia de Eucharista* (On the Eucharist in Its Relationship with the Church), April 17, 2003, no. 25.

who have made studying here a pleasure. But another big part of our life in Waco, Texas, is the Catholic community we were adopted into. On our first Sunday here, a colleague and his wife invited us to go to Mass with them and have lunch afterward. We quickly discovered that, a couple of years before, they had been through the same process we were going through. With them and some other friends from Baylor we started attending the Extraordinary Form of the liturgy. The Extraordinary Form is the Latin Mass that was celebrated by most parishes before the new Ordinary Form was put into place around 1970.[21] Although we began going for the community, we were drawn into the depth and contemplative nature of the Extraordinary Form.

I keep saying "we", but I haven't talked about my wife much. Although she had been along for the ride up to this point, she had mostly been forced to inquire through my inquiry. She would participate in discussions, meet with the priests, and go to Mass, but she just had not had the time, since she had a full-time graphic design job, to inquire on her own terms. Now, though, having moved to freelance, she had a lot more time to read. And read she did. When we arrived in Waco, she was at the point at which she did not really have any objections to Catholicism but had a lot of questions. So she set out to answer them.

I had been at a similar point for the last few months in Charlotte. I knew I would be leaving Protestantism and was pretty sure I would become Catholic. Yet, I had gaps in my understanding that I was uncomfortable with, and making this type of life change was intimidating. My first year at Baylor was a time for everything to settle in while I worked on school. I kept thinking, reading, and talking about Catholicism, and I kept getting closer. During my second semester, I realized that I already trusted the Catholic Church. When there was a question of doctrine or morals, I did not weigh the evidence on various sides and look for proof texts, but went to the *Catechism* first. At that point, I was still not convinced by the arguments for the Catholic side of one practical issue. I made a conscious decision to trust the Church, which was the first time I had

---

[21] See Pope Benedict XVI's *Summorum Pontificum* (July 2007), which explains why the Extraordinary Form is still celebrated.

done so on an issue with practical consequences that were not all desirable. It was freeing.

Although we had had many good Catholic friends at this point, we had never lived primarily in a Catholic community. In Cambridge we were too far from converting, and in Charlotte our friends were mostly either Protestant or in the process of becoming something else. At Baylor we found a Catholic community. I have already mentioned that fellow graduate students in the philosophy department took us to Mass our first week in town. During my second semester, we were invited into a SOCRG (the Super Official Catechism Reading Group—SOCRG), which met weekly around a meal, red wine, the *Catechism*, and a desire to live Catholic lives deeply and honestly. We also befriended a couple from Mass who became our confirmation sponsors. Although we were not yet Catholic, by being a part of these communities, we were living Catholicism from the inside in a new way we had not been able to. As I have mentioned, Catholic practice is incarnational. So, to understand Catholicism better, it was important for us to participate in Catholic life as much as non-Catholics could.

Sometime during Lent of my first year at Baylor, I realized I was ready to become Catholic. This did not happen through another inference, but through the realization that I trusted the Church and was ready to trust her completely. The interior light had formed. Before this, I had decided to wait for Andrea before converting because, judging by her trajectory, she was also on her way to becoming Catholic. It was definitely worth waiting to be able to enter the Church together, but I did not have to wait too long. Andrea decided she was ready in November. We talked to our priest, did catechesis with him, and became Catholic on February 10, 2013. We were received in the Extraordinary Form and had many friends and family and our wonderful sponsors there to celebrate with us. Maybe we are still in the newlywed phase, but being Catholic has been better than I even hoped. It is hard to explain the change in our mode of life. As my wife and I often say, it seems both barely and thoroughly different. Although Catholics have a reputation for living a life of rules and guilt, our experience (and the experience of many of our friends) has been that being Catholic is freeing. I do not have to build my own theology and way of life but can enter into the ordinary form of Catholic life and participate in the many devotions and practices that the Church encourages but does not require. The Church explains the clear boundaries of the Christian life and what is *required* and offers many other practices by which to become better friends of God. I do not have the space to expand on this, but the biggest surprise for me was how great confession is.

Although this has been fairly long, I have been able only to scratch the surface of my conversion. Converts are often written off through psychologizing by those who disagree with them. But if you have not carefully considered the reasons I have (Aquinas on grace, Newman on the development of doctrine, MacIntyre on traditions and rationality, the *Catechism* on the sacraments, Merton on the interior life, et cetera) and had similar experiences (gone to enough Masses to get past the strangeness and to understand what is going on, lived according to the Church calendar, prayed the Stations of the Cross or the Rosary, spent time with the Blessed Sacrament in adoration, et cetera), then be slow to think you are in a place to reject Catholicism. As Étienne Gilson says, "We must understand before we can criticize." One thing I have heard from many Evangelicals who think carefully about Catholicism—including those who do not convert—is that they had *many* misconceptions about what Catholicism actually teaches. These issues are not quick fixes that you can read an article on and be in the know; they are turns of mind that are deeply but subtly different. Thus, they require time to understand and get hold of. So please, take the time and effort to understand what Catholicism is and why so many of your fellow students, colleagues, and friends have come to believe it.

5

My Journey to the Catholic Faith

By Travis Johnson

Introduction

As with many who have followed a path similar to mine, my journey to the Catholic Church has been long, burdened with uncertainty and risk, speechlessly frustrating, and, among other things, lonely. I have upset my mother, argued with my sister, disappointed friends, and caused my boss to wonder from which planet I had descended. Despite some common feelings, and occasions of poor judgment and brash and awkward interactions, my journey home has been good. God has protected and provided for my family. Our Blessed Mother has unmistakably arranged and given grace in seemingly impossible situations. The prayers of Saint Joseph and Saint Thomas, among others, have undoubtedly strengthened me in my work, given me courage and wisdom in my weakness and worry, and sharpened me in mind and word.

Let me begin by stating clearly that I do not pretend to know all the answers or claim certainty beyond faith's prerogative. In many ways, my conversion to the Catholic faith rests upon that singular and indubitable fact, that it is faith—familiar to all yet enjoyed by few— that drew me and bound me to Christ and his Church. The story that follows goes back to the beginning, when I first encountered faith, and my ensuing struggle for certainty.

Foggy Beginnings

One of the troubles in telling my conversion story is being able to delineate its beginning. As an Evangelical, I always struggled, when asked, to identify when and where my faith actually began. Aside from occasions to "share my testimony" (a common exercise in Evangelical circles), it was not something I otherwise considered. My usual answer had something to do with my lying in bed one night, around the age of twelve, and saying a prayer. The content of this prayer was as vague as the event and in time would grow terrifyingly uncertain.

God only knows what arrested me in sleepless panic to consider the final destination of my immortal soul that night. The truth, however, is that I cannot recollect a day when I did not believe in the gospel, even before that hallowed night. Of course, what I believed developed and became more informed, but my faith, to whatever extent I understood it and possessed it, has always been an enduring memory. Along with my parents, my church played a significant role in the development and strengthening of my Christian faith. Whether it was my parents, my youth pastor, or my friends, I had tremendous influences throughout my teenage years who loved Christ, were devoted to the Scriptures, and genuinely desired for me to grow and flourish in the faith.

An Evangelical Upbringing

I was formed in the heyday of Evangelical Christianity. It was the '90s, and Christian music sounded like popular music; Christian T-shirts were fashionable, in abundance, and proudly bestowed and adorned at all youth-group events. Youth pastors looked and often behaved like their youth; and most importantly, the good-looking girls from the local high schools attended weekly Bible studies and youth-group retreats.

The church I attended was a nondenominational Bible church. From the high premium placed on evangelizing the lost to the practical guiding mantra that "it's not a religion but a relationship", the church was a prototypical Evangelical church, and the youth group was invariably and indisputably *on fire* for God. The fire, burning hot and bright from those summer youth-camp bonfires, which were fueled annually by passionate worshippers, zealous evangelists, and the abominable and guilt-inducing collections of secular CDs and smuggled-in packs of cigarettes, freed and set hearts on fire for the upcoming school year and the harvest that lay before them. In short, Christianity was cool, cathartic, and convincing.

Anecdotal descriptions aside, these experiences were of significant benefit to my formation. Along with the steadfast devotion and guidance of my parents, those youth ministers, friends, and events, and even *some* of the unoriginal and rebranded clichés of pop-Christian culture to the movement, had, by and large a positive influence on my faith. I was exposed to Scripture and prayer and was taught to cherish them deeply through study and practice. The church and lay leadership, to their credit, did not just exhort us to build friendships, serve others, and perform frequent and varied acts of Christian charity but provided us with opportunities for regular demonstrations of good works and community-enrichment efforts. Through mission and service trips, and through countless hours sharing common life with my friends and youth pastors, my devotion to Christ grew.

Searching for Certainty

Not being able to pinpoint my conversion to Christianity was something that began to trouble me during these formative years. I suppose that it was for this reason, in part, that I had multiple conversion or "rededication" experiences as a youth. Not only was the lying-in-bed-one-night story foggy, but it became less certain as I encountered new ideas and began to meet others and hear of their experiences of faith and conversion. These stories seemed to be substantiated with clear demarcations of conversion and were always dressed in the certainty of a future heavenly prize. What defined the origin and core meaning of my faith and what I was told to be the imperishable seed of "saving" faith were foggy memories and subjective experiences whose reality I had often doubted. I began to question not only the validity of my alleged conversion moment and my sincerity at the time but even whether the moment had occurred.

Outside my inner subjective feelings, beliefs, prayers, memories, and whatever inherited or learned proclivities I may have had was deafening silence. The most important decision in life was a decision made in quiet darkness. Aside from a level of authority and trust that I had determined to allow, there was no one standing outside my mind and feelings whose declarations were authoritative and whose words carried the weight of certainty. The verification of and surety of my faith depended, in large part, on me and my own spiritual energies and knowledge. I suppose it would be like getting married in a dark room. The person officiating might be a priest or a bum off the street, but you would not be sure and you would not know whether there were any guests to ask.

During this time, and as a public profession of my faith in Christ, I received the sacrament of baptism. I was taught to believe that baptism was nothing more than "an outward symbol of an inward reality". Although I was brought up to believe in the necessity of being baptized, this "necessity", I later discovered, was merely superficial, certainly had no objective power, and thus possessed no causal relationship between the baptism event and my salvation or life of faith. The theology of baptism would come to play a significant role in the early stages of my conversion to the Catholic faith. Thankfully God's grace is not bound by human ignorance. Regardless of what exactly transpired ontologically and spiritually that day, my baptism was, at the time, a watershed moment. For the first time, there were declarations and actions that were beyond me and to which I was submitting. There was concreteness and an audience to my profession of faith. Having silenced this interior doubt, I would eventually begin a journey that sought to silence all doubt of the Christian faith, at least my version of it.

Quest for Knowledge and the Road West

Despite having grown up in church and having spent a lot of time in Bible studies and at youth retreats, my knowledge of Christianity was shallow. I knew the general story of Scripture and was convinced that God loved me and wanted me to love others, and that was about it. Not bad, I suppose, but certainly deficient for someone whose faith in Christ was allegedly central to his life. With the encouragement of my parents, I decided to attend Ravencrest Chalet, a one-year Bible school in the mountains of Colorado. Or more accurately, I decided to attend the mountains of Colorado at a one-year Bible school. The choice was a no-brainer. I could flounder around in Northwest Arkansas, take community-college courses, and continue my job answering customer-service calls for Walmart, or I could live in the mountains of Colorado and study the Bible. Needless to say, I chose the mountains and Bible school over Walmart and college algebra.

My reasons for setting out on this solitary, western road were many. As I drove through Kansas, I remember feeling a rising sense of anticipation and excitement as I drew nearer to my mountaintop destination. This feeling was more than anticipation of the thought of seeing the Rockies slowly begin to rise in the sunset. It was a new sense of awareness and vision of the world that, I imagine, comes only as we experience those coming-of-age sort of moments. Those moments when our youth and all that we once were or considered important are momentarily forgotten as we gaze, perhaps for the first time, into that golden horizon of the future, which is bigger and more interesting than we once suspected.

As my horizon grew that year, so did my thirst for knowledge, for education, and, most importantly, for a greater understanding of my faith. That year of Bible school developed in me an earnest desire to attain an intellectual grasp of my faith, which had, by and large, been only an exercise in personal application. Up until that point, I figured, like many Evangelicals, that the Bible had been exclusively written for me and my life. I just had to read it, and then figure out how it applied to the current circumstances. I desired an understanding that could provide objectivity and surety that what I believed was capable of transcending worldly scrutiny and what-ever confidence I had in my spiritual energies and past memories and experiences. By the end of that year, I had set my trajectory on pursuing deeper theological study and formal training, which meant seminary. Of course, no such direction and passion comes without, at minimum, a curiosity in books. Although I had seen books before, was somewhat familiar with the concept, and had actually read one in high school, I had never given them much attention. My curiosity in these storehouses of knowledge, ideas, and creativity would grow that year and in the years to come. They would eventu-ally help to open my eyes to the glories of the Catholic faith as well as to the inherent problems with Protestantism.

Apologetics, Philosophy, and Confusion

Along the way I picked up an interest in Christian apologetics. The idea that one could provide intellectual arguments for the truth of Christianity appealed to my increasingly analytical mind and stubborn inclination for certainty. For this reason, along with my growing desire for theological training, I majored in philosophy in college. I had determined that studies in philosophy paired nicely with Christian apologetics and theology, and that spending three years encountering great minds and influential ideas would serve me well as I sought to engage and understand the greatest mind of all—the mind of God.

Despite the historical exposure and those maturing moments of faith, caused by intellectual nausea and spiritual anguish, my hopeful experience in philosophical study increasingly diminished and became disenchanting. If philosophy was attainment of the good life through the pursuit and love of wisdom, then I could hardly see how arguing the existence of the wall that I was banging my head against was related to or valuable to that end. Philosophy, as it was largely presented, seemed like nothing more than a mental exercise, intent only on solving riddles and logical conundrums, and thus, from my judgment, seemed altogether useless and was a project that I had no qualms about abandoning upon completion of my university studies and as I began to prepare for seminary.

Southern Evangelical Seminary

I enrolled in my first classes at Southern Evangelical Seminary in the fall of 2006, and it was a sweet breath of fresh air. My professors were smart, witty, and wise, and above all we shared a common faith and purpose. They spoke of truth and goodness as if they were real things, capable of being discovered, understood, and enjoyed. Most of my professors saw themselves as guides to life and the Christian faith, presenting deep philosophical and theological insights and questions whose answers were of paramount importance and consequence to all of life. Thankfully, these professors were never content merely to present ideas without providing the necessary tools for proper reflection and understanding. Many of them taught students to ask questions, pursue fair and honest reflection, uncover assumptions, and think soundly about faith and reality. Above all, they presented Jesus Christ as the singular and solid manifestation in which all truth and goodness was grounded.

Most of my time at SES was untroubled by questions of certitude of faith. Reason was on prominent display. No questions of theology or morals were left untouched by the power of apologetics and rational demonstration. SES' stated version of Evangelical Christianity was right, and others were wrong, and there were, at minimum, three points to support the former and three points to argue against the latter. To be sure, there were mysteries of the faith acknowledged, yet most of faith's contents were indubitable and rationally discoverable, so long as one had the proper metaphysic and employed the correct interpretation of Scripture. I slowly began to question some of these assumptions and would eventually become overburdened by the fact that it was ultimately up to me to determine what Christian faith was. Before these occurrences, there were things going on in the background that slowly began to shift my attention to the Catholic Church.

Evangelicals Evangelizing for the Church

Growing up in the Protestant South,[1] I encountered very few Catholics and thus knew very little about the Catholic faith. I knew that Catholicism was a variation of Christianity that held beliefs different from those of us real (i.e., Evangelical) Christians and that many of its followers might not be "saved" and should therefore be evangelized just as ferociously as the neighbor across the street. In fact, the only theological encounter that I had had with a Catholic dealt with prayers to the saints. A teenage Catholic girl, whom I met on a mission trip, was defending the notion to a gang of us Evangelicals. I found the idea biblically tenuous and uninteresting. Saints were made

---

[1] A phrase popularized by Flannery O'Connor, "The Catholic Novelist in the Protestant South", in *Mystery and Manners: Occasional Prose*, eds. Sally and Robert Fitgerald (New York: Farrar, Straus, and Giroux, 1969), 191–209.

only in heaven and praying to someone other than God seemed idol-atrous. Of course, I was wrong, and ironically, this Catholic belief has featured prominently in my daily Catholic life. That the bodily death of a saintly man or woman does not restrict our communion and the saint's prayers on my behalf speaks volumes of the eternal reality and transcendence of the Communion of Saints. Evangelicals, although they pray fervently for each other here on Earth, allow death to ter-minate communion and friendship and have unknowingly built walls around Earth so as to prevent heaven's saints from getting in to con-tinue their offering of prayers on our behalf. But I digress.

When I entered SES, Catholicism was therefore neither friend nor foe. For this reason, the introduction and indoctrination into Catho-lic thinkers and theologians was of little consequence when I arrived. Saint Thomas Aquinas, for example, was a name with which I was familiar but with which I had had very little interaction prior to SES. As odd as it sounds, his thinking would emerge as the dominant phil-osophical and theological approach of several SES professors at the time. Of course, by marrying oneself to Saint Thomas, one inevitably gets the whole family, which includes thinkers and writers such as Flannery O'Connor, G. K. Chesterton, Étienne Gilson, Jacques Mar-itain, Peter Kreeft, Eleonore Stump, Réginald Garrigou-LaGrange, and many, many others. My interaction with Catholic thinkers and writers was unlike anything I had experienced among my Protestant brethren. These Catholics wrote deeply and profoundly about reality, God, Scripture, and Christian virtue and living, and their writings seemed always to be accompanied by a sober, clearheaded, and mag-nanimous devotion to Jesus Christ and his Church. Reading these Thomistic thinkers and Catholic scholars placed me in an unfamiliar yet pleasant world of Catholic thought and tradition whose story did not begin in protest. Yet, despite this near-unanimous fervency for Catholic categories and thought among SES professors and students, there was an assumption that, regarding our Evangelical traditions and beliefs and these Catholic thinkers, we could have our cake and eat it too.

This notion that we could take what we liked of Saint Thomas' theology and discard the parts that were upsetting to our Protes-tant tastes grew increasingly suspicious during my time at SES. It seemed to me, at least intuitively, that this collective parsing of Saint

Thomas was unfair, and perhaps even dishonest. To my knowledge, no one ever pointed out that Saint Thomas penned the *Summa Theologiae*, his seminal work, in dedication to the Blessed Virgin Mary, Immaculate Seat of Wisdom, and submitted fully to the authority of the Roman Catholic Church and her teachings. How, I began to wonder, could this giant of Christendom and his great host of intellectual devotees be right about so many things—often providing the key to unlocking all philosophical and theological conundrums and difficulties—yet be fundamentally wrong about the most important things, such as the source of Christian authority and the nature of salvation? This oddity of SES would lead me to consider other oddities that went to the very heart of the Protestant movement.

To its credit, SES not only engendered in students an ardent passion for clear and orderly thinking about matters of Christian faith and scholarship, but they also rightly elevated Saint Thomas Aquinas, Church history,[2] and the Bible, encouraging students to approach them with grave seriousness and to let unmitigated truth be the guide to all their actions and commitments. So, when I came face-to-face with serious questions regarding the cogency of my Evangelical Protestant faith, I sought to pursue those questions with honest reflection and with great concern never to allow my projects to compromise Sacred Scripture and never to allow the voices of Church history to be drowned out by twenty-first-century Evangelical Protestant assumptions and traditions. This pursuit I began near the end of my time at Southern Evangelical Seminary.

Sola Scriptura and the Consequence of Disunity

My pursuit of the cogency of Protestantism and conversion to the Catholic faith was a three-year journey. It was, I suppose, not unlike other conversion experiences. It did not come on the heels of a conclusion reached through theological inquiry and studies of Church

---

[2] To provide historical support for his theological positions, Norman Geisler frequently cites Church Fathers and theologians within his four-volume theology book, which was the primary text used for systematic-theology courses at SES. This strategy seems to imply the importance of Church history as an arbiter of present beliefs. See Norman L. Geisler, *Systematic Theology*, 4 vols. (Minneapolis: Bethany House, 2005).

history alone. Nor did I arrive at Rome through a moment of existential crisis that pushed me out the door and sent me rushing to find the nearest priest. I recall no event or argument, no epiphanies, no direct answers from heaven, and no manifestations that removed all doubt and provided certainty of the Church's claims. My conversion was, by and large, a very normal, day-by-day encounter with questions, conversations, experiences, studies, and moments of prayerful pleadings for truth. While much of the intellectual wrestling found its form in reading authors who posed serious questions to Protestant assumptions, beliefs, and traditions, a fair amount of this wrestling was experienced and observed within the various communities that I was a part of during those years. Intellectual conundrums began to shift into real theological problems, whose disastrous consequences I would soon begin to notice in my church, myself, and within the Evangelical culture at large.

What began to act as a splinter in my mind was the indisputable disunity of Christians, which is no more evident than within the denominational system of the Protestant tradition. It became apparent to me that unity—one of the four distinctive marks of the Church and that for which Jesus prays—is not only absent within Protestantism but is fundamentally impossible to achieve due to the Protestant belief in sola scriptura. This intellectual puzzle of Christian unity and sola scriptura would be marked by events and discoveries that began to supply color and a live context to my thoughts, resulting in what I saw as serious problems in Christianity and the meaning and objectivity of my faith.

As I considered Christian unity and the source of Christian authority, I began to notice similarities between Evangelical churches and the American marketplace. It appeared to me that choosing a church was, for all intents and purposes, simply a matter of taste and personal preference. Protestant churches and the seemingly endless promotion of differences and offerings to interested parties and guests appeared to have more in common with the cereal aisle at the local grocery store than with that unified and Mystical Body established by Jesus Christ (Eph 4:4–5; Col 1:24). A theological commitment, an identification with a mission, the variety and offerings of church ministries and groups, the attraction to the personality and preaching abilities of the pastor, a preference for the style of music, comfortableness with the ambiance and physical layout, availability of coffee and pastries, a sense of shared social similarities and interests among parishioners, a vague and subjective appeal to individual needs uniquely being met, and many other factors were, it seemed, what drove people, including me, to choose which church to attend. It was a buyer's market, and churches seemed more engaged in passive, yet strategic competition rather than in unified purpose and worship of Jesus Christ.

The idea of belonging and being a part of my church community at the time, therefore, grew increasingly artificial. I belonged to the church so long as I felt as if they wanted me there and so long as I was benefiting from the relationship, which again, was based on my preferences and my beliefs and their meanings. The notion of "church", therefore, became confusing, unimpressive, and, aside from a cultural obligation, absolutely pointless for entering heaven's gates. I grew weary not only of my choice but of even having a choice, for it was not simply a matter of choosing a church, but a matter of continuing to choose that church week after week, month after month, and year after year. Every Sunday, I left judging the merits of the service, and thus the church, according to my own theological scruples and preferences. I slowly began to wonder if I was creating Christianity in my own image. My answer would soon be answered in a conversation about the Protestant-sanctioned practice of birth control.

I had recently been considering the nature and practice of birth control and had concluded that it seemed at best imprudent and at worst, and according to the majority of Christendom prior to the twentieth century, a wicked sin. A friend listened patiently while I opined reasons for my growing aversion to this practice. My friend's simple yet revealing response to me was that no one should be legalistic or too dogmatic about an issue such as birth control when there is no demonstrable biblical mandate against it. This response was perfectly sensible, given my friend's commitment to the authorial primacy of Sacred Scripture. Despite this common response, I could not help thinking how odd it was that something that was once universally condemned by the majority of Christendom could now be a matter resigned to personal conviction. What else, I began to wonder, has shifted from universal acceptance and belief to mere opinion? What is Protestant dogma? What is Christianity? What is faith? Above all, who decides? I realized that the ultimate and final answers to all these questions lay in one source: me. Due to sola scriptura, dogma is whatever is dogmatic for the individual, Christianity is whatever is deemed acceptable and believable by the individual, and faith is ultimately a submission to one's predetermined beliefs. This discovery showed me that the faith of my fathers and their fathers was not a faith that had been passed on and received, but rather a mere version of it. What the older generation believed as being inseparable from Christian belief, including matters of grave sin, now bore the reproachful labels of "being legalistic" or "too dogmatic". I could only conclude that it was, at least for now, the individual, modern science, and the ever-burgeoning pace and progress of twenty-first century life that bore the influence and final determination of the "faith which was once for all delivered to the saints" (Jude 1:3). I had come to a place where I had not only lost meaning and objectivity, but also Christianity. If I were to retain my Christian faith and live it honestly and authentically, then I had no choice but to abandon my self-made religion and the meaning that I gave it.

By this time, I had abandoned all hope in Protestantism. To be sure, there were other areas familiar to and fundamental to Protestantism that I had discovered to be rationally implausible and incompatible with both Sacred Scripture and the Church Fathers. Some of these areas have been addressed in detail in the appendices. My attention began to shift away from Protestantism to Catholicism. As providence would have it, I moved within three blocks of a Catholic church during this time. Soon after, and on the sage advice of my father, I began to attend daily Mass. My father, a committed Evangelical and faithful man of God, knew that for my questions to be answered and a sense of God's direction to be heard, I needed to "go, and experience it". So I went, not as a distant observer, curious about rites and rituals, but as someone who, upon entering for the first time, sensed the presence of something deeply real and transcendent.

I attended Mass many more times after that. I also began meeting and talking with the parish priests. Their profundity and clarity of Catholic doctrine was matched only by their patience and grace as they sat hour upon hour listening to a near total stranger. I recall one conversation with Father David Miller, a priest at the local parish and someone whom I would eventually come to know as a friend. After listening to my fears regarding the possible consequences of my conversion, such as the loss of my job, a fractious relationship with my parents and other family members, and most of all, leading my own family down the wrong path, Father Miller reminded me of two things. He first spoke of God's love. He told me that God loved my wife and my children more than I ever could or imagine, and that whatever is chosen, even if in error, is incapable of quenching God's love. Secondly, he reminded me that the possibility of suffering and hardship should never be used as an excuse for disobedience, and that whatever path I chose, it must be chosen by compulsion in obedience to the truth. These were the prayers that carried me during that final year before my conversion. I prayed that God would protect my family. I prayed that God would stop me if I were moving in the wrong direction. Finally, I prayed for the courage to follow truth no matter its leading or its cost. By the following year, my journey was complete. Truth had called me home to the Roman Catholic Church.

Receiving Christ's Church and His Body

One year before my journey began, five years ago, a friend and I decided to go to a Catholic Easter Vigil Mass at Saint Patrick Cathedral in Charlotte, North Carolina. I suppose we went out of curiosity. After all, we were both studying in seminary and we were encouraged to be curious about, to investigate, and to seek understanding of things and ideas with which we were unfamiliar. So we went. I write we "went", but in reality we were drawn. Of the many Catholic churches in Charlotte—and several, at that time, would have been just as convenient for us to go to—the church we attended would play a significant part in our lives.

Three years later, on June 29, 2013, at Saint Patrick Cathedral, my friend and his wife would be received into full communion with the Catholic Church. Later that same day and just a few feet from where my friend and his wife had become Catholic, my infant daughter, through the sacrament of baptism, would become the first member of my family to become a member of Christ's visible and unified Church on Earth. On the feast of Christ the King, November 24, 2013, my wife and I would join my daughter as we were finally received into full communion with the Holy Roman

Catholic Church. And it was at Saint Patrick Cathedral that I finally received the meaning and objectivity of my faith: Christ himself. I received not a symbol or an idea or a promise but Christ's Body and Blood. It wasn't something that I had attained through reason, nor was it something that I had determined to be true on my own. It was the mystery of the Church and the mystery of the Christian faith. It was Christ himself, drawing me finally to the banquet of his Body and Blood and to a real faith—a faith that acknowledges and receives, *by faith*, what has been handed down through the Catholic Church, beginning with Peter and the apostles. It is a faith that does not first ask for my understanding or promise rational certainty. It is a faith that submits to Christ and to the authority of his Church, the Roman Catholic Church, no matter the cost.

6

Carefree College Student to Catholic Convert

By Michael Mason

Introduction

Anyone who has undergone a profound conversion will assuredly admit that the experience can be very unsettling. A religious conversion can be especially troubling, for it forces one to call into question the very foundations of one's existence. If calling into question one's philosophy of life is not difficult enough, religious conversions include social, emotional, political, and occasionally vocational repercussions that can be far-reaching. But as difficult as a conversion may be, I have been blessed to have undergone two in my life. Each conversion was united with a crisis of faith that forced me to reassess much of what I had come to believe was true. This is the story of how I passed from being a carefree college student to a committed Catholic.

Carefree College Student to Committed Christian

I was raised in a family that embraced the Christian faith. Though my parents believed that I should be given the opportunity to form my own opinion regarding the Christian faith, they frequently took my brother and me to the local Methodist church and encouraged us to attend confirmation class. Amid such a positive Christian witness, I eventually embraced the faith and was baptized and confirmed. Notwithstanding the general affinity I had for Christ and his message, I discontinued practicing my faith when I moved to a new town during my freshman year of high school. Though I retained many of the values instilled in me through confirmation, I chose to spend my time and energy living the life of a typical Midwestern kid. I was an honor-roll student who spent time with friends, played baseball and football, and did not give much thought to the perennial questions of man's existence. When it came time for me to choose a university to continue my studies, I decided to pass on the opportunity to continue playing football at a small private school and chose to expand my horizons at Ohio University.

When I arrived on campus in the fall of 2000, I was determined to enjoy all the trappings of college life. Though class and study were a priority, I chose to spend the majority of my time exploring the nightlife at one of the top party schools in the country. Initially, the party lifestyle fulfilled all my expectations; nevertheless, by my junior year, my life of decadence began to take its toll. During my junior year, the nights I spent out on the town were followed by days filled with surges of overwhelming anxiety. Unexpectedly, my heart would begin to pound; I would begin to feel as if I were choking and eventually would feel as if I would pass out. Though these attacks filled me with terror, I could not bring myself to tell any of my friends or family. After three months of experiencing these attacks on a daily basis, I arrived at the conclusion that I must be going crazy. Eventually, I decided that I had to see a doctor.

As I tentatively sat across from a psychiatrist one cold and dreary March morning, I was convinced that I had lost my mind. When the doctor asked what brought me to the clinic, I confessed that I was going crazy. To my utter astonishment, he informed me that that was certainly not the case. Considering the fact that we had just met, I asked him how he could be so confident. He informed me that crazy people do not know they are crazy. The fact that I thought I was crazy was the clearest evidence that I was not. After talking for a few minutes, he informed me that I was suffering from panic attacks and the primary cause of this anxiety was the amount of alcohol I was consuming. Effectively, my body was going into shock when I eventually descended from the high associated with drinking copious amounts of alcohol. The counselor taught me some strategies to alleviate my anxiety when a panic attack ensued, offered to prescribe medication for me, and informed me that I would have to stop drinking so much. I declined to take medication, and though I knew that I should stop abusing alcohol, I was unwilling to do so. Hence, I decided to continue in my intemperate lifestyle and embrace the inevitable consequences. Fortunately, God had already begun orchestrating my deliverance from this licentiousness.

During my sophomore year, I was befriended by a girl named Korinne, who was involved in Campus Crusade for Christ. Though she and I did not share the same convictions, we developed a strong friendship. What impressed me the most about Korinne was her fun-loving disposition, her sense of purpose, and the joy she exuded. We regularly talked about the meaning of life, the existence of God, and the gospel. Though I believed that I was having more fun than Korinne, in time I began to realize that she was far happier than the people I met at parties and in bars. Though the rewards of the party lifestyle were instantaneous and powerful, eventually the life of decadence led only to heartbreak and despair. By the end of 2003, my anxiety attacks, my dissatisfaction with the party scene, and the overall meaninglessness of my life began to take their toll, and I realized that I needed a change. One cold, clear January morning in 2004, I sat in my room and read the parable of the sower in Matthew 13:1–23. As I sat and read this familiar passage, I was reminded that my proverbial soil was full of rocks and thorns. Though I always received the Word of God with joy, the worries and trappings of this life choked what God was trying to grow in my life. Notwithstanding my usual fatalistic reading of this passage, that morning a new possibility occurred to me. What if I was not destined ultimately to reject the Word of God time and time again? If I tilled the soil of my heart, would the seed of God's Word grow and produce fruit? The Scriptures undeniably taught that God loved me and wanted me to know and love him in return. Other than myself, what could possibly keep me from him? At that moment, I committed myself to seeking God with my whole heart, mind, and strength, and if he was real, he would certainly reward my obedience. Later that day, I called Korinne and asked her to help me find a good Bible study.

From that point forward, I began to attend Campus Crusade for Christ meetings and Bible studies regularly, and I even attended a mission trip to Panama City Beach, Florida, during spring break. Gradually, I began to overcome many of my bad habits, and eventually the fruits of conversion began to emerge. Furthermore, for the first time in my life, I was confronted by young people who had purpose, fulfillment, and joy. The life and witness of these young people instilled in me a desire to have a personal relationship with Jesus Christ and to share the Good News with the world. I not only made incredible friends, but I also met my wife during that time. I found her to be beautiful, smart, fun, and completely committed to living her life in service of our Lord. Our relationship progressed quickly, and we both knew that we wanted to spend the rest of our lives using the tools we learned through Campus Crusade to reach out to the fallen world around us.

Filled with the zeal of a new convert, I set out to evangelize the world. I shared my newfound faith with family, friends, and strangers. The vast majority of the people I talked with were cordial, and their responses to my message ranged from intrigued to dismissive. However, I met some people who were very antagonistic to the faith, and they raised objections to the Christian faith that had not previously occurred to me. These people questioned the very tenets of Christianity, including the existence of God, the historicity of the Bible, and the Resurrection of Christ. Coinciding with these intellectual challenges was a spiritual trial: six months after my conversion, the initial thrill of it began to wane, and the challenge of living the Christian life become evident. It also became acutely apparent to me that if the Christian faith were not true, I would not be able to continue in it. During this budding crisis of faith, I graduated from college, took a position teaching eighth-grade language arts in Charlotte, North Carolina, and got married.

Our new life in Charlotte was a happy one, though various objections and doubts continued to plague my mind. One night, while reading a book by Norman Geisler, I discovered that he taught at an Evangelical seminary in Charlotte where one could get a master's degree in Christian apologetics. I subsequently applied to Southern Evangelical Seminary and was accepted. My studies commenced in the summer of 2006, and thus began one of the best seasons of my life. I had the profound blessing to study philosophy and theology with professors and students who loved God, were passionate about Christ's Great Commission to preach the gospel to the world (see Mt 28:18–20), and were not afraid to confront the most difficult questions of our time. The professors and students at Southern Evangelical Seminary encouraged me to think deeply and carefully about the Christian faith and instilled in me the value of study and prayer. They taught me to take the Bible seriously, to defend the historical Christian faith, and to read Saint Thomas Aquinas. Though I could not foresee it at the time, these invaluable lessons would eventually lead me to the second major conversion of my life.

My conversion to Christianity in college and my subsequent crisis of faith had led me to study philosophy and theology at Southern Evangelical Seminary. The relevant peace of mind that ensued was a welcome respite from the confusion and doubt that had plagued my mind during the latter years of my undergraduate studies. I learned that there were compelling arguments for God's existence and that the objections that critics raised against the possibility of miracles, the Resurrection of Christ, and the reliability of the Bible quickly lost all rhetorical force when one understood the philosophical assumptions on which they were built. However, I also began to notice troublesome issues in the theology and apologetics that I was being taught. Initially, I attributed them to my lack of theological vision, but the longer I studied at Southern Evangelical Seminary, the more I realized that the Evangelical theology I was being taught was susceptible to some disastrous objections.

Energized Evangelical to Catholic Convert

While studying at Southern Evangelical Seminary, I was encouraged to ask difficult questions, demand cogent answers, and look to the best and brightest Christian thinkers in theology and philosophy for aid. I began to gravitate to various Catholic authors, including Étienne Gilson; Jacques Maritain; Father Réginald Garrigou-Lagrange, O.P.; Father Brian Davies, O.P.; Eleonore Stump; Peter Kreeft; Father James Schall, S.J.; G. K. Chesterton; and Josef Pieper, for I began to see that these brilliant men and women were capable of answering man's most pressing questions. Though one would assume that my Evangelical professors would have warned against reading such authors, I was actually encouraged to read them. What struck me about their work was the rigor of their argumentation, the charitable way they engaged their interlocutors, and the humility and likeness to Christ that permeated their material. Though I was encouraged to separate the Evangelical wheat from the Catholic chaff in their work, slowly but surely I began to see that the Catholic faith of these authors did not equate to the straw-man view of Catholicism that the Evangelical world had presented to me. These authors were committed Christians who loved God, were prayerful and holy, and had an Evangelical zeal that rivaled their Protestant counterparts.

Coinciding with my discovery of the richness of contemporary Catholic theology and philosophy was an equally powerful impression of a negative sort. Though my time at Southern Evangelical Seminary was extremely fruitful both intellectually and spiritually, as my studies began to come to a close, I began to question seriously the tradition in which my walk with Christ had been nurtured.

Since my conversion to Christianity in 2004, I had been steadfast in my Evangelical faith. In 2010, I was finishing my degree at SES, was teaching theology and apologetics at an Evangelical high school, had just given two lectures at a prominent Evangelical apologetics conference, and was a member of a thriving Evangelical church. Everything that I desired when I entered seminary was coming to fruition, and my future looked very bright. But my soul was not at peace, for I began to be troubled by a variety of issues. It had become increasingly and tragically apparent that Evangelicalism was inextricably divided on a variety of issues that are essential to the gospel message. Evangelicals have no common, authoritative moral or spiritual theology, and they do not agree on the relation of faith and reason, the extent and nature of man's fallen state, justification, the atonement, salvation and works, the nature of baptism and communion, the nature and mission of the church, church leadership, or the role of the laity, to name but a few. Further, Evangelicals believe that it is the responsibility of the individual Christian to decide for himself the correct position regarding these topics. In fact, it is common to hear Evangelical leaders encourage the members of their congregation to read the Bible for themselves and decide what the Bible teaches on these and other subjects of monumental significance to the Christian life. Moreover, even highly educated, well-meaning, prayerful Evangelical professors, pastors, and leaders arrive at radically different conclusions on these topics. Though one may conclude that I would have merely abandoned Evangelicalism for a more reformed, confessional brand of Protestantism, I realized that those denominations have no advantage in this area, for they were divided over the most central questions of doctrine and morals as well. I shared my unease with my wife, and she was also deeply troubled by the veritable sea of confusion and contradiction that is the Evangelical universe. Our subsequent discussions led us to question the two fundamental guiding principles of the Protestant Reformation: sola scriptura and sola fide.

Sola Scriptura

Even the most casual observer of Protestantism generally and Evangelicalism specifically would be immediately struck by the sheer number of Protestant sects. Initially, I believed that the issues outlined above could be overcome by careful philosophical argumentation and good biblical exegesis. However, as the conclusion of my studies drew near, I began to consider the possibility that the very foundation of the Protestant faith was fundamentally and hopelessly flawed. I knew when I turned my attention to the formal cause of the Reformation that I was treading in very dangerous waters. If sola scriptura were not true, I knew I could no longer be Protestant. The gravity of this truth was immediately evident to me, and I knew there would be no turning back should I find the principle of sola scriptura wanting. Ultimately, I realized that this principle was untenable, for the Bible did not teach it, history did not testify to it, and it could not unify Christians or establish an authoritative canon.

Evangelicals are hopelessly divided on matters of doctrinal creed, moral code, and liturgical practice. Though this disunity could at best be unfortunate, at worst it could hinder the desire of the Lord, whom I had committed to follow and serve. As I considered the fact that Jesus and the apostle Paul taught that the unity of the Church is a visible reality (Jn 17:23; Rom 12:4–5; 1 Cor 12:12–30; Col 1:18, 24; Eph 1:22; 4:15–16; 5:23), I began to question seriously whether Protestantism could provide a way to unite Christians. In the summer of 2011, I came to the conclusion that the principle of sola scriptura effectively makes unity in moral code, doctrinal creed, and liturgical practice impossible, for every appeal to Scripture is an appeal to an interpretation of Scripture, and men interpret the Scriptures in radically different ways. Second, I realized that the principle of sola scriptura cannot give one a list of the authoritative books that belong in the Bible, for no Protestant believes that the table of contents of his Bible is part of the inspired text. Finally, the Bible does not teach sola scriptura. In fact, the Bible teaches that both the *written* word of the apostles and the *spoken* word of the apostles (tradition in Catholic theology) are equally authoritative (Mt 28:19; Mk 16:15; Jn 21:24–25; 1 Cor 11:2; 15:3, 11; 2 Thess 2:15; 3:6; 2 Tim 1:13; 2:2). Furthermore, the Scriptures do not teach that the Bible is the pillar of truth; rather, the *Church* is called the "pillar and bulwark of the truth" (1 Tim 3:15). For an expansion on these and other detrimental objections to the principle of sola scriptura, I refer the reader to appendix 3, "Facing the Issue of Sola Scriptura".

Sola Fide

Though I was convinced that the Protestant principle of sola scriptura was false and that the Catholic view of authority could be defended biblically, I was not convinced that I should abandon the initial motive for the Reformation—namely, sola fide. From my earliest days in Campus Crusade for Christ, I had learned that a man was justified before God by grace alone, through faith alone, in Christ alone. I was told that this principle was clearly taught in the Scriptures and that abandoning this principle could spell certain doom for my salvation and that of my wife and children. However, upon closer reading of the Scriptures, I realized that the Bible does not teach the Protestant view of salvation but clearly teaches the Catholic view.

Protestantism holds that faith is the only element required by the Christian in order to be justified before God. Catholics believe that faith alone is not the only thing necessary, but one must also love God—for only faith accompanied by love of God is a living faith. In Catholic soteriology, one is justified by faith alone, and not by works, so long as one's faith is accompanied by love of God, for love of God is what makes friendship with God possible. The primary difference between Protestants and Catholics in this respect is Paul's use of the word *faith* in his epistles. Protestants understand Paul to be using the word *faith* or *believing* apart from the other two theological virtues of hope and love, whereas Catholics believe that Paul is using the term in a wider sense to include both hope and love with faith.

Most passages of the Bible are neutral in regard to the relationship between faith and justification, for they can be interpreted by both Protestants and Catholics in such a way as to align with their respective positions. The question, however, is whether the Bible ever claims that one is justified by faith alone or whether there are passages indicating that one is justified by faith working through love. Catholics have the advantage here, for all the passages that seem to support the Protestant position can easily be interpreted by Catholics, and a number of other passages clearly teach the Catholic position (Jn 14:23; Gal 5:5–6; Jas 2:21–23; 1 Pet 1:8–9; 1 Jn 3:14; 4:8; 5:3–4).[1]

Through a great deal of struggle, thought, and prayer, my wife and I decided to leave our thriving Evangelical church in June 2012 and began moving toward the Catholic Church. Though we were both excited about the future, the gravity of our move became far more evident, and a certain degree of doubt and trepidation began to emerge in our minds and hearts: most of our family and friends were Evangelicals, I knew that my job teaching at an Evangelical high school would come to an end, and we were unsure whether we would ever fit into the Catholic world.

The Joy of Catholicism

Our first son was born in July 2012, and my wife and I began attending the Rite of Christian Initiation of Adults (RCIA) class at Sacred Heart Catholic Church in Salisbury, North Carolina, in September. Though our intentions were expressly directed toward entering the Church at the Easter Vigil, we were by no means moving forward with unshakable confidence. We believed that we were following

---

[1] I am indebted to Bryan Cross, PhD, for this insight. See Bryan Cross, "Does the Bible Teach Sola Fide?", Called to Communion, September 3, 2008, http://www.calledtocommunion.com/2009/09/does-the-bible-teach-sola-fide/.

the call of the Holy Spirit, who had been faithfully directing our lives since we met at Ohio University, but we also began to realize that our crisis of faith might not be cooled until we were in full communion with the one, holy, catholic, and apostolic Church. We began attending Mass regularly, prayed for good council regarding our decision, and asked God to give us the faith to follow his lead.

RCIA is a program designed to help potential converts investigate the Catholic faith. Jenni and I were blessed to have a young, newly ordained priest teach our class, and we were immediately taken with his sense of humor, pastoral presence, and passion for the Catholic faith. He and the pastor of our parish were always willing to meet with Jenni and me to answer questions regarding the faith. Not only did our priests ease our conversion, but the wonderful people of Sacred Heart welcomed us into the Church with open arms. Many of them sacrificed their time to go through RCIA with us, and their prayers, encouragement, and friendship helped us to embrace our newfound faith more fully. Further, as we began to worship in the presence of the Holy Eucharist, through fellowship with Catholics who loved Christ and his Church deeply, and under the teaching of holy and noble priests, our faith began to grow exponentially and the truth of the Catholic faith became indisputable. By December, Jenni and I decided to inform our family and friends that we intended to enter the Catholic Church. Consequently, our son was baptized at Sacred Heart on January 12, 2013, and my wife and I were received into full communion with the Catholic Church at the Easter Vigil later that year.

When my wife and I began attending Sacred Heart in the summer of 2012, we were, in a manner of speaking, reluctant converts. Though we believed the Catholic Church was the Church that Christ founded, we could not envision our life as Catholics. We knew that I would eventually have to find new employment; we were uncertain about how our family's spiritual life would evolve; and we were unsure whether we would ever feel at home in Catholic culture. Jenni and I were not lukewarm Evangelicals, and we knew we would not be lukewarm Catholics. We were just unsure whether we would find likeminded people to share our lives. As our formation in the Catholic faith unfolded during our time at Sacred Heart, it became abundantly clear that we would have no trouble finding our place in the Catholic Church.

Though our time at Sacred Heart was overwhelmingly joyful, God continued to bless our reception into his Church by providing us not merely with new employment but with new employment in our home state: both Jenni and I were able to secure teaching positions at Catholic schools in Cincinnati. After our move, we began attending Saint Gertrude Catholic Church, a strong and vibrant Catholic community in the Dominican tradition. Saint Gertrude has been a spectacular parish home. From our earliest days in Campus Crusade for Christ, Jenni and I knew that a true Church would be strikingly Christ centered, have a distinct Evangelical zeal, and would be markedly Bible based. The passion with which the priests, Dominican sisters, and laypeople at Saint Gertrude pursue friendship with God through the Catholic Church is an inspiration to us both. We have found not only a parish community to call home but fellow brothers and sisters in Christ who will encourage and inspire us to grow in holiness and virtue.

Conclusion

Though all the reasons I listed above played a very important role in leading Jenni and me into the fullness of the Christian faith, ultimately it was God himself who drew us into his Church. Although our journey was long and arduous, God, in his infinite grace and mercy, abundantly provided all that we needed for reception into his Church. My wife and I are grateful for everything we learned in our Evangelical faith, for when we became Catholic, we were not required to leave behind much of what we learned as Evangelicals. A zeal for a personal relationship with Jesus Christ; fidelity to him, to his Church, and to the Word of God; and the desire to see others come to know Christ in a meaningful way had been forever impressed on our souls. However, by God's grace, we chose to break through the glass ceiling of our Protestant faith into the eternal heights of the Catholic Church, the Mystical Body of our Lord Jesus Christ. The thrill of being Catholic has not worn thin, and the great adventure, which is the Catholic life, has only begun.

7

A Story of Conversion:
Trusting in the Authority of Christ

By Brian Mathews

[I]f I am delayed, you may know how one ought to behave in the household of God, which is the Church of the living God, the pillar and bulwark of the truth.

— 1 Timothy 3:15

Beginnings

Baptism

One of my fondest memories from childhood involved standing in my mom and dad's bedroom, preparing for baptism. My father, an ordained Southern Baptist minister, coached me on how to hold my nose when being immersed. Shortly thereafter, I walked into the baptismal font at Sagemont Baptist Church, ready to be baptized by my dad. Little did I know that I would be participating in divine life on that special day, a day on which God would use my father in an extraordinary way to adopt me into his covenant family.

Looking back on my childhood experience, naturally some of the details are a bit vague, but I distinctly remember that, at one point, my father knelt down to talk with me about the most important thing in life, Jesus Christ. The most loving thing a father could do for his son was to lead him to Christ. These childhood moments fill me with joy, knowing that my mom and dad were greatly concerned with my eternal well-being, wanting to share with their son the love of God that they had experienced. Being drawn to the heavenly Father by the grace of the Holy Spirit, embracing Christ as a child brought a unique hope to my life.

Eternal Life

When I was growing up, the most important thing for many Evangelical Christians was to receive Jesus Christ into one's life, so that one could have eternal life. "For God so loved the world that he gave his only-begotten Son, that whoever believes in him should not perish but have eternal life" (Jn 3:16). Eternal life meant that, due to the sacrifice of Christ on the Cross on behalf of sinners, a person was able to go to heaven, escaping eternal separation from God. Since eternal life was a gift from God that could not be earned, once a person made the decision to trust in Christ for eternal life, that person would go to heaven. Eternal life is not based upon the performance of good works, but instead it is the work of Christ on the Cross that saves a person once they have believed.

From the time I was a young child and into my adolescent and early adult years, this was my understanding of what it meant to be saved. Salvation was not contingent on church attendance, receiving communion, being baptized, or performing good deeds. Even where one attended church was irrelevant with respect to being saved. The most important thing was whether a person had ever made the decision to trust in Christ and have a personal relationship with him. Although most of the other things mentioned above, such as being involved in a church that taught the Christian faith as taught by the Scriptures, were important, they were secondary matters that did not determine a person's eternal destiny, although for many Evangelical Christians, subsequent obedience is important in indicating whether someone is truly saved in the first place.

I am very thankful for being raised in a spiritual tradition with a strong emphasis on having a personal relationship with Christ. It is vital in the life of a Christian. While having a personal relationship with Christ is crucial, another pressing question for the disciple of Christ concerns how a person is to live out this relationship, a question with which I would eventually struggle.

Church Background

My mom and dad were from two denominational traditions, one Methodist and the other Southern Baptist. Even though my dad was an ordained Southern Baptist minister, by the time I was eight years old, my family had moved to New Jersey and began attending a charismatic Assembly of God church. After my mom and dad served there in ministry for a year, we headed to California and participated once again in a Baptist congregation. By the middle of my fourth-grade year, we moved back to Texas, where my parents had grown up, this time becoming members of a Methodist community. The pastor who married my parents was now the person my dad would work with in music ministry for many years to come.

During these early years, participating in many denominations was never a confusing ordeal, for once again, the most important thing was not the particular denomination to which a person belonged but trusting in Christ. Denominational differences did not become challenging until I was later confronted with the reality that the disparities concerned more than just secondary matters, but this was not even a blip on my radar at the time. For now, being involved in different kinds of churches implicitly reiterated the primary emphasis on having a personal relationship with Jesus, not a personal relationship with the Methodist or Baptist denomination.

The University

When I entered college and throughout my early adulthood, my life was filled with spiritual highs and lows. I remember struggling to discern my calling in life, but the word *calling* entailed the difficulty of attempting to discern a career path. Was I supposed to become a doctor or a businessman or enter into vocational ministry and teach or preach? What exactly was it that God wanted me to pursue? I did not have any clear direction on the answer to this all-important question, and the fear of missing out on God's calling for my life nagged at me. Instead of enthusiastically engaging in my studies with clear goals, I slowly began to be confronted with doubts in addition to making some very poor decisions in my personal life.

The Reliability of the Bible

During my freshman year of college, I enrolled in an Old Testament course. Students were required to take this class due to the religious nature of the university. However, instead of encouraging me in the Christian faith, this course challenged me with matters (or difficulties) pertaining to Scripture. I remember my Old Testament professor giving the impression that the Bible contained contradictions. But if the Bible had contradictions, how could it be the Word of God? Truth does not contradict itself, and God does not make mistakes. And if the Bible is not reliable because of contradictions, how can one be confident that Christianity is actually true? I did not really know much about apologetics at the time, but I was already being confronted with apologetic issues that brought discomfort.

The Bible and Science

During my sophomore year, my biology professor attempted to debunk the opening chapters of Genesis by showing that the information provided in the text of Scripture did not match the truths gleaned from observing nature. Once again, I remember being irritated by this, but I did not have a thoughtful response. Of course, there are various ways in which the opening chapters of Genesis can be harmonized with the truths found in natural science, but I was clearly ignorant of such things. One thing was for sure, though: doubts concerning some of the truths of the Christian faith crept in, and throughout my college and early adult years, I faced significant struggles with being faithful to God.

Theological Curiosity

After graduating from college with a business degree in finance, I started working as a loan officer in the mortgage industry, which lasted only a short while. Discontented, I continued to grapple with God's will for me as it pertained to a career. I had struggled with putting other things and people before God, and now I was ready for a change. I remember at one point thinking, "God, if only I could do something in ministry, then I would be happy." I had an immature understanding of what it meant to be truly happy, but despite this, being blessed by God with musical abilities and having grown up in a musical family, I pursued a part-time ministry job as a music leader of a small Evangelical congregation. Over the next few years, I led the music ministry at two churches, with a keen interest in apologetic questions. I remember special relationships with two pastors, enjoying their friendship and engaging in theological discussions. They both blessed my life, and I eventually started graduate school at Dallas Theological Seminary (DTS). Even though I really was not sure what I would do with a theological degree, I knew that I wanted to know more about God and pursue various theological questions in greater depth.

Calvinism

It was around this time that I became more exposed to the theological system known as Calvinism. I will never forget one of my best friends, a friend from childhood, conversing with me concerning some of the doctrines of Reformed theology. A Calvinist and DTS student himself, he thoughtfully articulated some of these doctrines, one of them being the idea that Jesus did not really die for the sins of the world—that is, for the sins of every man. From a Reformed theological standpoint, one of the reasons for this position is a seeming universalism that would follow if Christ had indeed died for every single man. In other words, if Christ paid for the sins of all mankind and really wanted every single person to be saved, then, in light of the doctrines of grace in the Reformed tradition, everyone would ultimately make it to heaven. Not only would there be no reason for anyone to go to hell (since everyone's sins have been accounted and paid for by the Crucifixion), but also God, as sovereign, is in control and will not be denied in what he ultimately wills.

Although my good friend did not intend this, I became very disturbed, as this seemed to call into question the very love of God, leading to the thought that Christ does not really desire that all men be saved, nor does he provide the opportunity for everyone to be saved. In this framework, God does not *offer* sufficient grace to every person so that every individual has at least the opportunity to be saved.

Norman Geisler

It was through this theological issue that I first became familiar with Dr. Norman Geisler, the cofounder of Southern Evangelical Seminary. My father-in-law, a strong Christian who was in seminary at DTS, introduced me to one of Dr. Geisler's books that responded to the soteriology of Calvinism. Of course, like many theologians,

Dr. Geisler attempts to refute limited atonement by citing scriptural passages that point to the universal salvific will of God, but he also uses philosophy to lend credence to the view that Jesus really did atone for the sins of the world. Not only did Dr. Geisler appeal to me theologically, but I also learned of his credentials in the field of apologetics.

While living in Dallas, I listened to a radio interview with Frank Turek, a student and colleague of Dr. Geisler. Dr. Turek winsomely and convincingly articulated strong evidence in favor of Christianity. Inspired by this newly discovered discipline, I began reading apologetic books, as I was becoming more interested not only in believing the truth as it pertained to the Christian faith but in knowing why I believed what I believed, and I wanted to be equipped to be used by God in defending these truths. Because DTS did not offer an apologetics degree, my theological studies there lasted only one semester. So after prayerful consideration as well as meeting and talking with Dr. Geisler, my family and I set our sights on Charlotte, North Carolina, so that I could attend Southern Evangelical Seminary under the tutelage of Dr. Geisler.

Southern Evangelical Seminary

Apologetics and Philosophy

At this point, Catholicism continued to be a nonissue, although God had already brought thoughtful, godly Catholics across my path while I lived in Texas. I really never gave Catholicism much thought, nor was there a need to, as my spiritual upbringing was not explicitly anti-Catholic, and I was, in a sense, content in my Evangelical circles. So, during my first couple of years of seminary, I enthusiastically learned and became better equipped to defend the Christian faith. SES provided me with access to a wide array of resources, but philosophical reasoning was particularly stressed and emphasized in being foundational to defending and understanding the Christian faith. I was introduced to the importance of metaphysics and, more specifically, the philosophy of Saint Thomas Aquinas in undergirding one's theology and biblical exegesis, especially as it pertained to the nature and attributes of God.

Saint Thomas Aquinas

The school's emphasis on and profound respect for the thought of Saint Thomas Aquinas would later be of great significance to my entering into full communion with the Catholic Church, but during these early formative years, Saint Thomas Aquinas was never presented as a Catholic philosopher or theologian. Instead, he was portrayed as more of a proto-Protestant believing doctrines such as sola scriptura that were in line with the Protestant Reformers. For example, Dr. Geisler writes, "Aquinas agreed with the later Protestant principle of *Sola Scriptura*, the Bible alone as the Word of God, the totally sufficient norm for our faith."[1] Although my SES education was in no way limited to the thought of Saint Thomas Aquinas and my professors disagreed with him at times, such as on the doctrine of transubstantiation, the school had garnered a reputation as being Thomistic, hence Dr. Geisler's label of "Evangelical Thomist".

Theological Struggles

Calvinism versus Moderate Calvinism

Even though my early years were marked with great progress in learning and understanding many of the truths of the faith, the seeds of doubt regarding sola scriptura were being planted as I continued to struggle with the issue of Calvinism. I spent hours upon hours studying the scriptural arguments related to these doctrines but was never completely satisfied with the "moderate Calvinist" position according to Dr. Geisler, nor was I convinced by the arguments in favor of Reformed soteriology. This was quite bothersome because how I witnessed to others was contingent on which theological position was true. For example, if Christ really did not desire that all men be saved, and instead a person's free will was more of an afterthought as it applied to salvation, since God irresistibly provided salvific grace only to the elect who would persevere in the faith as a result, then a presentation of the gospel that included the notion that God loves every single person unconditionally and wants every person to come to the knowledge of the truth and be saved would be a distortion

[1] Norman L. Geisler, *Systematic Theology*, vol. 1 (Minneapolis: Bethany House, 2002), 294.

of the truth. Not only would this impact how one witnessed, but it would also significantly influence one's view of God in general.

Lordship versus Free Grace

Also on the horizon during my studies at SES was the controversy between the Lordship view of salvation and the Free Grace understanding. The Lordship position stresses faith for salvation as being essentially connected to turning away from sin, surrendering one's life to Christ, and following him as Lord. The Free Grace position emphasizes that salvation is a gift from God conditioned on simple faith in Christ, and by *simple* is meant a faith that is not essentially related to good works or turning from sin. In other words, a person's obedience or lack thereof has nothing to do with his entering into heaven, and it is even possible for a believer to reject the faith and die in this state and still go to heaven, because salvation is conditioned on a single moment of believing in Christ. But according to Lordship proponents, saving faith will entail at least perseverance in faith until the end of one's life, which should also involve obedience. If a person ended up rejecting the faith later in life and even died in this state, this was evidence that a person was never saved in the first place.

As you may recall, my spiritual background leaned more toward the Free Grace side, although there was still room for other elements, such as the possibility that a person would think he was saved when in reality he had never had a personal relationship with Christ. At SES, the professors in residence, with the exception of one, were either firmly in the Free Grace camp or leaned toward this understanding of salvation. At first, being exposed to the interpretations of Free Grace theology was freeing, as this seemingly provided a means of reconciling difficult passages that, at first glance, did not appear to teach that we are saved by grace through faith alone. For example, Matthew 16:24–27:

> Then Jesus told his disciples, "If any man would come after me, let him deny himself and take up his cross and follow me. For whoever would save his life will lose it, and whoever loses his life for my sake will find it. For what will it profit a man, if he gains the whole world and forfeits his life? Or what shall a man give in return for his life? For the Son of man is to come with his angels in the glory of his Father, and then he will repay every man for what he has done."

Instead of the words *save* and *life* referring to salvation from hell, or life as it relates to going to heaven, through sophisticated argumentation, Free Grace interpreters explain that in this context, which is a discipleship context involving persons that already believe in Christ and are saved as opposed to a witnessing context for unbelievers, the terms in question refer to salvation in some other kind of sense. In other words, the kind of salvation in question in this passage has nothing to do with whether a person enters into heaven when they die. Arguing from contextual factors and in light of the conviction that eternal salvation is not dependent on works and is eternally secure for those that have believed in Christ, this passage is teaching about the concept of rewards in eternity, not whether a person enters into heaven. Repaying every man according to what he has done has to do with what kind of rewards one has in the future Kingdom of God, which will vary based on the works of each Christian. To say that entering into heaven is based on following Christ, denying oneself, and suffering for Christ is to imply that salvation is conditioned on works, which in their minds is a giant step toward agreeing with Catholics.

Free Grace versus Free Grace

However, what began as a seemingly hopeful adventure in understanding truly what the Bible teaches based on sound hermeneutical principles, which involved taking into account grammatical and contextual factors in addition to having a decent understanding of the biblical languages, eventually became an exercise in futility. Even though Free Grace theologians were united in combating the Lordship position, I would soon gain exposure to the controversies within their own circles, controversies that have come to be associated with the phrase "crossless gospel". This conflict concerned not merely secondary issues but essential foundational matters of the Christian faith—namely, the very gospel itself.

What Is the Gospel?

To summarize the conflict, Free Grace biblical exegetes do not agree on the contents of saving faith. In other words, although they might all express that one is saved by believing in Jesus, exactly what it means to believe in Jesus for eternal life is not agreed upon and is hotly contested. For example, does one have to believe that Jesus is God or simply that Jesus is a person who will save him from hell if he believes in Jesus? Does one have to believe in the death and Resurrection of Christ in order to go to heaven, or can one be saved while being completely ignorant of the sacrifice of Christ on his behalf? To be saved, does a person have to believe that the gift of eternal life is something that can never be lost, or can someone disagree with eternal security and still go to heaven? Does a person have to believe that Jesus was human and divine, or can a person be saved without any understanding of the humanity of Christ?

Even though each Free Grace theologian used the same methodological principles in attempting to interpret Scripture correctly, at least five competing positions resulted, indicating at least five positions on the nature of the gospel itself, the bedrock of the Christian faith. I did not realize it at the time, but sola scriptura was becoming more and more practically unworkable. I graduated with my first master's degree in apologetics from SES, but I honestly felt somewhat bewildered, as I did not really know what someone truly needed to believe to be saved and receive eternal life. And if I did not know the contents of saving faith, how could I witness and lead others to Christ? It is one thing to teach basic apologetic issues, such as defending the existence of God or giving arguments for the Resurrection of Christ, but how could I actually engage in vocational ministry as a job if I did not understand what it meant to believe in Jesus for eternal life? After spending grand amounts of time in attempting to resolve these difficulties, I could not reach a resolution and eventually downplayed the controversy.

The Catholic Question

Rather than seriously pursue a vocational ministry position after my first degree, I decided to continue my education at SES to become better acquainted with the original biblical languages. Since many theologians appealed to the original languages in order to justify their particular theological viewpoints and since being familiar with Greek and Hebrew was considered an important factor in coming to the correct interpretations of Scripture, my desire was to become better equipped in this area. In my second round of studies, the Catholic question would soon come to light.

During my theological studies, I taught private piano lessons to a number of students, sometimes in their homes, and in the course of instructing these children, I developed a special friendship with a Catholic family, especially with the father. This father would meet with Jehovah's Witnesses in his home, enjoying theological conversations while giving reasons for the truths of the Catholic faith. Inevitably and quite naturally, he and I engaged in theological discussion. In explaining one of his meetings with Jehovah's Witnesses, he stressed the importance of the Church in giving Christians the Bible. In other words, Christians would not have a Bible to study or read if it were not for the Church handing down this authoritative book. Other issues we discussed included the Protestant doctrine of sola fide and the conversion story of Scott Hahn. From my perspective, the thought of a Protestant converting to Catholicism based in large part on his studies of the Scriptures sounded completely foreign. After all, Catholics believed all sorts of things not found in the Scriptures, or so I thought. When my friend learned of my affinity for the Angelic Doctor, Saint Thomas Aquinas, he eventually said something that I will never forget: "I bet within five years you will become Catholic." I just sort of laughed and shrugged off the suggestion. Little did I know that his prediction would eventually become a reality.

Toward the end of my education at SES, I enrolled in a course solely dedicated to studying the letter to the Romans. After spending multiple years in seminary, I had already completed numerous apologetics, theology, philosophy, and Bible classes in addition to becoming more acquainted with the biblical languages. The stage was set to study one of the most important books of the Bible, a foundational book for understanding the doctrine of salvation. One of my assignments was to write a paper that outlined Saint Paul's main arguments throughout his epistle. Instead of making significant progress, I found that the problem of having to decide between competing interpretations of Scripture reared its ugly head again, with one major exception.

Sola Fide Questioned

One day, while working from my computer at home, I came across a debate between a Catholic and a Protestant over the issue of salvation or justification. Instead of listening to the debate casually, I decided to take notes. What would ensue during the debate was unpleasantly shocking, as this Catholic apologist made strong biblical arguments in favor of the Catholic position on justification, the very important soteriological doctrine having to do with how a person becomes saved and enters into a right relationship with God. I had never heard the Catholic position persuasively articulated in such detail from the Scriptures, and even if this apologist did not necessarily win the debate, it was another interpretation of Romans, and the Scriptures in general, with which I was forced seriously to contend. Now, in addition to the Free Grace and Lordship salvation interpretations as well as N. T. Wright's New Perspectives on Paul, which is another contrasting view of the doctrine of justification from one of the most respected New Testament scholars in the world, a thoughtful Catholic interpretation on the doctrine by which the Church stands or falls, according to Martin Luther, had entered the fray. It is not as if I had never been exposed to some of the Catholic arguments prior to this moment in my education at SES. The difference is that I was hearing more in-depth, plausible arguments and responses from a Catholic scholar himself.

Distress came upon me once again, as I was feeling the heavy burden of having to interpret the Bible correctly on this all-important question. Foundational questions and doubts flooded my mind, and for the first time, the Catholic question was becoming a serious concern. What if the epistle of Saint James really does teach that justification is not merely a one-time forensic event but is instead a process by which a Christian grows in justification by works as a result of God's grace already at work in a person's life? What if Saint Paul's teaching in Romans that justification is by faith apart from works of the law did not exclude another sense in which works are a part of justification? What if Saint Paul was not speaking hypothetically in Romans when he wrote, "For it is not the hearers of the law who are righteous before God, but the doers of the law who will be justified" (Rom 2:13)? Or earlier in the chapter, when he expressed the coming judgment of God, "For he will render to every man according to his works: to those who by patience in well-doing seek for glory and honor and immortality, he will give eternal life; but for those who are factious and do not obey the truth, but obey wickedness, there will be wrath and fury" (Rom 2:6–8)? What if the concepts I had learned regarding eternal life, rewards, and salvation were mistaken? These were just some of the questions that were grabbing my attention.

Justification before Men?

One of the most salient points in the debate concerned the Protestant response to the kind of justification that Saint James espoused in his famous epistle. "You see that a man is justified by works and not by faith alone" (Jas 2:24). Some Evangelicals attempt to reconcile the apparent contradiction between Saint Paul and Saint James over the issue of justification by reasoning that James puts forth a different kind of justification altogether, one that is before men as opposed to before God. Theologians might maintain that, in his letter to the Romans, Paul argued for justification by grace through faith alone before God, but James communicated a different kind of justification by works before men. Since one cannot be justified by works before God, due to God's standard of perfection, of which we all hopelessly fall short, James cannot be implying that works before God can justify a person. This is how some of the Protestant biblical scholars attempt to reconcile Saint Paul and Saint James.

A Catholic response to this claim involves going back to the Old Testament to help inform one's interpretation of these seemingly contradictory books. Since Saint James refers to Abraham's offering his son Isaac on the altar as support for his instruction on justification, the account in Genesis 22 is paramount to understanding his statements. But a major difficulty for the Protestant explanation is that when Abraham offered up Isaac, no other persons were present to witness such obedience. If Abraham was showing his faith before men by his works, why are no men present to see his good deeds? Isaac does not seem to be a good candidate to fulfill this criterion because he was the one to be sacrificed. There is also good evidence to suggest that Isaac was actually an adult who willingly allowed himself to be sacrificed by Abraham, which makes sense in light of Isaac's being a type of Christ, who willingly allowed himself to be sacrificed on behalf of the world in submission to the will of the Father. So it looks as though both Abraham and Isaac were engaging in incredibly righteous actions with no one else present to witness such actions, which would indicate that the justification taking place in Genesis 22 is a justification before God and not men.

Genesis 22 provides further support for the Catholic position, as it
is God who responds to Abraham's righteous actions, not men:

> But the angel of the LORD called to him from heaven, and said, "Abra-
> ham, Abraham!"
> And he said, "Here am I." He said, "Do not lay your hand on the
> lad or do anything to him; for now I know that you fear God, see-
> ing you have not withheld your son, your only-begotten son, from
> me." ... And the angel of the LORD called to Abraham a second
> time from heaven, and said, "By myself I have sworn, says the LORD,
> because you have done this, and have not withheld your son, your
> only-begotten son, I will indeed bless you, and I will multiply your
> descendants as the stars of heaven and as the sand which is on the
> seashore. And your descendants shall possess the gate of their enemies,
> and by your descendants shall all the nations of the earth bless them-
> selves, because you have obeyed my voice." (Gen 22:11–12, 15–18)

Saint Paul and Saint James

So then how do Catholics reconcile Saint Paul and Saint James with
regard to the important doctrine of justification? Although both
authors of Sacred Scripture describe a justification before God, they
show the different senses in which a person can be justified. Saint
Paul teaches that a person is initially justified by a living faith apart
from works. In other words, persons cannot merit this initial justification, which entails a person's coming into friendship with God
and being adopted into his family. Prior to being adopted into God's
family, persons are separated from God, lacking participation in the
divine nature. Initial justification takes place through baptism, by
which a person receives the supernatural virtues of faith, hope, and
love (Rom 5:5; 6:3–4; Tit 3:3–7; 1 Cor 6:11). So the faith that saves
is a living faith, a faith informed by love, and this is all made possible
and actual by the sacrificial atonement of Christ on behalf of sinners.
A person cannot earn this standing before God. It is a gift.

Saint James, on the other hand, does not describe how an unbe-
liever becomes accepted into God's family; Abraham believed in God
long before Genesis 22 (cf. Gen 12, 15). On the contrary, Saint James
describes how a believer, who has already received supernatural life,
grows in his participation in the divine life. Because of the sacrifice of
Christ and the grace of God already at work in the person's life, he can

continue to cooperate with God's grace by doing good works in correspondence with the living faith he exercises, and, in effect, his works become meritorious so that eternal life is simultaneously a reward and a grace. When confronted with the difficulty of the notion that eternal life is a gift of God, so that no one can boast, yet also, in a sense, a reward for one's works, Saint Augustine wrote the following:

> This question, then, seems to me to be by no means capable of solution, unless we understand that even those good works of ours, which are recompensed with eternal life, belong to the grace of God, because of what is said by the Lord Jesus: "Without me you can do nothing" (Jn 15:5). And the apostle himself, after saying, "By grace are you saved through faith; and that not of yourselves, it is the gift of God: not of works, lest any man should boast" (Eph 2:8–9), saw, of course, the possibility that men would think from this statement that good works are not necessary to those who believe, but that faith alone suffices for them; and again, the possibility of men's boasting of their good works, as if they were of themselves capable of performing them. To meet, therefore, these opinions on both sides, he immediately added, "For we are his workmanship, created in Christ Jesus unto good works, which God has before ordained that we should walk in them" (Eph 2:10).... Now, hear and understand. "Not of works" is spoken of the works which you suppose have their origin in yourself alone; but you have to think of works for which God has molded (that is, has formed and created) you.... We are framed, therefore, that is, formed and created, in the good works that we have not ourselves prepared, but God has before ordained that we should walk in them. It follows, then, dearly beloved, beyond all doubt, that as your good life is nothing else than God's grace, so also the eternal life which is the recompense of a good life is the grace of God; moreover it is given gratuitously, even as that is given gratuitously to which it is given. But that to which it is given is solely and simply grace; this therefore is also that which is given to it, because it is its reward—grace is for grace, as if remuneration for righteousness; in order that it may be true, because it is true, that God shall reward every man according to his works.[2]

So even the works that a believer performs by the grace of God are gifts from God, not originating from ourselves but having God as their source, yet they are rewarded with eternal life as

---

[2] Saint Augustine, *On Grace and Free Will* 20.

believers freely cooperate with that grace. As Saint Augustine insists in the next passage, free will is not taken away. The reason a person's works can have such value is because they are connected to the sacrifice of Christ, being accomplished through the supernatural grace and virtue of love that is gratuitously infused into the believer in baptism. As Saint Paul says in Galatians 5:6, "For in Christ Jesus neither circumcision nor uncircumcision is of any avail, but *faith working* through *love*" (emphasis added). The armor of sola fide experienced a compelling crack.

Doubting Sola Scriptura

Now that a thoughtful, persuasive case for the Catholic position on salvation broke into the theological arena, what was I to do with all the conflicting interpretations of the Scriptures on this essential doctrine? Seemingly godly, brilliant, educated scholars and theologians who were all attempting to be faithful to the biblical text were arriving at incompatible theological conclusions. I imagine that many of them also were praying for the Holy Spirit to lead and guide them, yet somehow, even though they all invoked the same Holy Spirit, mutually exclusive conclusions still resulted. In addition, these Protestant scholars were using the same principles of interpretation to arrive at their decisions. Avoiding taking a passage out of context and violating the grammatical structures of language, paying attention to the historical factors, and interacting with the original biblical languages were all stressed by the same biblical interpreters, yet on foundational and essential doctrines, such as what it means to believe in Jesus for eternal life, conflicting outcomes still resulted. And concurrently, what was I to make of Catholicism's persuasive case from Scripture concerning the nature of salvation? Soon I would providentially be introduced to a way out of the seemingly insurmountable dilemma.

An SES Catholic?

In discussing theological issues with close friends from SES, I discovered that an SES alum, who also had a background in Free Grace theology (and is a contributor to this book), had joined the Catholic Church. Although I was not acquainted with him personally, I learned of his contributions to the website Called to Communion, which is dedicated to effecting reconciliation and reunion between Protestants and Catholics. This website is filled with articles that charitably and thoroughly articulate the Catholic faith, but uniquely, the contributors did not grow up Catholic. Instead, they arrived in the Catholic Church only after being spiritually formed within the Reformed Protestant tradition. My curiosity was piqued as I began reading some of the articles.

Solo versus Sola Scriptura

One of the first articles I saw caught my attention: "Solo Scriptura, Sola Scriptura, and the Question of Interpretive Authority". Keith Mathison, a respected Reformed Protestant scholar, wrote a book criticizing *solo scriptura*, a term used to indicate that the only authority for the Christian is Scripture. This is contrasted with sola scriptura, which is the notion that Scripture is the only infallible authority, but there is also the true authority of the Church and the regula fidei (the rule of faith), although these authorities are still subordinate to the Scriptures. Mathison criticizes solo scriptura as something that causes hermeneutical chaos and anarchy. One notices the myriad of conflicting, competing interpretations within Protestantism, harming the unity and witness of the Church for which Christ prayed in John 17. Instead of hearing the Church preach the gospel of Christ, the world is "hearing an endless cacophony of conflicting and contradictory assertions by those who claim to be the Church of Christ".[3] So how does an Evangelical Christian normally deal with such challenges, according to Mathison?

The usual response involves the examination of each competing position according to the Scriptures. In other words, one attempts to decipher which position is more faithful to the Bible, but, in embarking on such an endeavor, inevitably what transpires is that

---

[3] Keith Mathison, *The Shape of Sola Scriptura* (Moscow, Ida.: Canon Press, 2001), 274–75, cited in Bryan Cross, "Solo Scriptura, Sola Scriptura, and the Question of Interpretive Authority", Called to Communion, November 4, 2009, http://www.calledtocommunion.com/2009/11/solo-scriptura-sola-scriptura-and-the-question-of-interpretive-authority/.

each Christian decides for himself, according to his own interpretation of the text, which interpretation is correct. Because Scripture does not interpret itself but needs to be read and interpreted by someone, Scripture ultimately ceases to function as the final interpretive authority in deciding theological matters. Instead, a person's individual reason and judgment becomes the final authority, resulting in a kind of subjectivism and theological chaos. Mathison voices his concerns:

> Ultimately the interpretation of Scripture becomes individualistic with no possibility for the resolution of differences. This occurs because adherents of solo *scriptura* rip the Scripture out of its ecclesiastical and traditional hermeneutical context, leaving it in a relativistic vacuum. The problem is that there are differing interpretations of Scripture, and Christians are told that these can be resolved by a simple appeal to Scripture.... The problem that adherents of solo scriptura haven't noticed is that any appeal to Scripture is an appeal to *an interpretation* of Scripture. The only question is: *whose* interpretation? When we are faced with conflicting interpretations of Scripture, we cannot set a Bible on a table and ask it to resolve our difference of opinion as if it were a Ouija board. In order for Scripture to serve as an authority at all, it must be read, exegeted, and interpreted by somebody.[4]

According to Mathison, many Evangelical Christians are no longer interpreting Scripture within its ecclesiastical and traditional hermeneutical context. They are no longer allowing the Church or the regula fidei to be their interpretive guide, which severely limits Scripture's ability to function as an actual authority. As notable theologians are now denying parts of historical Christianity, such as parts of the Nicene Creed, based on their own interpretations of Scripture, it is evident that solo scriptura as a methodology naturally leads to theological error, divisions, and confusion. Each individual interprets Scripture as it seems right in his eyes, and the result is thousands of denominations teaching all sorts of conflicting ideas about Christianity.

---

[4] Mathison, *The Shape of Sola Scriptura*, 246, cited in Cross, "Solo Scriptura, Sola Scriptura, and the Question of Interpretive Authority"; emphasis in the original.

Mathison also points out that solo Scriptura runs counter to early and medieval Christian practice, given that councils were convened by true bishops to solve theological disputes. Persons did not go home, read their Bibles, and then come to their own conclusions regarding Christian doctrine. And to make matters worse, denying the authority of the Church undercuts one's reliance on Scripture as an authority because it is the Church that gave Christians the Bible. Without the Church, one could not have any certainty regarding which books are to be included in the Bible.

Solo Scriptura Abandoned

Mathison's critiques of solo scriptura resonated deeply with my experience. The theological confusion in my life resulting from my attempts to understand Christianity according to my interpretations of the Scriptures considerably hampered my progress in the Christian life. The lack of clarity due to endless theological disputes with no practical solution stifled my ability to witness, teach, and live out the Christian faith. Foundationally speaking, I did not really have a confident or authoritative answer to the question "What exactly is the Christian faith?" Is the Christian gospel what is taught by proponents of Free Grace theology, and, if so, which brand of Free Grace orthodoxy? Is Christianity what is taught by advocates of Lordship salvation, or are they preaching a false gospel, as some would claim? The conflicting interpretations concerned not just secondary matters but the very essence of Christianity.

For the first time in my spiritual life, the divisions within Protestantism, in which there are thousands of denominations filled with persons attempting to be faithful to the Scriptures, struck me as antithetical to Christianity itself. At SES, I spent considerable time researching and studying various theological positions or topics in preparation for future ministry, but I do not recall much of an emphasis on denominations being a problem in and of themselves. Maybe it was taken for granted that this is just an unfortunate reality with which Christians are faced, with no hope of resolution until Christ returns. I distinctly remember my biblical-language professor stressing that Scripture does not interpret itself and that it must be interpreted by persons using sound hermeneutical principles, yet the resulting problem of multiple individual authorities did not enter the discussion, at least as far as I can remember. Regardless of my recollection, I felt illuminated in understanding that Christianity was never intended to be a giant theological puzzle for each Christian to solve by way of individual scholarship, yet with practically no hope of putting the foundational theological pieces in place.

Sola Scriptura Reduces to Solo Scriptura

Even though the problems uttered by Mathison in regard to solo scriptura were enlightening, did his solutions provide a viable alternative to the seemingly insurmountable problems? One of the chief purposes of the article on Called to Communion was to demonstrate that there is no principled difference between solo scriptura and sola scriptura, and if there is no principled difference between the two, then ultimately Mathison's criticisms of solo scriptura would also apply to his own position—namely, that of sola scriptura. So it is argued that the very thing that Mathison and other Reformed Christians attempt to avoid—the problem of final interpretive authority being located within each person—is the very predicament in which their own position ends. How is it the case that sola scriptura in reality reduces to solo scriptura?

To mitigate the problem of private interpretation within Protestantism, Mathison's solution is to rely on the church as a higher interpretive authority to which each person should submit, and Catholics in principle agree with this. But the difference lies in the way in which Mathison locates and defines the church. Reformed Christians define *church* by wherever the true gospel is found, but how does a Reformed Christian know of the true nature of the gospel to begin with? For Reformed theologians, the gospel is discovered by interpreting Scripture, but leaning on one's own interpretation of Scripture is the very thing that is problematic of the solo scriptura paradigm, is it not? If one is told to submit to the church as an external, higher authority meant to inform and guide his interpretations of Scripture, yet the determination and definition of that church is based on his own interpretation of Scripture, then the final interpretative authority still resides within the individual. This is illustrated whenever persons switch churches, denominations, or confessional traditions based on their personal interpretive decisions in regard to Scripture.

The Catholic Resolution: Apostolic Succession

So how does the Catholic position substantially differ from Mathison's and from that of Reformed Christians in general, offering a way out of the conundrum of final interpretive authority residing in the individual? Although Catholicism teaches that individuals are to submit to the Church as a higher authority when it comes to interpreting Scripture and understanding the Christian faith, *Church* is not defined according to one's interpretation of Scripture. Instead, the Church is defined by apostolic succession, which involves an unbroken chain of bishops extending from the present all the way back to the original apostles, who were ordained by Christ himself. In other words, Christ gave the apostles authority to teach in his name, and the apostles passed on to others, by the laying on of hands, this divine authority to teach in his name; in effect, they appointed bishops as successors, who in turn appointed successors, and this process extends to the present day. If a person does not have apostolic succession, he is not divinely authorized to teach, preach, and govern Christ's Church. So one locates the Church through apostolic succession, and it is through the successors of the apostles, the Magisterium, that a person understands the true nature of the gospel, which means that the final interpretive authority indeed rests with the Church, not with the individual believer.

I must admit, while the article profoundly resonated with me on a personal, intellectual, philosophical, and theological level, such a solution was also incredibly foreign to my thinking. Up to this point, confessions, creeds, and even Church history were afterthoughts, being secondary to my efforts to interpret the Scripture rightly. Even though I was mired by the theological confusion of competing biblical interpretations, it was still somewhat comfortable serving in a Southern Baptist church, the denomination in which my beautiful, loving grandmother taught Sunday school for years. All I had ever known and experienced was Evangelical Christianity, which, even though it did not contain the *fullness* of the faith, contained many beautiful, spiritual, godly beliefs, practices, and persons, most notably my family and its deep emphasis on Scripture. To enter into full communion with the Catholic Church in order to provide an intellectual solution to the problem of sola scriptura, although extremely important, would not be enough. It would take much more. Ultimately, it would have to be a work of grace from the Holy Spirit.

Ongoing Conversion

So I continued seeking by reading and studying for extensive amounts of time. I prayed to God, asking him to lead me to the truth. Regardless of what that would mean for me, that is where I wanted to be. Eventually, I had to inform the pastor of the church we were attending of my need to take a break from serving. I could no longer in good conscience lead a small-group Bible study or teach apologetics at our local church with such doubts and concerns. I was in my last year of seminary, usually a time for embarking on job searches or filling out applications for doctoral work, but instead, I was seriously contemplating a profound paradigm shift in the direction of the Catholic Church—a change that would also impact my wife and our three kids.

In my studies, I began discovering the importance of apostolic succession in Church history. The succession lists of bishops, the grave importance of being submissive to the bishop, the manner in which the Church would resolve theological disputes (councils), the way in which the early Christian apologists would respond to heretics and schismatics by pointing to apostolic succession, and the significance of the primacy of the Bishop of Rome captured my thoughts. God did not establish his Church only for her to fall into apostasy a short time later. Instead, the successors of the apostles were given a special charism of infallibility, meaning that, ultimately, the Church could not be lead astray and teach error concerning faith and morals. Not only did history point to the Bishop of Rome as having a unique authority over the entire Church, but the biblical evidence for the Catholic interpretation of Matthew 16:16–19 concerning Saint Peter in correspondence with the Old Testament backdrop of Isaiah 22 provided a firm foundation for the Church's claims regarding the hierarchical structure of the Church.[5]

Canon Question

In addition to seeing Church history's witness to apostolic succession, I realized that sola scriptura could not account for another key ingredient of the Christian faith: the biblical canon. The list of books that were to be included in the Bible is not in the Bible itself, and if the Bible is the only infallible authority for matters pertaining to the faith, then the list of books that make up the Bible is itself fallible and could be in error. Is the Bible supposed to be composed of seventy-three books or only sixty-six? Catholics, Eastern Orthodox, and Protestants do not have the same list. So how does one adjudicate between the competing canons? When looking into Church history, one notices that there are differing lists. And, interestingly enough, the early Christians used the Septuagint, the Greek translation of the Old Testament, which included all the books that are part of the Catholic Bible. Regardless, the canon problem posed another difficulty for sola scriptura; yet, once again, Catholicism had an authoritative answer to the difficulty.

Sola Scriptura Not Scriptural

One of the more notable critiques of sola scriptura is that Scripture itself does not teach it, implying that the doctrine is self-refuting. Not a single verse of the Bible (Protestant or Catholic) says or teaches that Scripture is the only infallible authority for the Christian faith. Instead, in verses such as 2 Thessalonians 2:15 Saint Paul speaks of another kind of tradition that is put on the same comparative level as written tradition: "So then, brethren, stand firm and hold to the traditions which

[5] In Matthew 16:19, Jesus gives Peter "the keys of the kingdom of heaven". This does not imply an innovative New Testament teaching. Rather, the relevant notion of "the key" is mentioned in Isaiah 22. There, Eliakim is placed in charge of the house of Judah, a unique position of authority that has only the king as a person with higher authority. The key also denotes succession as the key was passed from one servant to another. In the New Covenant, Peter receives a name change, indicating a special purpose for him in God's plan of salvation history, and is given the keys to a new kingdom, implying that Peter was given a unique authority to act as a kind of prime minister in accordance with the Davidic King, Jesus himself.

you were taught by us, either by word of mouth or by letter" (cf.
1 Cor 11:2). The doctrine that Luther used to justify breaking off
from the Catholic Church had crumbled before my very eyes.

Saint Thomas Aquinas: A Proto-Protestant?

In light of my education at Southern Evangelical Seminary, with its
fitting emphasis on the philosophical thought of Saint Thomas Aquinas, my journey toward the Catholic Church inevitably involved
interacting with the Angelic Doctor. It became apparent that his
thoughts were very hard to reconcile with historical Protestantism on
matters pertaining to soteriology and ecclesiology. In addition to his
emphasis on the sacramental life as instrumental to growing in righteousness, his view of authority caught my attention. Just prior to the
his death, Saint Thomas expressed: "But if I have written anything
erroneous concerning this sacrament or other matters, I submit all to
the judgment and correction of the Holy Roman Church, in whose
obedience I now pass from this life."[6]

If the Holy Roman Church were a fallible institution, capable of
error in matters pertaining to faith and morals and of leading others
astray, why would Saint Thomas submit his writings to that Church?
To give a modern-day analogy, would it make sense for a Protestant
theologian to submit his theological writings to the Southern Baptist
Convention for correction? Aquinas held to the Catholic Church
as an infallible authority, submitting his writing to that Church. To
illustrate the point further, he states:

> Now the formal object of faith is the First Truth, as manifested in
> Holy Writ and the teaching of the Church, which proceeds from the
> First Truth. Consequently whoever does not adhere, as to an infallible
> and Divine rule, to the teaching of the Church, which proceeds from
> the First Truth manifested in Holy Writ, has not the habit of faith, but
> holds that which is of faith otherwise than by faith.[7]

For Saint Thomas, the habit of faith involves adhering to the
teaching of the Church precisely because she possesses an infallible

---

[6] *Catholic Encyclopedia*, "Saint Thomas Aquinas", http://www.newadvent.org/cathen
/14663b.htm.

[7] Saint Thomas Aquinas, *Summa Theologiae* II-II, 5, 3.

and divine authority, being protected from error in regard to the articles of the faith. The final interpretive authority does not rest with a person's private judgment, which is fallible. Instead, the Church is the divinely authorized instrument of God to interpret the Scriptures and teach the faith. Since the Church is the authority that Christ established, to trust in that authority is to trust in the authority of Christ. To submit to that authority is essentially to submit to Christ. Multiple quotations could be cited, but one more will suffice to show that Saint Thomas Aquinas held to the Catholic understanding of authority as opposed to sola scriptura.

> The universal Church cannot err, since she is governed by the Holy Ghost, who is the Spirit of truth: for such was our Lord's promise to his disciples (Jn 16:13): "When he, the Spirit of truth, is come, he will teach you all truth." Now the symbol is published by the authority of the universal Church. Therefore it contains nothing defective.[8]

Saint Thomas Aquinas submitted to the Catholic Church, believing that Christ passed his authority on to his apostles, who then passed that teaching authority on to their successors, so that when the Church exercises this teaching authority, she is governed by the Holy Spirit and cannot err. Although Saint Thomas is not himself considered infallible, he is known as one of the brightest Christian thinkers in history, not to mention that he is a saint because of the holiness that he exhibited during his life. SES rightfully taught me to respect such a profound Christian theologian. In light of his unparalleled theological acumen and godly example, it is not surprising that Saint Thomas Aquinas influenced my move in the direction of the Catholic Church.

The Eucharist

Obviously Symbolic?

By this time, the two pillars of the Protestant Reformation, sola fide and sola scriptura, had undergone irreversible, significant damage, but the discovery that would burst wide open the doors into the Catholic Church was something completely unforeseen and remarkably

[8] Ibid., II-II, 1, 9, sed contra.

missed in all of my theological inquiries. In fact, Christ drew me to him in a manner that I would have never thought possible: through the Eucharist.

My own spiritual heritage regarded communion as only symbolic. The Lord's Supper was a time to remember what Christ had gained for us on the Cross. He had achieved salvation by paying the penalty for our sins, and communion was a time to give thanks. When I was growing up, communion was celebrated once a month, at the most, in my Evangelical congregations. It was never considered the focal point of any service.

While the Lord's Supper was a solemn, special occasion, it never garnered any special attention in my theological studies. The merely symbolic nature of communion seemed so obvious as not to cause any hesitations about it in my mind. Clearly, Jesus did not mean that the bread was literally his body. Such an idea seemed foolish, for at the Last Supper, his own body was behind the table, holding the piece of bread. How could he be pointing to his own body in his own hand when his body was the thing that was holding the bread? Was his body holding his own body?

What If?

Admittedly, such an idea does seem nonsensical, except for one all-important caveat. What if the person saying such a seemingly nonsensical thing actually predicted and accomplished his own Resurrection from the dead, something that seemed, and still seems, absurd to many people? What if this person actually claimed to be God himself, a remark considered preposterous and blasphemous to many during the time of Christ? And what if this person claiming to be holding his own body in his own hands is really God himself?

Regarding such a possibility, Saint Augustine writes, "For Christ was carried in his own hands, when, referring to his own Body, he said, 'This is my Body.' For he carried that Body in his hands."[9] In taking the claims found in Church history more seriously, I discovered one of the most important teachings in Christianity. Bishops, apologists, theologians, and Church Father after Church Father stressed the reality of the real presence of Christ in the Eucharist. From the

---

[9] Saint Augustine, *Explanations of the Psalms* 33, 1, 10.

earliest times, Christ's literal Body and Blood took center stage, indicating that it was the focal point of Christianity. Just mentioning the literal presence doesn't do justice to its significance, as it is not only the case that Communion is not merely symbolic, but the very sacrifice of Calvary becomes present when the bread is transformed into the Body of Christ, and, by extension, what the priest holds in his hands is the whole Christ—Body, Blood, Soul, and Divinity. Jesus is not sacrificed over and over again, as if he dies every time a Catholic Mass occurs, but the Mass makes present the one sacrifice of Christ on Calvary. When a Catholic receives the Eucharist, it is the glorified Christ that he receives, resulting in a more powerful participation in the divine life, the very life of God. He grows in righteousness, meaning that the merits of Christ are further appropriated to him.

Historical Witness

Although the scriptural arguments in favor of the Catholic interpretations of passages such as John 6, 1 Corinthians 10 and 11, the Gospel accounts of the Lord's Supper, and many others convey solid support for the real presence, the historical reasons for accepting this beautiful teaching of the Church had a significant effect on my transition toward the Church. A few quotations are worth citing:

> Take note of those who hold heterodox opinions on the grace of Jesus Christ which has come to us, and see how contrary their opinions are to the mind of God.... They abstain from the Eucharist and from prayer because they do not confess that the Eucharist is the flesh of our Savior Jesus Christ, flesh which suffered for our sins and which the Father, in his goodness, raised up again. They who deny the gift of God are perishing in their disputes.[10]

> We call this food Eucharist, and no one else is permitted to partake of it, except one who believes our teaching to be true and who has been washed in the washing which is for the remission of sins and for regeneration [i.e., has received baptism] and is thereby living as Christ enjoined. For not as common bread nor common drink do we receive these; but since Jesus Christ our Savior was made incarnate by the word of God and had both flesh and blood for our salvation,

[10] Saint Ignatius of Antioch, *Letter to the Smyrnaeans* 6:2–7:1.

so too, as we have been taught, the food which has been made into the Eucharist by the Eucharistic prayer set down by him, and by the change of which our blood and flesh is nurtured, is both the flesh and the blood of that incarnated Jesus.[11]

The bread and the wine of the Eucharist before the holy invocation of the adorable Trinity were simple bread and wine, but the invocation having been made, the bread becomes the body of Christ and the wine the blood of Christ.[12]

You ought to know what you have received, what you are going to receive, and what you ought to receive daily. That Bread which you see on the altar, consecrated by the word of God, is the Body of Christ. That chalice, or rather, what the chalice holds, consecrated by the word of God, is the Blood of Christ. Through those accidents the Lord wished to entrust to us His Body and the Blood which he poured out for the remission of sins.[13]

It is not man that causes the things offered to become the Body and Blood of Christ, but he who was crucified for us, Christ himself. The priest, in the role of Christ, pronounces these words, but their power and grace are God's. "This is my body", he says. This word transforms the things offered.[14]

You will see the Levites bringing the loaves and a cup of wine, and placing them on the table. So long as the prayers and invocations have not yet been made, it is mere bread and a mere cup. But when the great and wondrous prayers have been recited, then the bread becomes the Body and the cup the Blood of our Lord Jesus Christ.... When the great prayers and holy supplications are sent up, the Word descends on the bread and the cup, and it becomes his body.[15]

Due to space constraints, I am not able to mention in any detail other notable factors that influenced my embrace of the Catholic Church, such as the beauty of the liturgy; the sacramental life; the

---

[11] Saint Justin Martyr, *First Apology* 66.
[12] Saint Cyril of Jerusalem, *Catechetical Lectures* 19, 7.
[13] Saint Augustine, *Sermons* 227.
[14] Saint John Chrysostom, *Against the Judaizers* 1, 6.
[15] Saint Athanasius, *Sermon to the Newly Baptized*.

Communion of the Saints; the tradition of prayer; the rich intellectual tradition; the *Catechism*; the Church's being the largest charitable organization on earth; the Church's leading the way in defending vital moral and social issues; the list of impressive converts and reverts—persons such as Blessed John Henry Newman, G. K. Chesterton, Dr. Peter Kreeft, Dr. Scott Hahn, Dr. Francis Beckwith, and Dr. Bryan Cross—the courage of prior SES converts, such as Joshua Betancourt, Andrew Preslar, Jeremiah Cowart, and Dr. Jason Reed; the Catholics who have exhibited impressive godliness and generosity, which have combated unflattering Catholic stereotypes; the Catholic priests who met with me privately—Father DeClue, Father Matthew Kauth, Father Timothy Reid, Father David Runnion; Pope Benedict XVI and Saint John Paul II; being blessed with another son and a stronger family because of the Church's unpopular teaching on contraception; and the Blessed Virgin Mary.

Although even more could be listed, it must especially be reiterated that in becoming Catholic, as so many have expressed before, I have not left my Evangelical Christian faith behind. Rather, I have found its fullness in the Catholic Church. The many beautiful, good, and true gifts I have received and been taught through the witness of family, friends, Evangelical church families, and the SES family will not be cast aside. Instead, they will only be further deepened and solidified in living out the Catholic faith.

The Mass

In the fall of 2010, my family and I attended our first Mass in a small parish in Lancaster, South Carolina. Although many might look at this church from the outside and consider it an old, run-down building whose days were numbered, we caught a glimpse of the inside. Although we did not know any of the liturgical responses, we heard the Sacred Scriptures read aloud. The music might not have sounded particularly delightful or "relevant", but a calm reverence marked this house of worship. After the priest finished his homily, what would transpire would be none other than heavenly and supernatural. Persons quietly knelt down, respectfully waiting as the priest continued with the liturgy. Eventually, the priest leaned on the altar and uttered the words "Take this, all of you, and eat of it, for this is my body, which will be given up for you." With an intense focus, the priest lifted up what appeared to be common bread, but, in reality, Christ was present before our very eyes. The reverence and awe that so characterized this beautiful, small parish was none other than a response to the miraculous presence of our Lord and Savior, Jesus Christ.

In December of 2012, my family and I were able to partake of the divine nature, being nourished by Christ's miraculous presence in the Holy Eucharist; we entered into full communion with the Catholic Church, our home.

> For in the Catholic Church, not to speak of the purest wisdom, to the knowledge of which a few spiritual men attain in this life, so as to know it, in the scantiest measure, indeed, because they are but men, . . .—not to speak of this wisdom, which you do not believe to be in the Catholic Church, there are many other things which most justly keep me in her bosom. The consent of peoples and nations keeps me in the Church; so does her authority, inaugurated by miracles, nourished by hope, enlarged by love, established by age. The succession of priests keeps me, beginning from the very seat of the apostle Peter, to whom the Lord, after his Resurrection, gave it in charge to feed his sheep, down to the present episcopate. And so, lastly, does the name itself of Catholic, which, not without reason, amid so many heresies, the Church has thus retained; so that, though all heretics wish to be called Catholics, yet when a stranger asks where the Catholic Church meets, no heretic will venture to point to his own chapel or house.[16]

[16] Saint Augustine, *Against the Epistle of Manichaeus* 4, 5, in *The Nicene and Post-Nicene Fathers: First Series*, eds. Alexander Roberts, James Donaldson, Philip Schaff, and Henry Wace (Peabody, Mass.: Hendrickson Publishing, 1996), 130.

8

To Enter the Sanctuary by the Blood of Jesus

By Andrew Preslar

What follows is the story of how I became a Catholic, as best as I can remember it. Only the first section is predominantly autobiographical. The next four sections are devoted to describing the contours of the biblical, liturgical, and ecclesiological considerations that would lead me to Catholicism. In the sixth section I recount the final steps that I took toward and then into the Catholic Church, including the process of navigating through some of the confusing and troubling aspects of her recent history. The concluding section contains a synopsis of the development in my views on salvation and how this relates to the liturgical life of the Church.

Searching for Holy Ground

My father is the cofounder and head pastor of an independent Bible church in Charlotte, North Carolina. In our family, "the church" meant both this particular community of believers and, eventually, the place where our religious services were held. Our theological doctrine of the church involved a different and more inclusive definition of the term, but the church in this wider sense was something so abstract that for all practical purposes and in regular conversation "the church" simply meant our church.

In the early days, we gathered for worship in the home of one of the church elders. (Our polity was Presbyterian, though doctrinally and culturally we were closer to Baptists.) As the church grew, we moved from this house to various rented locations and eventually began making plans to purchase our own place of worship. At that point, my father was constantly on the lookout for buildings or undeveloped land suited to our needs. A place did not even have to be up for sale for him to remark fervently on its potential as we drove past. Sometimes, if the place was for sale, we would stop and take a look around. His enthusiasm was contagious, and to this day I am drawn to every church I see, desiring to stop and get to know it, from the land to the liturgy.

We eventually purchased several acres of land, the bulk of which is set in a dell a good distance from the road. The property is bordered on one side by a large creek and backed by extensive woods. Here we constructed a small church building. Although we did not believe that there was anything particularly sacred about this or any other place on earth (other than the land promised to Abraham and his descendants), looking for a place to worship as a church felt (to me) like searching for holy ground, and moving into the place, we found, was like entering the promised land. I can remember my father, grandfather, and other church leaders turning over clods of earth with a shovel as we ceremonially dedicated the ground to its new use.

The following narrative is not an account of how I walked or drifted away from these beginnings, because I do not believe that that would be an accurate depiction of events or their outcome. Rather, I believe that I am still living in the same land into which, as a young boy, I was reborn by faith and baptism in the name of the Father, and of the Son, and of the Holy Spirit. What follows is an account of how I went on to explore this land and how I came to see it as an essentially Catholic country. Over the years, there have been significant changes in my theology and ecclesial life, but my respect, admiration, and affection for the church of my childhood and young adulthood, the people and the place, is undiminished.

Another childhood experience also fostered an incipient concept of sacred space. When I was eleven or twelve years old, a friend lent me his copy of J. R. R. Tolkien's fantasy novel *The Lord of the Rings*. This was the three-volume Ballantine Books paperback edition, with Tolkien's own watercolor paintings on the front covers and, on the back covers, a delightful photograph of the author in profile, laughing and holding his pipe. This book turned out to be my ticket not only to a new fictional world but to a new way of seeing the natural world of everyday experience. I came to see the things of Earth through the lens of Middle Earth and so became convinced that the world is enchanted, in the sense of having an inherent meaning and significance. I was already familiar with the biblical depiction of the heavens and the earth as having been spoken into existence, duly arranged, and filled with lights and creatures (Genesis 1) that in turn "utter speech" to the glory of God (Psalm 19). Tolkien subtly encouraged me to "listen" for these words, creating and created, in nature.

Of course, one does not have to read fantasy to awaken to the beauty and mystery of the natural world, but in my case it was *The Lord of the Rings* that gave rise to and fostered this sensibility. It was in Middle Earth that I first learned to walk in wonder. I still reckon this to have been more than (though not less than) an aesthetic experience. Reading Tolkien elicited in me something that C. S. Lewis called joy—that is, an acute longing that does not exactly correspond to any finite thing. According to Lewis' interpretation of this experience, joy is a signpost directing us to our ultimate, eternal home. I did not come across Lewis' account of joy until some ten years after my first reading of *The Lord of the Rings*, but from that time I had often had the experience exactly as Lewis described it.

Although I did not at first perceive the connection between joy and heaven, Tolkien's novel served as a kind of anchor for my soul during a period of my life (late boyhood to young adulthood) in which I began to care less and less about Christian faith and obedience. I had accepted the basic tenets of Christianity as these were presented in my home and church, in much the same way that I accepted my parents' views on other matters from the time that I first understood them. As I began to make up my own mind about more and more things, it never once occurred to me to question the content of my religious instruction. I simply did not spend much time thinking about or trying to live by my beliefs. Nevertheless, through my reading and rereading of *The Lord of the Rings* and other books by Tolkien, an important (though relatively obscure) connection was maintained with something that I instinctively knew to be not only beautiful but holy.

Encountering God and Rediscovering the Bible

This is where Southern Evangelical Seminary (SES) comes into the picture. When I was about twenty-one, several students from SES started visiting our church. One of these students, an older, married man, formed a "college and career" group and began teaching Christian apologetics. I had been attending church services more often than not, mostly from a sense of family obligation. Now, at the prompting of my parents, I began going to the "college and career" meetings, during which the teacher recapitulated the content of his SES apologetics courses in a manner suitable for this church group. The philosophical arguments for the existence of God and the historical evidence for the claims of Christ and the reliability of the Bible appealed to me on an intellectual level. I had always believed that Christianity is true, but now I wanted to know about the evidence for Christianity and the relation of revealed truth to truth discovered by means other than Bible study, including observation, intuition, philosophy, mathematics, empirical science, and the liberal arts. Although I had no intention of changing my behavior, I became interested in Christianity in much the same way that one might become interested in any other subject.

Eventually, however, the thesis and corresponding evidence that the claims of Christ are true began to bear down on me, and I was brought face-to-face with the fact that I had built a barrier between faith and life. Now I began to think seriously about the implications of the gospel as truth, reasoning that if the gospel is indeed true, it cannot be confined to the realm of subjectivity but is instead a statement of the way things really are, regardless of what anyone thinks or feels about it. On one level, this was a straightforward and prosaic bit of philosophy. But on another level, and by the same token, it was breathtaking because this simple piece of reasoning introduced into the realm of my personal experience something like what is expressed in the 139th psalm. One night, while alone in my apartment, I was unexpectedly overwhelmed by the presence of God, and the barrier between faith and life was removed. A few months later, I went off to Bible college with the intention of earning a degree in theology and then returning home to obtain a degree in apologetics at SES. I had no clear idea of what I wanted to do with this education; I only wanted to know more of the truth that is in Christ Jesus.

I had a wonderful time in college, learning much, making good friends, and enjoying the natural beauty of the mountains, hills, and rivers of West Virginia. I spent much of my time in the library, reading theological journals and thereby being introduced to new perspectives on and various ways of engaging divine revelation. The *Westminster Theological Journal* and the *Christian Scholar's Review* were among my favorites. I appreciated the former particularly for the articles on the Old Testament that elucidated aspects of salvation history as well as the relation between modern science and the Genesis narratives. The *Christian Scholar's Review* enriched my developing theological views by exploring in myriad ways the relationship between theology and other kinds of learning, especially philosophy and literary studies.

In this way, I started to develop a "catholic", or at least eclectic, frame of reference for exploring theological matters. I became willing to engage (and learn from) other kinds of Christians at the level of dialogue rather than mere disputation. Eventually my circle of reading would take in Catholic authors, including some of the classics in Western theology (Augustine, Anselm, and Aquinas) along with a few twentieth-century philosophers, especially Étienne Gilson and Jacques Maritain. The inclusion of Catholic theologians and philosophers in my increasingly diversified reading might be seen as a preamble to my eventual conversion, but it was not until I had been at seminary a few years that my own biblical-theological convictions began perceptibly to take a turn that would eventually lead me to the Catholic Church.

During my time at SES, the ethos of the school was definitely more speculative than practical, and I am entirely grateful for that. Quiet study in pursuit of truth as a good in itself was (and is) for me a welcome contrast to the bustling pragmatism and soul-constricting relativism of American society. Other aspects of seminary life, especially the number of remarkable people (among both students and faculty) I met there, are worth recalling in their own right, but here I will comment on only two general aspects of my education that helped me along the path to full communion with the Catholic Church.

The first and most obvious of these was the high regard in which Saint Thomas Aquinas was held at the seminary. That several of our professors took Aquinas to be a reliable guide in some fundamental philosophical and theological matters helped to break down my prejudice against the Catholic Church, much of which had already been dissipated by the aforementioned reading, along with the discovery that Tolkien was a faithful Catholic. Not every professor at SES was a Thomist, but the classes in philosophy, apologetics, prolegomena to theology, and theology proper were definitely taught from a Thomistic perspective. Through reasoning along with Saint Thomas, we discovered the inadequacy of reason regarding the mysteries of God, which must be received by faith on the basis of divine authority. We also learned, however, that faith does not abolish reason; rather, reason can help us to distinguish between genuine and spurious claims to divine authority and to understand better both the nature of what God has created and the meaning of what he has revealed, so as to love, obey, and adore him better. Thomism is not the only helpful school of Christian theology, but it is a deep well of biblical, theological, and philosophical wisdom. While making no claim to have personally explored its depths, I have tasted the water and found it to be cold and refreshing.

The second thing that brought me closer to Catholicism was learning to read the Bible as literature and canon. In my Old and New Testament seminary courses, we were helped to see and appreciate that the sacred authors used various literary genres and devices to convey their meanings, which were to be discovered in their respective contexts. But at the same time we were encouraged to understand this diverse set of writings in relation to one another as the written Word of God, such that the Bible could and should be read as a cohesive whole rather than a mere collection of disparate parts. Thus, my introduction to the Bible as literature was coupled with my introduction to what has been called "canonical" hermeneutics. Reading the Bible as canon, as a complete book, enhanced my budding appreciation of the Bible as literature. By paying attention to the canonical context of each portion of Scripture, I became more sensitive to both the direct and the allusive narrative weaving by which the inspired authors invoked, interpreted, and even anticipated other important events in sacred history. In this way, I discovered new depths in the long-familiar texts, with the result that I once more began really to enjoy reading the Bible.

Although I did not recognize it at the time, consciously reading the Bible as canon and deliberately employing the "analogy of faith"

(Scripture interprets Scripture) was my first step in reading the Bible with church tradition as a guiding light. By reading the Bible as a complete and internally consistent book, I was tacitly assuming that fidelity to tradition—in this case, the traditional Protestant list of the books of the Bible—is a sound hermeneutical principle. It took a couple of years for this to become apparent to me, at which point I began consciously to accept tradition, more broadly construed, as hermeneutically essential and authoritative. From that point, it would be a few more years before I finally submitted to the ecclesial authority by which apostolic Tradition (2 Thess 2:15) is definitively distinguished from merely man-made traditions, opinions, and schools of thought.

While in college, my most absorbing interaction with Scripture had consisted of trying to reconcile various "problem texts" with the tenets of the theological system I had inherited from my home church and the teaching institutions with which we chose to associate—namely, classical Dispensationalism with particular emphasis on the doctrine of eternal salvation by belief alone. I was treating the biblical texts like puzzle pieces, and my doctrine of salvation was the picture into which those pieces must be fitted. Thus, I spent a lot of time reading the Bible at arm's length, in a kind of defensive posture, not wanting to take the risk of discovering something that would lead me to reconsider my own theological convictions. Although the professors of biblical studies at SES held to more or less the same doctrine as I did, they were not as defensive about it as I was; at least, their interest in biblical theology was much broader than mine, which had been mainly confined to a few texts as either proving or threatening my doctrine of salvation.

Now, I began to appreciate those teachers and authors who seemed to be more interested in understanding the Bible itself than in underwriting a particular doctrine or school of thought. Following their example and instruction, I began to engage the Bible with a less polemical and more inquisitive mindset. One summer, I gave myself completely over to Scripture reading, my only goal being to engage the texts in a spirit of discovery. I bought a cheap, paperback Bible and read it from cover to cover, scrawling notes over every page, and so began to discover firsthand the unity, coherence, and beauty of the Bible from beginning to end.

By the time I finished seminary, my biblical theology could be summarized by the age-old aphorism "the New Testament is hidden in the Old, and the Old is revealed in the New". Dispensationalism, which in its classical form features a dichotomous reading of Sacred Scripture (Israel versus Church, law versus Gospel, even Gospels versus epistles), was part of the official doctrinal position of the seminary I attended, but that framework was not an important part of my educational experience there or my renewed, personal engagement with the Bible. On the other hand, neither was my developing biblical theology much influenced by Reformed Covenant theology, which in the Evangelical world is often contrasted with Dispensationalism. I read several books on the subject and found much in them that was helpful, but it never seemed to me that the Reformed brand of Covenant theology, featuring a "covenant of works" and a "covenant of grace", was especially biblical; at least, I could not find any compelling reason to adopt that particular way of reading Scripture. One thing that was settled in my mind at that time, relative to those categories and debates, was that I could no longer accept the Dispensationalist thesis that the time of the Church is a parenthesis in the overall biblical narrative. Instead, I was beginning to see in Sacred Scripture a pattern of anticipation (Old Testament) and fulfillment (New Testament), with Christ being the crux of the narrative, and the Mystical Body of Christ, the Church, being an integral part of the story.

The primary application, generally speaking, of my rediscovery of the Bible was that the most important hermeneutical question for me was no longer, "How does this passage apply to my life?" as though my life were the touchstone by which the value of Sacred Scripture was to be tested. Rather, I began to ask, "How do I apply my life to this passage?" such that the biblical narrative was taken to be the context in which my life made sense and found direction. From this standpoint, I found many direct and indirect applications of Scripture to my life, but the perspective on my life was now provided by the whole of salvation history, not merely the twentieth- and twenty-first-century American milieu. Because I now found the Church to be an integral part of the whole, the story of redemption ceased to be regarded as something confined to a text, the remote past, and an immanent but presently unrealized eschaton. Certainly, I believed that salvation history had been inscribed as divine revelation in the canonical texts, which preserve a record of events that occurred thousands of years ago, and that the end of the story carries us beyond this world to a "new heaven and a new earth" (Rev 21:1). But I was also beginning to discover that, as implied by the Great Commission (Mt 28:19–20) and the gift of the Holy Spirit (Jn 14:15–29), redemptive history also includes the Christian centuries, the ongoing (according to one vivid characterization) "aftershocks" of the seismic victory of Christ over death and Hades.

Thus, without clearly recognizing or consciously desiring it, I was moving from an individualistic and contemporary form of Christian belief, focused on my life and immediate cultural background, to a more communal and traditional form of Christian faith, focused on the ongoing story of the presence and mighty works of God on behalf of, in, and through his chosen people across the world and throughout history. This growing interest in an expanded "sacred history" brought me directly to the threshold of Church history, including the 1,500 years that had passed between the end of the Acts of the Apostles and the beginning of the Protestant Reformation.

Worshipping God and Discovering the Liturgy

Closely related to my rediscovery of the Bible was my growing interest in the shape, content, and significance of the church's corporate worship. This would eventually lead me carefully to consider the sacramental and liturgical aspects of worship, with a special focus on the Lord's Supper. The first time I entertained more than a passing thought about the Supper was during one of my Bible college classes, in which a professor raised the question of whether the Lord's Supper should be celebrated in any context other than a church worship service. My first thought was that the Lord's Supper can be celebrated anywhere by any Christian. My subsequent thoughts, in justification of the first, were that every believer in Christ is a priest (1 Pet 2:9; Rev 1:6), that no believer is a priest in any sense besides the priesthood of every believer, and that consequently no specially ordained ministers were necessary to do anything that the church was supposed to do. Thus, if any two or three believers were gathered anywhere at any time in Jesus' name, they could legitimately celebrate the Lord's Supper in memory of him.

Of course, I had just associated the ordinance of the Lord's Supper with the Christian priesthood, which is a bad move for a Protestant to make, since the connection between the Lord's Supper and the priesthood has sacerdotal connotations. My intention, however, was simply to apply an egalitarian conception of the church's ministry to the observance of the Supper. But I soon put the question aside and did not think about the matter again until some four years later, just before I graduated from seminary, when I spoke to a Reformed pastor about the requirements for receiving communion in his church. In my experience up to that point, studying and teaching were high spiritual priorities, while prayer, corporate worship, and the sacraments (or "ordinances") were secondary considerations. When I considered the "assembling of ourselves together", it seemed to be primarily a means to the end of hearing an informative sermon. But toward the end of my time in seminary, prompted by something that I was beginning to notice in the Bible, I began to look for a church with an emphasis on liturgical worship, prayer, and the sacraments.

What I was starting to see in Scripture is that the ritual or sacrificial worship of God is a major theme that can be traced from Genesis to Revelation—from the Garden of Eden (which some biblical theologians have described as the "holy of holies" in the temple of creation), through the altars of Abel, Noah, and the Patriarchs and the Tabernacle and Temple liturgies of Israel, to the Upper Room, the Christian assembly, and the Heavenly Sanctuary and Throne Room, all of which center on Calvary. The "tree of life" underscores and encapsulates the sacramental aspect of redemptive history by linking Eden (Gen 2:9; 3:22), the Cross (Gal 3:13), and the New Jerusalem (Rev 22:1–2). I began to think that Christian worship that aspires to be biblical should be deeply informed by these biblical examples and themes of worship.

I had previously assumed that because the New Testament does not include detailed rubrics for worship, the apostles were tacitly condoning a "free-for-all" approach to church services (within the limits of generic propriety). Clearly, the New Testament offers few instructions concerning the structure of Church services, but it is also clear that these early services included the ritual action of celebrating the Lord's Supper in obedience to Christ's command. In addition to instructions on the Supper provided in the New Testament, there were other indicators that the liturgical forms of Christian worship that developed in the early Church are rooted in apostolic authority. The Gospels themselves, in addition to being theologically significant historical records and resources for private contemplation, serve as a kind of manual for worship. The Christian liturgy—in particular, Sunday worship (the Lord's Day) and the Church year—is patterned after the life of Christ as presented by the four evangelists. In addition to this, and given the relation of anticipation and fulfillment between the Old Covenant and the New, it seemed to me that Israel's now fulfilled and superseded cultus could legitimately be drawn upon by the Christian Church, not as a binding code but as a kind of template for liturgical worship, with the sacrifice of the Lamb of God standing in the place of animal sacrifices (Rev 5:6).

From the Christian perspective of the New Testament authors, the religious rituals and symbols of the Old Covenant were shadows and types of something greater—namely, the New Covenant in Christ Jesus. In the New Testament it is stated that the Old Covenant has been fulfilled by Christ, who is the substance or reality of those former things, which, being fulfilled, have now "passed away" (cf. Col 2:17; Heb 8:13). There is, however, a resemblance between the lesser and the greater, type and antitype, anticipation and fulfillment. The self-sacrifice of Christ at Calvary and the liturgy of the Heavenly Throne Room, featuring Christ's present priestly session administered with his own blood (Heb 7:23–25), is the fulfillment of the Tabernacle and Temple liturgies, which featured the Aaronic priesthood administered with the blood of bulls and rams (Heb 9:11–15). This principle applies to baptism and circumcision (Col 2:11–12) as well as the Lord's Supper and the Passover (1 Cor 5:7–8). Thus, the life, death, and Resurrection of Christ, as ritually remembered in the sacraments and through the course of the Church's liturgical year, fulfills but also somewhat resembles Israel's divine worship, including her seasonal feasts and fasts. Precisely because the New Covenant fulfills the Old, these resemblances do not involve a repetition or prolongation of the former Covenant, nor do they entail that the efficacy of the New Covenant rites is no greater than that of the Old. But the similarities between the covenants, as embedded in the very

relation of anticipation and fulfillment, do suggest that the relation
between the liturgical life of Israel and that of the Church cannot be
reduced to mere opposition.

I was vaguely aware that the Church's communal worship, like
the divine worship of Israel, has historically been liturgical, following a set pattern of rituals, prayers, and seasons. This tradition now
began to appeal to me as being distinctly Bible based. For me, drawing primarily upon biblical examples and images, the word *liturgy*
evoked the notion of a beautiful, reverent, and ritualized form of
public worship that is handed down by tradition and rooted in divine
revelation—worship marked less by the transient forms of the secular
world and more by the permanent things of heaven, insofar as they
have been revealed to the people of God. I still had no clear doctrinal ideas about the sacraments, and no knowledge of the history of
the Christian liturgy, but there was a growing sense that I had been
missing out on something important—and I wanted in. Of course,
I knew that the Catholic Church and the Orthodox Church feature liturgical worship and sacraments, but I was not prepared to go
exploring that far afield from Evangelicalism. Among confessional
and (more or less) liturgical Protestant churches, the Presbyterian and
Reformed tradition was more familiar to me than either Lutheranism
or Anglicanism, so it was there that I chose to begin searching for
"something more".

Apostolic Succession and the Eucharist

A few months before receiving my seminary degree, I began attending a traditional Presbyterian church. During a private meeting, the
church's pastor told me that according to the bylaws of the denomination I needed to be a member in good standing of an "Evangelical"
church in order to receive communion (in this context, I think that
Evangelical simply meant Protestant, or perhaps conservative Protestant). I had always been taught that a person is a member of the
church simply by virtue of having been saved through believing the
true gospel—neither baptism nor profession of faith nor anything
else was required for church membership. But that teaching referred
primarily to an invisible "universal Church", whereas in stating the

requirement for receiving communion, this Reformed pastor clearly had in mind membership in a visible church. As I considered the matter, the first thing that came to mind was that I had never formally become a member of any visible church, not even the church in which I grew up. I had been baptized with water in the name of the Father, and of the Son, and of the Holy Spirit, but I was not sure how this event related to church membership.

Now I was being encouraged to join a visible church formally in order to receive communion. This again raised the question that I had briefly considered in Bible college: What was the essential difference, if any, between receiving communion in this or any other "Evangelical" church and receiving it at home alone or with two or three fellow believers, having myself recited the "words of institution" (Mt 26:26–28) over a piece of bread and a cup of wine? The difference between raising the question at this point and asking it four years earlier was that I was no longer cocksure about the principle of ministerial egalitarianism in the Christian church. The New Testament clearly teaches the priesthood of all believers, but it is just as clear that the apostles received a special kind of power and authority directly from Christ. For one thing, Christ himself had given the apostles the commission to celebrate the Lord's Supper, or Eucharist: "Do this in memory of me." In their turn, as they went about establishing churches and setting things in order, the apostles ordained other men to distinct positions of service and authority in the churches and conferred upon those churches the commission to celebrate the Eucharist: "For I received from the Lord what I also delivered to you" (1 Cor 11:23).

Still, so far as I could tell, the New Testament did not give a clear answer to the specific question of who was authorized to celebrate the Eucharist. But as previously indicated, I was beginning to be convinced that Church history should inform Christian faith and practice, such that a question not answered in the Bible (either directly or by deduction) did not necessarily have to be chalked up as an indifferent matter or as something perpetually and in principle unresolvable. So I turned to the history of the early Church to see if there was any information on this particular question. The epistles of Saint Ignatius of Antioch, written around A.D. 107, provided me with an answer: a valid Eucharist is one celebrated by a bishop or someone whom the bishop has appointed to celebrate this sacrament. Thus, the Eucharist, which originated at Christ's own hands, was received and handed down in the Church through the apostles to the bishops and those whom the bishops ordained to celebrate this sacrament (i.e., the presbyters). Further investigation revealed this to be a deeply historical and, for 1,300 years, universal form of Church polity. But I was still not quite convinced that this "episcopal" ministry was biblical. I thought that "Presbyterian" (or else "congregational") polity might have mistakenly died out at the end of the first century or the middle of the second century, to be replaced by an episcopal polity that Christ and the apostles never intended.

As is generally acknowledged, in the New Testament and other early Christian documents the terms *bishop* and *presbyter* were not used, or at least not clearly and consistently used, with reference to two distinct offices in the Church. Rather, *bishop* and *presbyter* were deployed descriptively and interchangeably in referring to ordained Christian ministers (including apostles). It was only after the time of the apostles that these terms began to be clearly and consistently used in reference to two distinct offices,[1] so that by the end of the second century, episcopal polity featuring three distinct grades of ministry—bishop, presbyter, and deacon—is clearly evidenced throughout the Church, which has remained the case everywhere throughout history (with the exception of a few sects and the Protestant ecclesial communities).

Nevertheless, because of the way the words *bishop* and *presbyter* were used in the earliest Christian writings, I had always assumed that the distinction of the offices of bishops and presbyters was an illegitimate development within the Church. I never paused to consider how the Church after the time of the apostles could have almost immediately and universally lapsed into error on this fundamental point of polity, with no record of a general outcry in protest or any Church council called to deal with the ubiquitous mistake. Now I did pause to consider the matter and wondered if perhaps it was I, rather than the universal Church, that had been missing something. It seemed only fair to take another look.

The first thing I noticed was that in maintaining that the Christian ministry in the New Testament comprised only two grades

---

[1] Cf. Ignatius, *Epistle to the Magnesians*, chap. 6.

of ordained ministers, (1) bishop-presbyters and (2) deacons, I had been overlooking something both obvious and essential: (3) the ministry of the apostles themselves. The apostles clearly had distinct authority over their fellow bishop-presbyters. They had authority to establish orthodoxy and otherwise set things in order in the churches, including ordaining other men as bishop-presbyters and deacons. This apostolic authority in the Church is evidenced by the commission of our Lord to the apostles (Lk 10:16; Mt 28:19–20), the book of Acts, and the contents of the New Testament epistles, most of which were written by apostles and provide authoritative instruction on a variety of matters. Furthermore, and this was the crucial point, although it soon came to be widely acknowledged that the time of new, public revelation had come to an end with the deaths of the apostles, we can see evidence in the New Testament that distinctively apostolic authority was passed down to men such as Titus and Timothy, who, in addition to being bishop-presbyters themselves, exercised distinctive pastoral oversight among other bishop-presbyters in preserving the tradition of the apostles (1 Tim 6:20), setting things in order in the churches (Tit 1:5), and ordaining other bishop-presbyters and deacons (1 Tim 5:22). Eventually, the term *bishop* came to be used exclusively of this type of ministry, and *presbyter* was used to refer to those ministers who did not exercise such oversight, but were ordained by a bishop to celebrate the Eucharist, teach, and provide pastoral care in unity with the bishop.

Thus, the apostolic structure and authority of the Church's ministry, together with the integrity of her liturgical and sacramental life, was preserved in the transition from the apostles with their fellow bishop-presbyters and deacons to bishops with their fellow presbyters and deacons. Pastoral authority in teaching, governing, and sanctifying (administering the sacraments) was given by Christ to the apostles and by the apostles to the bishops, who, along with the presbyters and deacons, minister to the lay faithful. The Christian laity, being "a royal race of priests", serve God by cherishing and faithfully continuing in this living tradition in unity with their pastors, whereby the Church is built up from within (Eph 4:11–16) and becomes "salt and light" to the world (Mt 5:13–16).

While inquiring into the origin and development of episcopal polity, I also learned more about the early Church's understanding of the

Eucharist, not only with reference to who was authorized to celebrate this sacrament (namely, bishops and presbyters in apostolic succession), but also with regard to the real presence of Christ in the consecrated species, per his own words of institution: "This is my Body.... This is my Blood." Taken as a whole, from East to West and throughout the centuries, it is evident that the universal Church has believed and taught that in the celebration of the Eucharist the bread and wine really become the Body and Blood of Christ, which communicants who are rightly prepared receive unto their souls' health and salvation. It is also evident, not least through the appropriation of sacerdotal terms to the offices of bishop and presbyter and the sacrament of the Eucharist itself (e.g., *priest, altar, oblation*), that the Church has every-where believed that the Eucharist is in some way a true sacrifice pleas-ing to God, even though it does not involve the repeated death of the Victim. In becoming acquainted with the teaching of the historical Church on these matters, I became more aware of the sacrificial terms and allusions in the New Testament, with reference to Christ's Pas-sion and present priestly session as well as the Lord's Supper, the apos-tolic ministry, and the people of God as a whole. In this way, I came to believe that the Church's ordained priestly ministry, far from being opposed to or in addition to the work of Christ, depends entirely on that work for its efficacy, as being a participation in that work (Rom 15:16; 1 Cor 5:7–8; 10:14–22; 2 Cor 5:11–21; Heb 13:10).

While investigating these matters, I also, by way of comparison, became more familiar with how the various Protestant denomina-tions have historically understood the nature of Christian worship, particularly the sacrament of the Lord's Supper. From what I could tell, all of the leading Protestant Reformers rejected the traditional understanding that the Eucharist is a propitiatory sacrifice, and they also denied that the Eucharistic bread and wine are invisibly changed into the Body and Blood of Christ. Furthermore, all the Protestant churches rejected the sacerdotal ministry of bishops and presbyters (priests) as passed down in a sacramental succession from the apostles and instead developed their own forms of ordained ministry. Nev-ertheless, some of the first Protestants had ideas about the nature and benefits of sacramental communion that were miles away from any form of Evangelicalism to which I had been exposed. I did not know quite what to believe and confess regarding the Lord's Supper, but I desired to be united to Christ in whatever way he had intended when instituting the sacrament of his Body and Blood.

The Church of England and the worldwide Anglican Communion seemed to allow the greatest latitude in belief relative to most matters, including the Eucharist, which perfectly suited my growing interest combined with my (as yet) lack of conviction regarding the truth (or falsehood) of many important points of doctrine. I also appreciated that Anglicans had an episcopal church polity and an elegant form of liturgical worship enshrined in the Book of Common Prayer. What I had experienced of the Presbyterian and Reformed tradition was very admirable in its own way, but as I became more familiar with Church history it seemed to me that many of the treasures of the Christian tradition had been lost upon that way. I thought that at least some of those lost treasures might be found in Anglicanism.

Anglo-Catholicism

I soon discovered a traditional Anglican church less than a mile from my apartment. This community was more of the Anglo-Catholic persuasion, which is distinguished from other Anglican beliefs and practices by its emphasis on the continuity of the Church of England after the Protestant Reformation with the Church in England before the Reformation. My first visit to this church was for a midweek, noonday holy communion service. I will never forget kneeling in the dimly lit, Gothic-style church building, surrounded by stained-glass images of our Lord with angels and saints, while the priest stood (facing East) at what was clearly a high altar, complete with crucifix and tabernacle, and read the holy communion service from the Anglican Missal. (This missal comprised the Anglican Book of Common Prayer supplemented with prayers, in English translation, from the traditional Roman Missal.) Afterward, I spoke with the priest, briefly explaining my situation. I continued to visit, and we continued to talk. He told me that joining a "sacramental church" involves a "serious commitment" and that I could not receive communion until I had been "confirmed by a bishop in apostolic succession".

In the course of subsequent conversations and reading, I learned that, from an Anglo-Catholic point of view, the Church is hierarchical at the local level, being made manifest on Earth primarily in the Eucharistic assembly over which the bishop, or a presbyter ordained by and in communion with the bishop, presides. (In this way, Anglo-Catholicism follows the teaching of Saint Ignatius of Antioch.) The universal Church is supposed to be manifested (1) in each of these local assemblies in union with their respective bishops and (2) in the communion of all such assemblies with one another. Anglo-Catholics further believe that the universal, or catholic, Church has been divided into three branches: Roman Catholic, Eastern Orthodox, and Anglican (the "branch theory"). What these branches are supposed to have in common is the episcopal ministry preserved in apostolic succession and with it the fullness of the Church's sacramental life. What divides the branches are ecclesiological and cultural differences and disagreement over various doctrines and practices.

I became an Anglo-Catholic and a member of this particular Anglican parish for three reasons. First, there was the testimony to the beauty of holiness inscribed in the church building and the liturgy. Second, I thought that being Anglo-Catholic was a genuine way to be "catholic", which to me meant embracing the fullness of the Church's life from the beginning down to the present day, rather than simply stopping at the end of the first century and picking back up with Martin Luther or John Calvin or whomever in the sixteenth century or later. Anglo-Catholics claim to accept and abide by the teachings of the "undivided Church of the first millennium". Due to my growing awareness of and regard for the Church of these centuries, this was an important point in favor of Anglo-Catholicism. Third, the Anglo-Catholic branch theory of the Church, coupled with the long-standing disunity and doctrinal divergences among the branches, guaranteed that I would not have to receive the teaching of any presently unified and visible Christian community, including the Anglo-Catholic communities, as being in itself the settled teaching of the universal Church that Christ established. Thus, I could have the orthodoxy of history (up to a time) without the undivided Church of history and could rely on my private judgment for discerning the truth or deciding that the truth was unknowable in matters where the various branches of the divided Church disagreed with one another.

The third reason for becoming Anglican, however, was like a swinging door—it could as easily lead one out of as into the Anglican

Communion. The personal autonomy from magisterial teaching built into the Anglican branch theory granted me the freedom, in good faith, to question the branch theory itself, since, by the nature of the case, that theory could not be considered a binding article of faith. Granted that a visibly unified and authoritative universal Church once existed and that two of the three genuine "branches" of the putatively divided Church consider themselves still to be that one Church, it is natural if not inevitable for an Anglo-Catholic to wonder whether Anglo-Catholicism's own criterion of catholicity might rule out the branch theory. This methodological consideration was brought into greater focus by Church history (when did "schisms from the Church" become "branches of the Church"?) and biblical theology ("is Christ divided?"), which gradually led me to believe that the one, holy, catholic, and apostolic Church, though undoubtedly wounded by schism, still abides in her integral existence and operation such that the promises of Christ to the apostolic Church ("whatever you bind on earth will be bound in heaven" [Mt 16:19]) continue to be practically applicable at the universal level. It seemed to me that neither a divided church nor an invisible church could bind or loose at the universal level.

I knew that to look for and (if she might be found) enter into full communion with the one, visible Catholic Church would in effect mean abandoning every form of Protestantism, including Anglo-Catholicism, because the various Protestant denominations (and non-denominations) for the most part did not even claim to be the one universal Church that Christ founded, and the few that did make such a claim (along with some of the cults) were manifestly late arrivals on the historical scene, so they could not possibly be the universal Church founded in the first century. In this way I ceased to be Protestant sometime before I became Catholic.

As with liturgical worship and the Eucharist, my desire to find the universal Church and the local churches in full communion with the universal Church was in essence a desire to be more fully and deeply united to Christ. In both cases, my reasoning was fairly simple, and my premises were based on the words of Scripture. If the Eucharist truly is Christ's Body and Blood, and if the Church truly is "the fulness of him who fills all in all", "the pillar and bulwark of the truth" (Eph 1:23; 1 Tim 3:15), the Mystical Body and Bride of

Christ, then someone who loves Christ and has a sufficient awareness of and conviction about these things will be diligent in securing them for himself, like a trader who finds a pearl of great price or a man who discovers treasure in a field (Mt 13:4–46).

The Catholic Church

In setting out to look for the universal Church that Christ founded, I was immediately faced with a long-foreseen difficulty: I would have to consider the mutually exclusive claims of two churches, each being ancient and alive, each abiding throughout history in material continuity with the first-century Church, each claiming to be the one universal Church established by Christ. These two churches are, of course, the Catholic Church and the Orthodox Church. It was apparent to me by this time that if the universal Church that Christ founded still exists visibly on Earth, and if I were to find and join that Church, I would have to choose a side (i.e., join one church or the other) in the thousand-year-old schism between Orthodox and Catholics. I was no longer receiving communion or making aural confession at my Anglican parish, because I could not do so in good conscience. But neither could I in good conscience become either Catholic or Orthodox, because I knew that to join either of these churches would require a profession of faith that I could not yet make.

I longed, however, to receive Christ in the Eucharist, and I wanted to confess my sins and receive absolution through the ministry of his Church. So I prayed that the Holy Spirit would lead me to the Church that Christ founded and enable me to accept this Church's teaching by faith, on the basis of the authority that our Lord had given her. I admired the Orthodox Church for its emphasis on tradition and the corresponding richness of its liturgical life. I was also well aware that the Catholic Church is presently suffering from some serious maladies in this regard. Still, there were a variety of factors that drew me toward Catholicism. My Protestant background suggested the necessity of reconciliation with the Catholic Church because that had been at least our most proximate point of departure from the historical Church.

Furthermore, as an Anglo-Catholic I had come to appreciate, along with the Church Fathers in the period of Late Antiquity, medieval history, theology, literature, and devotions. To me, the Middle Ages on the whole represented an enrichment of Christian life and learning. Above all, my liturgical formation had been based on an Anglicized version of the traditional Roman Missal, Roman Ceremonial, and Church calendar. The Western tradition felt like home, intellectually, culturally, and liturgically. The Orthodox Church, by contrast, was unfamiliar. I admired Eastern iconography, and I knew by report that Orthodox liturgies were theologically richer and more beautiful than the contemporary liturgy of the Catholic Church. Still, I never visited an Orthodox church. I thought that choosing Orthodoxy would involve a general repudiation of Catholicism and consequently a loss of much of the rich theological, intellectual, and cultural heritage of the historical Church and the Christian centuries. On the other hand, I believed that the Catholic Church was in theory and in practice open to the spiritual riches of Orthodoxy and the Christian East. Thus, my propensity for catholicity further inclined me toward Catholicism. Finally, the local Church of Rome itself exercised something like a magnetic pull upon me, as it has upon so many Christians going back to the earliest times.[2]

Despite these predilections for Catholicism, my initial visits to Roman Catholic parishes were discouraging. I could not enter into the spirit of the liturgy but was instead disoriented by the new form of the Roman Rite, which, as I experienced it, was disappointingly different from both my biblical-theological vision of liturgical worship and my liturgical experience as an Anglo-Catholic. It seemed to me that the Tabernacle / Temple dimension of worship with its emphasis on the Eucharistic sacrifice and the "mystery of godliness" had been pushed to the background by the introduction of an *ordo* in which the unity of the liturgical action along with the "vertical" and numinous dimension of worship are rendered (relatively) obscure. Furthermore, although it is the Catholic Church's express intention that every Mass be celebrated reverently, it is commonplace for Catholics to tell stories of post–Vatican II liturgies that have purposely been anything but reverent. I certainly did not come in for the worst

---

[2] Rom 1:11–12; 15:23–24; "Inscription of Abercius"; Irenaeus, *Against Heresies* 3, 3, 2.

of things, but my trek toward Catholicism was initially stymied by my encounters with the new liturgy.[3]

Nevertheless, the growing conviction that I ought to become a member of the Catholic Church proved durable. This conviction was based partly on the biblical, theological, and historical evidence concerning the distinctive role of the apostle Peter, the Church of Rome, and the papacy in the life of the universal Church. (Vladimir Soloviev's *Russia and the Universal Church* was helpful on this point.) But it was also, as previously stated, based partly on something harder to define, something like a spiritual compass coupled with personal, intellectual, and cultural associations and affinities, largely fostered by literature and theological reading. I did consider the possibility that the Catholic Church to which I was drawn was in no small part the product of my imagination, or else a thing of the past, with the present reality being essentially different. Some of the strongest points made in favor of the Catholic Church in some of the books I had been reading seemed largely inapplicable in the situation following Vatican II. Still, I had learned from Aristotle via Saint Thomas that there is a difference between a substantial change and an accidental change, so I was open to considering the possibility that the Catholic Church remained substantially (in identity and essence) the same Church after the Council and the promulgation of the new form of the liturgy, despite being much altered in appearance.

Being an Anglican, specifically an Anglo-Catholic, John Henry Newman became very dear to me during this transitional period. Because of my concerns about the teaching of the Second Vatican Council and the "spirit of Vatican II" that pervaded the Catholic Church in the ensuing decades, I could somewhat identify with Newman's difficulties in the ideological atmosphere surrounding the First Vatican Council (1869–1870), even though that atmosphere or prevailing climate of opinion was in some ways the polar opposite

[3] It bears mentioning that many of the Catholics I know, including converts, have had a much more positive experience with the new form of the Roman Rite. Many of them heartily approve of the reformed liturgy as being more accessible for the laity and, in general, less of a barrier or stumbling block to Protestants. I do not wish to quarrel with them, and it is evident that on some points and in many cases they are right. For the purpose of this narrative, suffice to say that my initial impressions were what they were, and they played a large part in determining the timing and mode of my conversion.

of the one that permeated Vatican II. Newman's response to the situation, including his full acceptance of the dogmatic declarations of Vatican I, provided me with a good example of fidelity to the Church as well as a context for understanding why Vatican II was needed and what it achieved, particularly in correcting the unhealthy and extreme tendencies toward clericalism, centralism, and authoritarianism that had plagued the Church during Newman's lifetime.

To gain some understanding of the context of Vatican II, I did, of course, carefully read the Council documents themselves. Although some of these documents contained what appeared to me to be boilerplate affirmations, intentional ambiguities, and other things difficult to understand (in some instances being relative to my own ignorance), most of the material I found to be biblical and traditional. Furthermore, the teaching of the Council is saturated with a sense of Christian joy and gratefulness for the good things of God on the levels of both grace and nature. I very much appreciated this point of emphasis. So, while I struggled with some things in the conciliar documents and some of the changes in the Catholic Church following the Council, I was encouraged by other changes in emphasis and outlook (including some of the proposals for organic development of the liturgy) leading up to and introduced by Vatican II.

It is undeniable that in the fields of academic theology and biblical studies, as well as in some forms of pastoral practice, the so-called spirit of Vatican II is invoked to justify and advance the kind of liberalism that has marked many mainline Protestant denominations over the past century. But the Council documents and, just as importantly, the postconciliar teaching of the Magisterium itself are a different matter. Even supposing that some statements in the Council documents were intended, by some of the individuals who helped draft them, to be a Trojan horse by which to import non-Catholic ideas into the Church, it would not follow that those private intentions constitute the meaning of the statements in their public, ecclesial context (i.e., their meaning as taught by the Catholic Church). Furthermore, the sense in which such ambiguous and potentially problematic statements are to be interpreted would be (and in some instances has been) established by the ongoing teaching of the Magisterium as well as by prior teaching and tradition. As I read the encyclicals of Pope Paul VI and Pope John Paul II, along with many of the documents published after the Council by the Vatican's Congregation for the Doctrine of the Faith, it became apparent that the Catholic Church still spoke as the unique and authoritative bearer of the ancient and universal Christian tradition. Whatever experiments in banality and infidelity might be at work within the Church, it was clear to me that she still maintained a sense of her identity in continuity with the past.

Along with the writings and example of Newman, the Council documents themselves, and the postconciliar teaching of the Magisterium, two other things helped me a great deal in overcoming my reservations about the Catholic Church consequent upon the changes introduced by and following the Second Vatican Council:

1. I discovered that there is a school of thought within orthodox Catholic circles that, though in no way denying the teaching of Vatican II or the validity of the sacraments celebrated according to the new form of the Roman Rite, has been quite critical of the liturgical reforms (not to mention liturgical abuses) that followed the Council. Among the leading lights of this school, Joseph Cardinal Ratzinger is preeminent, not least because of his elevation to the papacy as Benedict XVI. I was pleased to find that there are people in the Latin Church, from the grassroots to the highest level, who maintain a comprehensive, inclusive, and active appreciation of their own liturgical patrimony.

2. The "hermeneutic of continuity" advocated by Pope Benedict XVI appealed to me as the most reasonable way to interpret the teaching of Vatican II, particularly for anyone who believes that the Catholic Church is the universal Church that Christ founded. Since, for reasons independent of the Council, I was coming to believe exactly that, the hermeneutic of continuity followed almost as a matter of course; in which case, whatever difficulties I had in harmonizing the teaching of the Council with other instances of the Church's teaching ought to be met with faith in Christ and the expectation of a bountiful theological harvest, consequent upon careful, submissive, and sustained engagement with the whole of the Catholic Church's tradition. (It helped that I had long been used to taking this same approach when considering apparent internal inconsistencies or points of tension in the canon of Sacred Scripture.)

After three years or so of investigating the matter, I concluded that the apparent rupture in the Catholic Church, between the present and the past, while it could be fairly characterized as a crisis, did not constitute a change of identity. Much that is true, good, and beautiful has been obscured in recent decades (a problem not unique to our time), but nothing has been irrevocably lost or repudiated, and some important things have been, or are being, restored. All things considered, and with a few exceptions, I could not pretend to be attracted to the contemporary Catholic Church insofar as I had experienced it, but neither could I honestly deny that this is the same Church that has existed throughout the Christian centuries. The Church had survived the Arian crisis, the iconoclast controversies, the infamous "pornocracy" of the tenth century, the Western Schism (1378–1418), the Renaissance popes, and many other upheavals and scandals. My sense told me that she would likewise survive naturalistic higher criticism, narcissistic liturgical and theological experimentation, and the general influence of the cultural revolution of the 1960s, though these troubles, being nearer, weighed more heavily on my sensibility.

Among other matters that I took some time to investigate before becoming Catholic were those grievous enormities that have been referred to collectively as "the sexual abuse scandal". I read a few books on the history of the scandal, beginning with *Betrayal: The Crisis in the Catholic Church*, by the Investigative Staff of the *Boston Globe*. I also read many reports and articles as more and more grievous facts were brought to light, pertaining not only to the United States but also to many other parts of the world. I had to accept that if I were to become Catholic, along with receiving an inheritance in the great truth, goodness, and beauty that has been manifested throughout the Church's long history, I would be coming in for a share of the shame that pertains to notorious evils that have been perpetrated by Catholics, particularly those in ecclesial office. I am ashamed by the facts that some Catholic priests, using their office as a cloak, have sexually molested children and young persons, and some Catholic bishops have covered up these crimes instead of pursuing justice. I can understand that, for some people who would otherwise be open to considering the claims of the Catholic Church, these facts can form an all-but-insuperable barrier to conversion or even conversation. Certainly, there can be no excuse for these sins. I would simply encourage people to learn what they can, not just about the Catholic sexual abuse scandal but about the whole of the Catholic Church's life, including the ministry of her priests, the vast majority of whom are guiltless in this matter. Most especially, I hope that people will take the time to become familiar with the great Catholic saints who shine with the light of Christ throughout the Church's history. That is what I tried to do, and in the end I found that I was able to follow my conscience and enter into full communion with the Catholic Church.

A short time before I formally withdrew from membership in my Anglican parish, I became convinced that full participation in the life of the Body of Christ normally includes being in full communion with the Pope, the successor of Saint Peter in Rome, the same Peter to whom our Lord Jesus Christ made those promises recorded in Matthew 16. The decisive moment came while I was attending a clergy conference of the Anglican province to which I belonged. (I was preparing for ordination and so was invited to attend.) On the way to the conference, I told my pastor about my intention to leave the Anglican Church for the Roman Catholic Church. He gave me counsel and encouraged me to talk to other priests at the conference. I did so after dinner that evening, and their advice in response was both helpful and kindly delivered. Then I stayed up to read G. K. Chesterton's short book *The Catholic Church and Conversion*. There was nothing in this particular book that was especially decisive, objectively speaking, for the Catholic Church's claims, but before I went to sleep that night, I had come to accept those claims. I finally believed in the one, holy, catholic, and apostolic Church, as I had long been confessing in the Nicene Creed. The next day, I said a final good-bye to the Anglican priests whom I had come to know and respect during four years in their communion.

Now it was time to seek entrance into the Catholic Church. For a few months after the Anglican clergy conference, I continued to visit Roman Catholic parishes, but I was daunted by the size of the parishes, which in my area ranged from several hundred to a few thousand families. (Each church that I had previously been part of was quite small, such that the members all knew one another. This made for a strong sense of family with corresponding affection and accountability.) Besides this, I still could not adjust to the new liturgy.

Finally, I visited a small community listed as Saint Basil the Great Ukrainian Catholic Mission, which was meeting in the chapel of the local Catholic high school. The chapel had been booked by another group on the evening of my first visit, so the Mission had temporarily arranged to use the school's library for the liturgy. There, in a small space cleared out among tables and rows of books, I encountered for the first time in person the ancient Eucharistic liturgy of the Byzantine Rite, the Divine Liturgy of Saint John Chrysostom.

Earlier in this story, I mentioned my love for Middle Earth, but the Divine Liturgy called to mind *Perelandra*, C. S. Lewis' paradisiacal depiction of the planet Venus. Even in the incongruous setting of a high school library, the liturgy was overflowing with beauty and reverence. But there was nothing either starched or stifling about it. The liturgical action was a free and organic unity, a living whole, both ancient and full of life, both ordered and extravagant. It made me think of the Garden of Eden, which is likewise recalled by the Tabernacle and Temple of ancient Israel. The Divine Liturgy made sense on an intuitive level and filled me with a peace beyond understanding. The priest who celebrated the liturgy, the bishop of this eparchy (diocese), and the particular Eastern Church to which they belong, the Ukrainian Greek Catholic Church, are in full communion with the Pope, for whom the celebrant prays by name at each liturgical service. Here the door was opened, and about two months later I was received into full communion with the Catholic Church by a solemn profession of faith, receiving the sacraments of chrismation (confirmation) and the Holy Eucharist according to the Byzantine Rite.

In some ways, my transition from West to East has been almost as slow and difficult as my transition from Evangelicalism to the Catholic Church. Despite the immediate appeal of the liturgy, understanding and embracing the Greek / Slavic Christian tradition was not something that I could do overnight. In fact, at first I was only canonically a Byzantine Catholic, being at heart an Anglicized Roman Catholic pining for something like a medieval country parish, or a Catholic village clustered around an old seaside monastery, or just a small Roman Catholic church in Charlotte that worships according to one of the older rites of the Western Church.

Over the past few years, however, the Ukrainian Greek Catholic Church has become my home, in my heart as well as in canon law. My native romanticism has gradually been taken up (without being destroyed) into something more concrete and more edifying— namely, participation in the distinctive liturgical life of this particular church with the fellow believers at Saint Basil's. As Eastern Catholics, we are committed to both our unity with Rome and our own tradition, with its distinctive liturgy, theology, spirituality, discipline, and history, most of which we share with the Orthodox Church. However, as someone who came to the Catholic Church from Protestantism through Anglo-Catholicism, as a North American of Western European descent, and as a longtime admirer of the Middle Ages in general and Saint Thomas Aquinas in particular, I have been and undoubtedly will continue to be formed by both Western and Eastern traditions. These two traditions (which Pope John Paul II likened to two lungs) are mutually enriching aspects of the Holy Tradition that comes to us through the centuries from the apostles.

Where Heaven and Earth Meet

Much of this narrative has been focused on liturgical worship in the Church, but this is not because I have lost sight of the promise of eternal life with God in heaven. Far from it. The orientation of my spiritual life as a Catholic and in my life's longing for "holy ground" has been distinctly heavenward, though I did not always clearly recognize this and have often, through sin, wandered in another direction. But always I have been called homeward by the promise of heaven, the hope of heaven, and a dim perception of the uncreated beauty of that eternal realm in the beauty of creation.

In college and seminary, I thought a lot and occasionally argued about the means by which we receive the gift of eternal life, but I did not often think about eternal life itself. The pivotal moment for my understanding of salvation came just before I left seminary, when I began to think carefully about the teaching of Saint John the beloved apostle to the effect that eternal life is knowing God (Jn 17:3), and knowing God consists not only of having faith but also of abiding in love through keeping the commandments of Christ (1 Jn 3:10–24). For Saint John, abiding in eternal life is incompatible with abiding in death, but this does not entail that everyone who abides in eternal life is sinless; there is sin unto death ("mortal sin") and sin not unto death (1 Jn 5:16–17). Only the former extinguishes spiritual life. Even when a baptized Christian commits sin unto death, the free gift of forgiveness, cleansing, and reconciliation is available through confession (1 Jn 1:9). When I followed Saint John from his Gospel to his first epistle and back again, it seemed to me that abiding in eternal life and abiding in death by committing and refusing to repent of mortal sin are mutually exclusive because eternal life itself is not merely an infinite duration of conscious existence (even the damned have that), nor is it merely a promise about the future; rather, eternal life is a particular kind of life given and received as a gift here and now. It is a participation in the very life of God, who is love; hence, to have eternal life is to abide in love, which both fulfills the law (1 Jn 4:7–21; Rom 13:8–10) and triumphs over death and darkness (1 Jn 1:1–7; 2:1–11; 4:4–21).

Understanding eternal life as a gift whose nature is to know God by abiding in love caused me to reassess several of the assumptions that had always informed my doctrine of salvation, including the sharp contrasts that I had drawn between a gift and a way of life, justification and sanctification, forgiveness and cleansing, and God's grace and man's participation in that grace. Now I began to understand these things as being involved one in the other, as various facets of the same gift. Understanding eternal life as a way of life also helped me better appreciate those parts of the Gospel of John, such as the "bread of life" discourse in John 6 and the "fruit and vine" analogy in John 15, in which our life in Christ is portrayed in sacramental and participatory terms rather than as something abstract and static. Thus, several years before I entered the Catholic Church, I came to embrace in a general way an understanding of salvation that has been held by Catholic and Orthodox believers throughout the Christian centuries, an understanding that has sometimes been described as "covenantal and sacramental realism".

From the standpoint of covenantal and sacramental realism, the gift of salvation is not characterized by or based on a purely legal arrangement in which "the righteousness of God" is an extrinsic and alien quality that is merely imputed to those who believe; rather, the gift of salvation is fundamentally a familial covenant relationship in which those who are by nature sinners and strangers to the covenant of promise are by grace, through faith, forgiven, cleansed, and made sons of God who really participate in their Father's righteousness. Through faith in Christ, by the grace of God given in the sacraments, sinners truly become what God declares them to be. This great salvation flows directly from and is realized in union with Christ, the only-begotten Son and Divine Word of God, who was born and lived among us, self-sacrificially died on the Cross for our sins, was raised from the dead for our justification, ascended into heaven, and is seated at the right hand of the Father. Those who believe in Christ are delivered from the dominion of death and darkness into the realm of life and light (Jn 3:16–21); having the love of God poured out into our hearts by the Holy Spirit, we are made partakers of the divine nature, living members of Christ Jesus, and fellow citizens of the Kingdom of heaven (Rom 5:5; 2 Pet 1:4; Eph 2:1–10, 11–22).

That is the gist of the development in my understanding of salvation. It was like hearing a familiar song in a new key.

This brings me back to the liturgy of the Lord's Supper and to the conclusion of this conversion story. Every Sunday in the Divine Liturgy, we sing (and in the icons, we see) that Christ has conquered death by death and has by his Resurrection from the dead broken the gates of Hades; he then ascended bodily to the right hand of the Father on high, thereby opening the door to heaven for all who believe in him. The Church's worship, including its visible expression in liturgy, ceremonies, buildings, images, and icons, flows from and leads to faith. Our liturgical life is a manifestation of our assurance of things hoped for and conviction of things not seen (cf. Heb 11:1) and a real participation in the same until the return of our Lord, when those who are in Christ will finally see him face-to-face. Faithful participation in the liturgical and sacramental life of the Church prepares us for that divine vision. Especially in the celebration of the Eucharist, we learn to cast aside all earthly cares, that we might receive the King of all. When the Eucharistic bread and wine are changed by the power of the Holy Spirit through the prayer of the priest so that they become the Body and Blood of Christ, we are mystically present with the Lord in heaven, with the angels and saints gathered in adoration of the Lamb of God, who takes away the sins of the world. Thus, there is even here and now sacred space, holy ground, where heaven and Earth meet and the faithful gather (Mal 1:11; Heb 10:19–22; 12:22–24; Rev 4—5).

9

Moved and Sustained by the Blessed Virgin

By Jonathan Sonantis

Turn then, most gracious Advocate, thine eyes of mercy toward us, and after this our exile, show unto us the blessed fruit of thy womb, Jesus.

—Salve Regina

My conversion from Evangelicalism to Catholicism started about seven years before I finally converted. I was a standard Evangelical who had a conversion experience around the start of middle school. A year or two into junior high, however, I began a journey that would take me to where I am today. I began reading Scripture and became confused because what was apparently revealed by Scripture seemed to conflict with what reason and science told me. With the help of family, I was put in touch with some very helpful resources to which I owe my ultimate entrance into academia. I resolved to investigate my faith fully and go where reason led.

Fast-forward four or five years to my first year of college at Iowa State University, where I was very happy with some amazing Evangelical campus ministries but continued in my insatiable quest for the truth (read this less in an arrogant Indiana Jones way and more in a tortured cognitive dissonance way). Luckily, Brandon Dahm and some other friends of mine put me in touch with the philosophical and theological work of Thomas Aquinas and the Thomistic school of thought (I think I owe my love affair with Thomistic philosophy in part to the early mentoring of Brandon; he has my deepest gratitude). It cannot be overstated how eye-opening this experience was. Before I was put in touch with Thomism, I had vague, so-so arguments for the various truths of the Christian faith, of whose soundness I was sort of convinced. After I had been shown the light of Thomas Aquinas I could *see* the truth of the faith and the integrated whole that the faith is. It was beautiful. Perhaps I was on an immutable course from this very discovery. Perhaps the cognitive dissonance I had had in being Protestant and having such a deep respect for Aquinas pushed me into the obsessive investigation that would be resolved on the feast of Pentecost in 2012. One might say that *this* is where my journey to the Catholic faith began.

Then again, a year later I discovered the free online audio library provided by Peter Kreeft. I suffered from mild insomnia and would often put one of his lectures on as a way to absorb some interesting facts while I was failing to sleep. (Check out "The Spirituality of the Sea"! It is life changing.) I listened to hours and hours of this and was greatly edified as a result. Then I noticed Kreeft's lecture on ecumenism. I first thought, "What the heck is ecumenism?" To get an idea of what ecumenism is, think of Pope Francis' papacy. If I were to attempt to describe his papacy in one word, that word might be *ecumenism*. *Ecumenism* refers to the attempt to unite the various sects of Christianity.

Kreeft's talk gave me a real passion for the problem of Christian disunity. During the Last Supper, Christ prayed for a much deeper unity among Christians than is in principle possible in Protestantism. How deep a unity, you ask? Well, Christ asked the Father "that they may all be one; even as you, Father, are in me, and I in you" (Jn 17:21). This is pretty intense unity. The Father and the Son have the *same* intellect and will. This is much more than a vague spiritual oneness that simply fades the moment any theological question of substance comes up. At this point, maybe I saw at some level the impossibility of this kind of unity in any Protestant sect and had some sort of implicit argument about Christ not desiring and praying for things that were impossible. One might say *this* is where my conversion began.

Around the same time, I was getting more deeply into my philosophy degree and looking for ways to keep reading and thinking about Aquinas in the midst of my many other classes. I met Ed while taking a philosophy of physics class, and we got to talking about our mutual interest in Aquinas and in starting some sort of discussion group. It was in this group that some of my deeply ingrained anti-Catholic bias came up against the brutal truth: Catholics are Christians, and devoted ones at that. The months I spent with that group interested in Thomas Aquinas (who would guess that they were nearly all Catholic?) made it impossible for me to continue to believe that Catholics are not Christians, and at the very least I had to abandon the view that Catholics are the bogeymen they are made out to be. This time cleared away many of the ridiculous misconceptions I had of the Catholic faith (e.g., that Catholics are idolaters) as I continued to deepen my understanding of Aquinas' philosophy. One might say that *this* is when my conversion to the Catholic faith began.

There are many other events that contributed to my conversion, such as my e-mail correspondence with Peter Kreeft and Jay Budziszewski on various issues and perhaps my reading of the resources with which they put me in touch. But I would classify none of those things as the *beginning* of my conversion. The beginning of one's conversion is different from the beginning of one's being *convinced* of the truth of Catholicism. All of the above were important events along the way to my being convinced of the truth of Catholicism. But my conversion began differently.

There is yet another Kreeft connection here, however. There was a moment in his lecture on ecumenism that nagged at me for a long time. Kreeft said, "Baptists are learning to love Mary and pray the Rosary, and Catholics are asking, 'Do you know Jesus Christ as your personal Savior?'" This line really bothered me. Really? Baptists are learning to love Mary and pray the Rosary? I needed to look into this. For the next few days (neglecting to go to class as often as I should have, as often happened in those days) I obsessively investigated the Mary thing. The first and easiest point to determine was whether praying the Rosary is worshipping Mary and therefore idolatry (hint: it is not). The Rosary is a very interesting devotional practice that centers on three things: (1) the Our Father, (2) the Hail Mary, and (3) meditation on important events in the lives of Christ and Mary.

The only thing that produces worry regarding Mary worship or idolatry at all is the Hail Mary. There are three parts of the Hail Mary to consider in discussing whether it is idolatrous. First, there are the nearly direct quotations from Holy Scripture. This part is easy. If it is okay for the angel Gabriel to say to Mary, "Hail, full of grace", and for Elizabeth to say, "Blessed are you among women, and blessed is the fruit of your womb" (Lk 1:28, 42), then it is okay for us. The second part of the prayer to consider is the "Holy Mary, Mother of God" part. As a Protestant, I thought Mary was special and set apart (though not yet convinced of her sinlessness), so it was no problem to call her holy. Further, it is a simple corollary of trinitarian theology that "Mother of God" is true of Mary.

Then comes the third and final part. "Pray for us sinners now and at the hour of our death." Well, there is no harm in asking someone to pray for you. This leaves the question of whether it is possible for Mary to pray for us. Well, at the time (because I did not understand the beatific vision) I thought this depended on Catholics' being right about the Assumption of Mary, so I was off down a rabbit hole. The biggest criticism of the doctrine of the Assumption is that it did not arrive early enough. The idea is that the doctrine arrived on the scene so late that it cannot be considered authentic apostolic Christian doctrine. It had to have come in due to other influences.

But this is not true, and there are some clues here. The first thing I noticed is that no one in the Church has ever claimed to have body parts of Mary. You can pick anyone else important in any way in Church history, and there will be numerous relics claimed for that person. The strikingly odd fact about Mary is that no one ever even claimed to possess knowledge of where Mary's body is. This is not a knockdown argument for the Assumption, but it makes it more probable and establishes the early origin of the doctrine. (I had not at this point been put in touch with the evidence that veneration of Mary dates back to the early second century.)

Further, I reasoned that Mary's being sinless and preserved from Original Sin would make a doctrine such as the Assumption fitting. But it stands to reason that Mary would be preserved from sin. Christ was put on Earth and is meant to have been morally perfect. In entrusting his divine Son to an earthly mother, God would certainly choose a very virtuous person, free from sin, if he wished his Son to be fully human and fully virtuous to the extent of going to the Cross for man's sin. Further, while pregnant with Christ, Mary *housed* the divine presence, and we know from the Old Testament that having sin made it impossible to survive even *being in the divine presence*, let alone *housing* it. Mary was probably sinless (assuming Christianity is true), and thus the Assumption is fitting, and it is fitting that Mary is in heaven.

This, along with the discovery that Jesus calls departed Old Testament faithful alive while defending life after death to the Sadducees (Lk 20:27–38), as well as some Thomistic philosophy, convinced me that it was possible for Mary to pray for me and for me to ask her to do so.

Satisfied that the Assumption was not crazy and that even if it were false, Mary could pray for me, I decided to give it a try. *This* was the start of my conversion. I prayed the Rosary for the first time. It was probably the most beautiful prayer and meditation of my life to that point. Contemplating the torture and death of Christ moved me to tears as I asked our Lady for her intercession. You see, the Rosary exemplifies beautifully one of the important truths about Mary. Always and in all that she does, she points past herself to her beloved Son, our Lord Jesus Christ. During the Rosary, one contemplates the Incarnation, life, death, and Resurrection of Christ. It is a beautiful devotional practice and moves one toward virtue.

Now, being the stubborn rationalistic fellow that I am (and, more frankly, fearing the consequences of taking the big Catholic leap), I found those few items of Catholic doctrine of which I was not yet convinced, used them as an excuse to squelch the spirit awakening in me, and stopped thinking about the issue. After all, I would soon be heading to one of the best Evangelical schools (Southern Evangelical Seminary) to further my studies.

While studying at SES, I repressed my changing views, although I see now that I tended to use humor as a defense mechanism. When having serious discussions about the nature of the Church, I would half jokingly say, for instance, "Obviously it's the bishops in union with the Pope", when discussing the nature of the Church. This was quite hilarious in context, but you will have to take my word for it.

This "ignore it and make jokes about it" strategy was working swimmingly as a defense mechanism, but over time the last remaining problems I had with Catholic doctrine eroded away. I became solidly convinced of the real presence by carefully reading Scripture, among many other things.

Then came the influence of a wonderful man and historian. Wayne Detzler taught one of my favorite courses at SES—a course in Church history with a concentration on theology. Detzler taught the course with such gentle scholastic aplomb that I felt comfortable voicing nearly all of my remaining questions on Catholicism and my doubts about the official Evangelical line on various issues. After his honest and frank discussion of my questions, I had almost nothing left to object to in Catholicism. By the end of the course my defenses were all but gone.

This all left me in a very precarious position. I was convinced of nearly every Catholic doctrine while desperately trying to suppress the allure the Church had for me. I felt that whatever I did, whatever convinced me, I certainly could not become Catholic, because Catholicism was the enemy. It was a bridge too far. I did not *want* to be drawn in by, and convinced of, Catholicism.

At the time, I was taking many interesting philosophy classes and working on my thesis, so I was able to ignore and push down the impulse to run home to Catholicism. I became more confident in my philosophical work. Little did I know that the universe had conspired (in consultation with God and, I am sure, with the intercession of our Lady) to shake me from my willful slumber.

A friend of mine was going through similar doubts about Evangelicalism and being drawn to the Church in a somewhat different way. He came to me in confidence, voicing some of these doubts, but I was not very helpful, as my answer to most of his doubts and questions was "I agree" or "The Catholic Church seems right on that one." This conversation, though, made me unable to continue in my slumber. I remembered how important a decision it was, and, further, I realized that, in my final objection, I had been holding myself to epistemic standards that were too high.

That final objection against Catholicism was the vague assertion that people have charged popes with contradicting each other. But I know people have accused the Bible of contradicting itself, and I have not required myself to investigate every extant or possible accusation before believing it. To be sure, I would have to look at several representative examples before placing much confidence in such a thing. That I did. Nearly all accusations of papal contradiction failed to understand the conditions of papal infallibility, and other cases misread one or another of the popes in question. The final puzzle piece was in place. I could no longer in good conscience stay away from the Church.

I began going to daily Mass and began the process of official conversion. It was then that I really discovered all the things that many attribute to being the cause of people's conversions. I noticed, for example, the beautiful connection to history and the amazing sense of the sacred in the liturgy that is missing in much of Evangelicalism. God had guided me to the right decision, and I had perhaps the greatest personal growth period in my life as a result of this conversion. I had found the truth, and I had found my home. Catholicism is the true Church, and now, I am happy to say that it is *my* Church.

Sunshine and Roses?

But it's not all sunshine and roses. The one thing I would like to change about my journey is to include my wife in the process. The case is a little more complex than that, but the upshot is that I failed to adequately keep my wife abreast of the growing developments in my consideration of the issues surrounding Catholicism. Part of this was because it was an uncomfortable subject to discuss, but the other part was because I was yet in denial about my budding conversion until very late in the process.

Part of it, I think, was also my misconceptions regarding how widespread anti-Catholicism was in Evangelicalism. Now, don't get me wrong. There are a lot of people out there who, if you begin discussing the issues surrounding Catholicism, will view you as going through a temptation or having a "struggle." These are not the people to talk to, but there are a lot of people who are very open to understanding what's going on with you, provided that they can be assured that you aren't doing any of the things that Catholicism is falsely charged with being. That is, there are probably many people in your life who, though you might worry that they will cut you off or stop talking to you if you convert or think seriously about converting, can be disabused of the caricature of Catholicism that many of us held at one time or another. It will take discernment, but I think finding these people and having serious discussions with them is also a very important part of the conversion process. It is a part of my conversion that I unfairly neglected, and it is one of my main regrets in this whole process. I pray that God will bless all of you wherever you are in your long salvation journey, and that, if you haven't yet considered seriously the possibility that Catholicism is actually correct, you will give it a long serious thought. Don't believe every charge you see in Evangelical circles. Search out the answers yourself, and, with God's grace, you will be on a similar journey to mine. God bless!

CONCLUSION

Why Evangelicals (Really) Become Catholic

Why do a few intellectual evangelicals become Catholics?
Many reasons are given. It is an older, deeper, richer, more intellectual
tradition. . . .
It is clear that none of these are a test for the truth of a religion, and by the
same logic one could argue for becoming a Hindu, Buddhist, or even an
atheist.

—Norman Geisler

Faith is a gift of God; do not believe that we said it was a gift of reasoning.
Other religions do not say this of their faith.
They only gave reasoning in order to arrive at it, and yet it does not bring
them to it. The knowledge of God is very far from the love of Him.
We know the truth not only by the reason, but also by the heart.

—Blaise Pascal, *Of the Means of Belief*

The Gates of Conversion

The foregoing conversion stories have involved many theological, philosophical, biblical, and historical arguments. That is to say, they all have had a large intellectual component. Although this is precisely what one would expect from a group of former seminarians, it is important to point out that other types of reasons—ancient tradition, beauty, family, and intellectual tradition—were operative and should be operative in a conversion.[1] As the Thomistic philosopher Gerald B. Phelan has said:

---

[1] Although I am not happy with the distinction between intellectual and nonintellectual reasons, I think it is clear enough for the purposes of this text.

Like a medieval city, Thomistic thought has several gates. Some persons prefer to enter by the portal of Being. Others choose the brilliant gate of Truth. Still others find their way best through the door of the Good or through that over which the name Unity is written.... Of late there has been loud knocking at the gate of Beauty.... Must he despair of integrating his urgent and persistent impulses and purposes in one consistent, rational whole?[2]

After considering conversion accounts and rejecting the intellectual reasons, some have concluded that the conversions really happen because of these other reasons and that the conversions are therefore not rational.[3] In this conclusion, we want to reply briefly to such a charge by defending the rationality of conversions involving these other types of reasons.

Reason

First, it must be emphasized that the nine conversions in this book all involved many intellectual reasons. If you have read them, you noticed the reliance on biblical, philosophical, historical, and theological arguments that convinced us of many Catholic truths. These types of reasons differ from the others in that they have a more direct connection with the truth. Although conversions come in all shapes, every conversion should involve some such reasons, as all conversions should be aimed at the truth. Yet, as a matter of fact, conversions also must involve other types of reasons, as all of ours did.

Testimony

One might worry that relying on reasons that are less directly connected with the truth—or are less intellectual—makes one's belief irrational. But this is just not the case. Instead, we cannot help but rely on many other types of reasons for our beliefs. For example,

---

[2] Gerald B. Phelan, "The Concept of Beauty in St. Thomas Aquinas", in *Aspects of the New Scholastic Philosophy*, ed. Charles A. Hart (New York: Benzinger, 1932), 121–22.

[3] Eg., Normal Geisler and Joshua Betancourt, *Is Rome the True Church?* (Wheaton, Ill.: Crossway, 2008), 196.

one relies on the testimony of those they trust for many important beliefs. Yet, people of other religions can also appeal to testimony. Does this mean it is irrational to rely on it? Philosopher Jennifer Lackey is clearly right when she claims:

> Our dependence on testimony is as deep as it is ubiquitous. We rely on the reports of others for our beliefs about the food we eat, the medicine we ingest, the products we buy, the geography of the world, discoveries in science, historical information, and many other areas that play crucial roles in both our practical and intellectual lives. Even many of our most important beliefs about ourselves were learned at an earlier time from our parents and caretakers, such as the date of our birth, the identity of our parents, our ethnic backgrounds, and so on. Were we to refrain from accepting the testimony of others, our lives would be impoverished in startling and debilitating ways.[4]

We must rely on testimony when forming beliefs. Similarly, we must rely on other types of reasons that do not guarantee truth. (Many epistemologists today think most of our reasons are like this.[5]) To deny that beliefs based on testimony are rational undermines the rationality of most beliefs of most people. But this is not yet the heart of the matter.

Implicit in such a criticism is an overly rationalistic account of human belief and conversion. Very few of our beliefs are attained through rigorous enough argumentation to be "rational" on this assumed standard. Now, I want to argue that very few of our beliefs are attained purely intellectually. And this is just as it should be. Although we have an intellect, we are not only intellects. Instead, we are embodied social creatures who love, feel, sense, desire, fear, grow up in a particular community at a particular time, et cetera. We are complicated knowers, and when it comes to making the biggest decisions that structure our entire lives, we do not, and should not, remove ourselves from all of this and run syllogisms limited to the "rational" reasons. In other words, a conversion story that included only such reasons would not be a human story. Surely the testimony

---

[4] Jennifer Lackey, introduction to *The Epistemology of Testimony*, eds. Jennifer Lackey and Ernest Sosa (New York: Oxford University Press, 2006), 1.

[5] Trent Dougherty, "Fallibism", *Routledge Companion to Epistemology*, eds. Sven Bernecker and Duncan Pritchard (2001).

of others, the beauty and history of a tradition, certain dazzling intellectual and spiritual thinkers, what our family believes, those things that satisfy an existential worry, the practical fruits of a tradition or belief, and the experience of God in worship and prayer should be a part of a conversion story. It is utterly reasonable for things such as these to play a role in conversion, even though they might not be adequate as isolated tests for truth.

Antiquity

Similar to testimonial evidence is the draw of antiquity. In Newman's introduction to *An Essay on the Development of Christian Doctrine*, he considers some Protestant theologians' attempts to connect their tradition further back in history than the Reformation, as Protestant theologians do today. He notes that history is not always clear but then explains that whatever history does say, it is at least clear that the "Christianity of history is not Protestantism."[6] In the next paragraph he famously claims that "to be deep in history is to cease to be a Protestant."[7] This deep history and unbroken connection to the early Church is something that draws many converts to Catholicism.

Of course, being old does not guarantee something is true. But it is natural and healthy for people to want a traceable connection to things they care deeply about. In some circles, people are traced by their degree of separation from luminaries in the field. Mathematicians, for example, have an Erdös number, which indicates the degrees of separation by collaborative distance between mathematician Paul Erdös and another mathematician. To think this is irrelevant to truth is silly.

Tradition

Would you rather hear from the students of your favorite thinkers from the past or someone who has only read their biographies? Of course, being a student of a student does not guarantee that one gets

---

[6] John Henry Newman, *An Essay on the Development of Christian Doctrine*, introduction, sect. 5.

[7] Ibid.

everything right, but the personal connection counts for something. It is similar with Christianity. One thing all Christians should want is to have a connection like this to Christ. The continuous visible Church is at least some evidence of Catholicism's truth. Being able to trace a line, as it were, all the way back beats having a 1,400-plus-year gap.

Tradition can also mean continuity of practice. Of course, such continuity does not guarantee truth, but a practice that was established in the early Church and continues to this day offers a strong motive to believe. I remember being utterly surprised to discover that we have some fairly detailed records of what Church services in the early Church looked like. In the seminary, in addition to trying to develop biblical reasons for what Christians should do during a service, we could have considered early-Church practice. But we never did this in class, and that is because the descriptions are so Catholic (or Orthodox). For example, in his *First Apology*, Justin Martyr describes the early Church's practice, and the Eucharist is featured.[8] Then there is the Didache, which describes how the early Christians worshipped. If you have been to Catholic Mass, you will recognize the description. It is obviously rational for such considerations to play a part in a conversion.

Intellectual tradition also draws people to Catholicism. The intellectual lights of the Catholic Church are unrivaled by any other tradition. To name just a few: Augustine, Boethius, Anselm, Bonaventure, Aquinas, Scotus, Newman, and John Paul II. Of course, being a good scholar or being really smart does not guarantee that a person is correct. These thinkers draw converts not because they have scholarly credentials, though, but because they offer profound, systematic, and unique answers to our deepest questions and problems. The deep truths articulated and defended by Catholic thinkers are what bring people into the Catholic Church. Obviously this is reasonable.

Family

It is not just ancient tradition and great minds that influence conversions. For most of us, our families also play an important role in what we believe about many important things. We have to start our

---

[8] Justin Martyr, *First Apology* 65–67.

search for the truth somewhere, and most of us start with whatever our family believed. If not family, then we rely on other people we respect. Of course, the fact that someone in our family or someone we respect believes something does not make that belief true. Yet, as pointed out above, we cannot help but rely on the testimony of others. It is only reasonable that the people one loves deeply and respects would have a special role in a conversion.

Beauty

Beauty is another reason many are drawn to Catholicism. There are different ways to think of beauty as a reason for conversion. On the one hand, someone could think, "This is pretty and fun. I'll become this." Of course, if that is the depth of his reason for conversion, something is wrong. But there is another way for beauty to be a reason. From the time of the Greeks, many have thought that beauty and truth are deeply connected. This does not mean that every view in which anyone finds beauty is true. Instead, it is a reason to think that a view that has profound and abiding beauty that satisfies our longing for beauty while simultaneously drawing us in deeper is true. Catholicism has this. Unfortunately, this kind of beauty is not something that can be explained in a few—or even many!—sentences. It is found by pursuing a deeper friendship with Christ in the sacraments, spending time with him in adoration, participating in his life in the liturgical calendar, and being devoted to those who were deeply devoted to him. There is a superficial beauty to the liturgy and architecture of many Catholic churches. But this is just the beginning; it is the apparent, exterior beauty of a deeper and more hidden beauty that one must get to know like a person. How sad it would be to miss out on the profound inner beauty of a person just because she is also pretty.

Conclusion

In short, very few of people's deepest beliefs are held for only "rational" reasons. But why would we want to rely only on intellectual reasons? We are not separated intellects, but social animals. Although the reasons considered above should not be taken as self-sufficient guarantors of truth, they should be a part of a human conversion story. To argue otherwise is to misunderstand the nature of conversion. Converting to a religion affects every aspect of one's life, and every aspect of a person should enter into his conversion.

RESOURCES

Ad Fontes

The authors of *Evangelical Exodus* hope our stories have been edifying to you, whether you are Catholic, Evangelical, or otherwise. Should the book prove popular, a sequel or two might be in order![1] Although the authors of this book are all trained in apologetics, our goal was not to provide a full defense of Catholicism (the appendices are included primarily to avoid repetition). Rather, the book's purpose was to give each of us a chance to answer personally and accurately the question we are frequently asked by our Evangelical brothers and sisters: *Why did you become Catholic?* (see 1 Pet 3:15).

The next question we often get is: *What should I read to learn more?* Listed below are several books that have been helpful to us in that regard. The questions that those who are discerning whether to enter the Catholic Church ask during their journeys are usually not the same as those simply looking for a new church to attend. Thus, this list includes conversion testimonies, theological issues, and comparative resources from non-Catholics.

Catholic Conversion

Return to Rome: Confessions of an Evangelical Catholic by Francis J. Beckwith
Journeys of Faith: Evangelicalism, Eastern Orthodoxy, Catholicism, and Anglicanism by Francis J. Beckwith, Christopher A. Castaldo, Lyle W. Dorsett, and Wilbur Ellsworth

---

[1] At the time of this writing there are already enough converts from Evangelicalism to Catholicism from Southern Evangelical Seminary to publish at least two similar books of the same size!

Born Fundamentalist: Born Again Catholic by David Currie

Rome Sweet Home: Our Journey to Catholicism by Scott and Kimberly Hahn

Evangelical Is Not Enough by Thomas Howard

Apologia pro Vita Sua by John Henry Newman

By What Authority?: An Evangelical Discovers Catholic Tradition by Mark Shea

How to Go from Being a Good Evangelical to a Committed Catholic in Ninety-Five Difficult Steps by Christian Smith

Catholic Theology

The Catechism of the Catholic Church

Summa Theologiae and *Summa Contra Gentiles* by Saint Thomas Aquinas

The Faith of Our Fathers by James Gibbons

Fides et Ratio by Saint John Paul II

Why Do Catholics Do That? by Kevin Orlin Johnson

Rosary: Mysteries, Meditations, and the Telling of the Beads by Kevin Orlin Johnson

Catholicism and Fundamentalism by Karl Keating

Catholic Christianity by Peter Kreeft

Any Friend of God's Is a Friend of Mine by Patrick Madrid

Understanding Fundamentalism and Evangelicalism by George M. Marsden

An Essay on the Development of Christian Doctrine by John Henry Newman

Jesus and the Jewish Roots of the Eucharist: Unlocking the Secrets of the Last Supper by Brant Pitre

The Spirit of the Liturgy by Joseph Ratzinger (Pope Benedict XVI)

The Protestant's Dilemma by Devin Rose

The Catholic Controversy by Saint Francis de Sales

Magisterium: Teaching Authority in the Catholic Church by Francis Sullivan

Not by Faith Alone: A Biblical Study of the Catholic Doctrine of Justification edited by Robert A. Sungenis

Not by Scripture Alone: A Catholic Critique of the Protestant Doctrine of Sola Scriptura edited by Robert A. Sungenis

Evangelical / Protestant Resources

A High View of Scripture?: The Authority of the Bible and the Formation of the New Testament Canon by Craig D. Allert

The Spirit and Forms of Protestantism by Louis Bouyer

Roman Catholics and Evangelicals: Agreements and Differences by Norman L. Geisler and Ralph E. MacKenzie

Is Rome the True Church?: A Consideration of the Roman Catholic Claim by Norman L. Geisler and Joshua M. Betancourt

The Shape of Sola Scriptura by Keith A. Mathison

Reasoning from the Scriptures with Catholics by Ron Rhodes

The Bible Made Impossible: Why Biblicism Is Not a Truly Evangelical Reading of Scripture by Christian Smith (Note: Smith was not Catholic when he wrote this book. He later converted.)

Are We Together?: A Protestant Analyzes Roman Catholicism by R. C. Sproul

The Roman Catholic Controversy by James R. White

Evangelicals and Tradition: The Formative Influence of the Early Church by D. H. Williams

Catholic Websites

CalledtoCommunion.com
Catholic.com
CatholicDefense.blogspot.com
EWTN.com
NewAdvent.org
Vatican.va

MEET THE AUTHORS

Douglas Beaumont

Doug has a PhD in theology from North-West University and a MA in apologetics from Southern Evangelical Seminary where he served as assistant to Norman Geisler and taught Bible and Religion for ten years before converting to Catholicism. Doug is the author of *The Message Behind the Movie* (Moody, 2009), and has contributed to *The Best Catholic Writing* (Loyola, 2006), *The Apologetics Study Bible for Students* (B&H, 2010), *Got Questions?* (Pleasant Word, 2009), and several articles in *The Christian Apologetics Journal*. He lives in Charlotte, North Carolina, with his wife and four children.

Francis Beckwith

Francis is a former SES professor and is now professor of philosophy and Church-State Studies at Baylor University, where he also serves as associate director of the Graduate Program in Philosophy and codirector (with Trent Dougherty) of the Program in Philosophical Studies of Religion. He holds five earned degrees, including an MA and a PhD in philosophy from Fordham University and a master of juridical studies (in law) from the Washington University School of Law, Saint Louis. He is the author or editor of more than fifteen books, including *Defending Life: A Moral and Legal Case against Abortion Choice* (Cambridge University Press, 2007) and *Return to Rome: Confessions of an Evangelical Catholic* (Brazos Press, 2009). Having published more than a hundred academic articles, book chapters, critical reviews, and encyclopedia entries in a variety of publications, he has held visiting faculty appointments at Princeton University, where he served as a 2002–2003 Madison Research Fellow in the Department of Politics, and at the University of Notre Dame, where he was the 2008–2009 Mary Ann Remick Senior Visiting Fellow in the Notre Dame Center for Ethics and Culture. He resigned his post as the fifty-eighth president of the Evangelical Theological Society in the middle of his tenure in May 2007, a week after returning to the Catholic Church of his youth. He and his wife, Frankie, live in Woodway, Texas.

Joshua Betancourt

Joshua received his bachelor of biblical studies from Calvary Chapel Bible College. He also holds an MA in apologetics from Southern Evangelical Seminary. He is the coauthor (with Norman Geisler) of *Is Rome the True Church?* (Crossway, 2008). Before his conversion to the Catholic faith, Joshua was an ordained Anglican deacon and served as a workplace chaplain at various businesses within Southern California. He has also worked for apostolates such as Saint Joseph Communications and Lighthouse Catholic Media. Joshua now ministers as a lay Catholic hospital chaplain. He and his wife, Carolina, enjoy serving as catechists at the parish level. They are the parents of three children.

Jeremiah Cowart

Jeremiah has an MA in religion from Southern Evangelical Seminary and a BA in philosophy from the University of Georgia. He was first enamored by the virtue ethics of Aristotle while at UGA and was able to explore the subject further via Thomas Aquinas at SES. His lay interests lie in the intersections of various fields: ethics and biology, aesthetics and theology, science and religion. He is now completely outside of academia, working as a federal agent for the Department of Homeland Security. He resides in Georgia with his five children.

Brandon Dahm

Brandon grew up in Pella, Iowa, and received his BA in philosophy from Iowa State University, where he met his wife, Andrea. He then pursued an MA in philosophy at Southern Evangelical Seminary. Taking a year off from SES, he was a visiting scholar at Wolfson College, Cambridge University, where he studied Thomas Aquinas' *Summa Theologiae*. He is pursuing a PhD at Baylor University. He has published articles in the *American Philosophical Quarterly, Journal of Analytic Theology*, and *Faith and Philosophy*. His work is primarily on Thomas Aquinas, although he also studies and writes on John Duns Scotus and John Henry Newman.

Travis Johnson

Travis grew up in Bentonville, Arkansas, where he attended and was heavily involved in a large Evangelical Bible church. Prior to and during his conversion process, he worked at an Evangelical seminary in Charlotte, North Carolina. He and his wife and two daughters reside in Cincinnati, Ohio, where he teaches English, language arts, and religion at Saint Gertrude School. He holds a BA in philosophy and English from the University of Mississippi, an MDiv from Southern Evangelical Seminary, and an MA in education from Appalachian State University.

Michael Mason

Michael has a BS in middle childhood education from Ohio University and an MA in philosophy from Southern Evangelical Seminary and is working toward an MA in theology from the Athenaeum of Ohio. Prior to being received into the Catholic Church, he taught theology at an Evangelical high school in Charlotte, North Carolina, for six years. He resides in Cincinnati, Ohio, with his wife and children, is a parishioner at Saint Gertrude Church, and teaches language arts and religion at Saint Gertrude School.

Brian Mathews

Brian has an MA in apologetics and an MA in biblical studies from Southern Evangelical Seminary, where he was a teaching assistant for one year during his graduate studies. After teaching numerous apologetics classes at various Evangelical churches and being ordained a Baptist minister, he began to discover the truth of the Catholic faith. Brian, his wife, Diona, and their four children entered into full communion with the Catholic Church on December 29, 2012. Since then, the Mathews Family has been blessed with another son, Dominic William. Brian teaches Sacraments and Liturgy, moral theology, and apologetics at Charlotte Catholic High School. He also sings with the Carolina Catholic Chorale, a group formed to continue the rich Catholic tradition of sacred music at Mass.

Andrew Preslar

Andrew has a BA in Bible and theology from Appalachian Bible College and an MA in apologetics from Southern Evangelical Seminary. He was studying for Anglican orders before being received into full communion with the Catholic Church (Byzantine Rite) on February 3, 2008. He is a founding member of Called to Communion: Reformation Meets Rome (www.CalledtoCommunion.com), a website dedicated to promoting reconciliation and reunion between Catholics and Protestants. Andrew lives in Charlotte, North Carolina.

Jonathan Sonantis

Jonathan obtained an MA in philosophy from Southern Evangelical Seminary. He is working on a PhD in philosophy, concentrating on epistemology. He enjoys long walks on the beach and mildly clever Kierkegaardian pen names.

APPENDIX 1

Facing the Issue of the Biblical Canon

I want to know one thing: the way to heaven. God himself has condescended to teach me the way. He has written it down in a book. Oh, give me that book! At any price give me the book of God.

—John Wesley

It is common for Protestant Christians to claim to rely solely on the Bible as their source of religious authority (a doctrine known as sola scriptura—"the Bible alone"). There is a strong intuitive appeal here: If the Bible is inspired by God, then it is without error and authoritative in a way that no other authority could be. This ideal is reflected in statements such as that of Norman Geisler: "When speaking of its divine authority, the Bible makes it clear that this is a final authority, the court of last appeal in everything that it affirms.... The Bible, and the Bible alone, is a supremely authoritative book in matters of faith and practice."[1]

This is a problematic statement on more than one level. First, the Bible nowhere claims to be "a final authority", "the court of last appeal", or "supremely authoritative in matters of faith and practice". Therefore, these descriptions come from some authority other than the Bible. Second, because the Bible is not *a book* but rather *a collection of books*, even if one of those books made such claims for itself, how would we identify the other books as being "in the Bible" without an inspired table of contents? Finally, even if every single book of the Bible identified itself as belonging to the canon of Scripture, why would we trust them? Any writer can claim his writing is Scripture.

The problem of the biblical canon is of supreme importance for the Christian, for if Scripture alone is held to be one's highest authority,

[1] Norman L. Geisler, *Systematic Theology*, vol. 1 (Minneapolis: Bethany House, 2002), 240–41.

then one must be able to identify Scripture. Before one can rely on sola scriptura, one must ask, "*Quae scriptura?*" (Which Bible?). Yet, with all the energy devoted to proving the accuracy and inspiration of the Bible, not much is spent on its *identification*. Many do not discuss the issue at all, and those who do are surprisingly brief.[2] As Craig Allert notes, however, "Surely what the Bible is has much importance for what the Bible says."[3]

The Formation of the Biblical Canon

Canon is a Greek term that originally meant a straight rod or rule—a criterion. It began to be applied by Christian writers of the later fourth century to the correct collection and list of the Scriptures. Unlike many other religions, Christianity does not have a Scripture written (directly) by its founder. The process of determining what counts as Scripture is thus of paramount importance.

The Christian New Testament was written over a period of at least forty years by the followers of Christianity's founder, Jesus Christ, and their associates. It had considerable authority and use by the time it was completed in the first century, but so did other books such as the Shepherd of Hermas, the Didache, and the letter of Clement. No official list of canonical Bible books existed. During the second and third centuries, the Church began to discern these books more clearly, and toward the end of the fourth century, official canon lists began to emerge. This formation took place in three basic phases with continuing debate following.

First Century

After the Resurrection, the stories about Jesus and his teachings were passed along orally by the apostles, who were committed to guarding

[2] For example, Norman Geisler and Frank Turek's popular apologetics book *I Don't Have Enough Faith to Be an Atheist* devotes approximately four of its fifteen chapters to arguing for the reliability of the New Testament, yet only three pages (one of which is a chart) are devoted to the canon question. Another example is Ed Hindson and Ergun Caner's *Popular Encyclopedia of Apologetics*, which has four pages on biblical inspiration but not even one full page on the canon.

[3] Craig D. Allert, *A High View of Scripture?: The Authority of the Bible and the Formation of the New Testament Canon* (Grand Rapids: Baker Academic, 2007), 11.

the message they proclaimed and were promised they would be able do so (Jn 16:13). The apostles' teaching (whether by word of mouth or by letter) was authoritative (Acts 2:42; 2 Thess 2:15; 3:6). The first apostolic documents were written to particular Christian congregations or groups of congregations. The teachings of Jesus continued to play an important role for those who had known the apostles and had been trained by them. By the end of the first century, most of the New Testament books were in use by the churches and were cited frequently by early Church Fathers such as Clement and Ignatius. The first letter of Clement was read at services of the Corinthian church for decades. Even the Hebrew canon was still being debated among the Jews in the first century.[4]

Second Century

This basic trend continued after the death of the last apostle, when written documents began to play an increasingly important role for Christians. The Church's usage of the New Testament writings now evened out with that of the Old Testament. The four Gospels were probably already circulating together at this time, and Paul's letters were circulating as a collection. These were regularly referred to authoritatively, as were other writings of the apostles. Based on citations, some books, such as Acts, Revelation, and some of the shorter epistles, seem to have been accorded second-class status. Other books, such as the Shepherd of Hermas, the Apocalypse of Peter, and 1 Clement were also used but were cited less frequently. Later in the second century, conflicts with three aberrant groups—the Marcionites, the Gnostics, and the Montanists—prompted discussions of which books were acceptable. Some writers began to conceive of the "New Testament" as an authoritative single collection. Melito, Bishop of Sardis (ca. 170), produced the first orthodox attempt at a Christian Old Testament canon following from the Septuagint minus the book of Esther.

Third Century

By the third century the Church's usage of the "second class" New Testament books had evened out with the "first class" texts. The

---

[4]F. F. Bruce, *The Canon of Scripture* (Downers Grove, Ill.: IVP Academic, 1996), chap. 2.

so-called Muratorian canon was written, listing most New Testament writings and rejecting known spurious writings. However this "canon" did not include Hebrews, 1 and 2 Peter, James, or 3 John and did include the Apocalypse of Peter (noting that some would not allow it to be read in church) as well as the Shepherd of Hermas, which was said to be allowed to be read but not in church. The author also includes the book of Wisdom in the Old Testament canon.

Fourth Century

In Athanasius' Festal Letter 39 (A.D. 367) the term *canon* was used for the first time to specify the content of the New Testament, and this list was the first to match the current twenty-seven-book list. Athanasius includes the Catholic deuterocanonical books (the Protestant Apocrypha), although Esther is left out and noncanonical writings are not excluded from use. This list did not, however, settle the discussion, and alternate lists continued to be drawn up later, especially in the Eastern churches. The first list to match the Catholic canon was the one decreed by the Council of Rome in A.D. 382. The later Council of Hippo (A.D. 393) and the Third Synod of Carthage (A.D. 397) approved the same list. These were local councils, however, and were not considered binding on the entire Church.

Fifth through Fifteenth Centuries

None of the first-millennium ecumenical councils ever pronounced a canonical list of the books of the Bible, but local pronouncements continued to match the list approved by local councils. Pope Innocent I produced the same list of canonical books of Scripture in A.D. 405, and the later Council of Carthage (A.D. 419) approved it. These lists, too, were never taken to be authoritative for the churches in the East, however, and thus canonical "fluidity" continued from the fifth century on. Anglican Bible scholar Brooke Westcott notes the existence of six different lists of the Scriptures even into the tenth century. The West, however, seemed to have settled on the fourth-century canon, and it continued unabated for over one thousand years (e.g., the same list was approved by the Council of Florence in 1441). Eventually the New Testament canon in the East was brought into concert with the West's after the East's long refusal to accept the book of Revelation.

Sixteenth Century

The canon issue might have seemed settled after one and a half millennia, but with the Protestant Reformation came renewed discussion. The Reformers produced a new canon devoid of the Old Testament deuterocanonical books, and Martin Luther's distaste for the epistle of James ("a right strawy epistle") and his questioning of the "disputed books" (antilegomena) is well known. In his commentaries, John Calvin mentioned conflicting opinions concerning the books of Hebrews, James, 2 Peter, and Jude. Zwingli also questioned parts of the New Testament canon. Even today, classical Lutheranism distinguishes the New Testament homologoumena from the antilegomena.

Lest this be seen as merely a Protestant issue, it should be noted that "Luther's opponent, Cardinal Cajetan, following Jerome, expressed doubts concerning the canonicity of Hebrews, James, 2 and 3 John, and Jude. Erasmus likewise expressed doubts concerning Revelation as well as the apostolicity of James, Hebrews, and 2 Peter."[5] Although Rome still followed the fourth-century canon, it was not until after the Reformation was under way that the various biblical canons began to be authoritatively decreed in their final form at the Council of Trent (1546).[6]

The Criteria for the Biblical Canon

Given the known history of the biblical canon, why not simply trust that the Church got it right? The Westminster Confession seems to sum up neatly why this would be of concern: "The authority of the Holy Scripture, for which it ought to be believed, and obeyed, depends not upon the testimony of any man, or Church; but wholly

---

[5] M. James Sawyer, "Evangelicals and the Canon of the New Testament", *Grace Theological Journal* 11 (Spring 2009): 45.

[6] Others soon followed: the Anglican Thirty-Nine Articles (1563), the Reformed Westminster Confession (1647), and the Orthodox Synod of Jerusalem (1672).

upon God (who is truth itself) the author thereof: and therefore it is to be received, because it is the Word of God" (chap. 1, no. 4).

In other words, the fear is that if the Church is credited with determining the canon of Scripture, she would somehow come to be in authority over the Bible itself. It is said that the Church only "discovered" the canon but did not determine it. This is true, of course—no Christian tradition claims to have made the books of the Bible to be the inspired Word of God![7] This is not the issue; the issue is how these inspired books were authoritatively discovered or determined (the words can mean basically the same thing).

Various criteria have been suggested to show how the Church could authoritatively determine the canon without being in authority over it. The problem is that although the history of the formation of the canon is fairly straightforward, attempts to "reverse engineer" the criteria used by the Church to determine its contents is not.[8] Even if the criteria were agreed upon, however, issues would remain.

Inspiration

Being inspired by God is, by definition, the only real criterion for a book's inclusion in the biblical canon. This is fine in the abstract, but useless when it gets down to brass tacks—for to respond to the

---

[7] Not even the Catholic Church makes this claim. See Yves Congar, *The Meaning of Tradition* (San Francisco: Ignatius Press, 2004), chap. 3.

[8] John Calvin said that God bears testimony to the canon through the voice of the Spirit in the hearts of the believer (John Calvin, *Institutes* 1.7.5). Biblical scholar Roger Nicole considers seven criteria: (1) apostolicity, (2) orthodoxy, (3) Christocentricity, (4) inspiration, (5) the testimony of the Holy Spirit to the individual Christian, (6) the authority of the Church, and (7) the witness of the Holy Spirit given corporately to God's people and made manifest by a nearly unanimous acceptance. Roger Nicole, "The Canon of the New Testament", *JETS* 40, no. 2 (June 1997): 200–7. Famed New Testament scholar F. F. Bruce considers six: (1) apostolic authority, (2) antiquity, (3) orthodoxy, (4) catholicity, (5) traditional use, and (6) inspiration. Bruce, *Canon of Scripture*, chap. 21. Evangelical apologist Norman Geisler asks five questions: (1) Was the book written by a prophet of God? (2) Was the writer confirmed by acts of God? (3) Did the message tell the truth about God? (4) Does it come with the power of God? (5) Was it accepted by the people of God? Norman L. Geisler and William E. Nix, *A General Introduction to the Bible* (Chicago: Moody, 1986), chap. 12. Eastern Orthodox philosopher Richard Swinburne lists just three factors: (1) conformity to Christian tradition, (2) apostolicity, and (3) widespread acceptance by the Church. Richard Swinburne, *Revelation: From Metaphor to Analogy* (New York: Oxford University Press, 2008). Reformed apologist James White lists only one: inspiration. James White, *Scripture Alone* (Bloomington, Minn.: Bethany House, 2004), chap. 5.

question "Which books are canonical?" with "The books that are inspired" is just to say that we can know the inspired books by their being inspired! The question just gets pushed back a step to "How do we know which books are inspired?" What the canon *is* does not tell us how to *identify* it.

Further, if we assume that those in the early Church knew which books were inspired and used this as their means of determining the canon, we run into several problems. First, noncanonical Christian writings were described as inspired in the writings of the early Church (e.g., Clement's epistle to the Corinthians and Ignatius' epistle to the Philadelphians). Second, non-Christian writings were described as inspired in the writings of the early Church (e.g., Clement's *Stromata* on pagan philosophers). Even the allegedly technical term for God's inspiration (*theopneustos* from 2 Tim 3:16) is used of other writings, such as Gregory of Nyssa on Basil's *Genesis Commentary* and the Council of Ephesus on its ruling against Nestorius.

Apostolicity

Another seemingly obvious and objective criterion is authorship: namely, if a book is written by an apostle of Jesus Christ, it is inspired and canonical. Even here, though, problems arise. First there is the issue of anonymous books. None of the Gospels name their author in the original text. There have been numerous suggestions as to the authorship of the letter to the Hebrews (the earliest being Paul). There were several Jameses in the New Testament who have been considered to be the author of the epistle of James. And the book of Revelation does not identify its author by name. Although Church tradition is fairly strong on most of these, can we trust that the Church did not lie or was not simply ignorant as to the original authors? Modern skeptics answer no!

Further, what about excluded books that claim to have been written by the apostles (e.g., the epistle of Barnabas or the Apocalypse of Peter)? Since these have named apostolic authors (and are not simply late spurious writings), why are they not considered canonical? The historical fact is that authorship was often a matter of Church tradition. Thus, even if apostolic authorship were a trustworthy criterion, one is still trusting Church tradition for authorial identification.

Spiritual Witness

Trusting that the Holy Spirit will confirm the canonical books to individual believers is fraught with problems. First, no such thing is promised in Scripture itself, and so the very idea is based in some tradition (some cite John 10:27—"My sheep hear my voice"—as a proof text, but this is about the call to salvation, not recognizing authentic Scripture). Second, if this criterion is legitimate, all Christians should be able to distinguish the canonical books (or even verses) from noncanonical ones. But the fact of the dispute shows this to be questionable (which group is hearing the Spirit's voice?). Finally, if the Holy Spirit really does guide the Church in this manner, why do Protestants not trust the Church of the first 1,500 years of history?

Orthodoxy

Another suggestion is that the canon was determined by comparing various writings to some standard of orthodoxy. It must be asked, though: If the canon was determined by its orthodoxy, would this result from its agreement with itself (i.e., other canonical books— which is circular) or something else (which would seem to place something other than the Bible in authority over the Bible, which is the very thing these theories seek to avoid)? Further, how are skeptics to be answered who claim that the New Testament conflicts with the Old Testament (e.g., Acts 15)? There might be a solution, but who would decide whether it was sufficient? Finally, this test has been used to exclude canonical books from the canon. Some were maligned due to noninclusion of particular doctrines (e.g., Luther advocated excluding Esther, Ecclesiastes, the Song of Songs, and James). Revelation was discounted because of its heretical use by the Montanists, and other groups were known to twist the Bible to their own ends. This led Tertullian to assert that "our appeal, therefore, must not be made to the Scriptures.... Wherever it shall be manifest that the true Christian rule and faith shall be, there will likewise be the true Scriptures and expositions thereof, and all the Christian traditions."[9]

[9] Tertullian, *Prescriptions against the Heretics* 19.

Self-Attestation

To say that the Bible is its own test is difficult to take seriously. First, any alleged holy book could make the same claim, and so such a test offers nothing in the way of religious discernment, much less a more detailed method of Christian scriptural determination. Second, even the most recent proponent of such an idea ends up including the classic marks of canonicity in his exposition of the "self-attesting" view.[10] But if the Bible's self-attestation requires an "epistemic environment" that includes most of the standard proposed criteria, why not just say that these are the criteria? Although the theological motivation for such a claim is clearly to avoid "subordinat[ing] the canon to outside authorities",[11] it ends up relying on the same external factors anyway.

Acceptance by God's People

The leaders of the Church are historically responsible for the canon. Other criteria are often proposed to mitigate the importance of this fact. The fear is that if the canon question is answered by appeal to the Church's tradition, then, well, "we should all be Roman Catholics today."[12] The problem with this inclusion is that either God's people used the other criteria in their determination (in which case, they are not really part of the criteria, but only an instrument for employing the criteria), or they did not (making themselves the authority). Thus, it seems that either God's people are authoritative and the other criteria are unnecessary, or they are redundant as far as criteria goes. Finally, even if this criterion did not reduce to, or do away with, the others, which group of "God's people" are to be trusted?

Christian Tradition

The biggest problem with this "reverse engineering" procedure is that all proposed criteria were apparently ignored (or simply failed) for (at least) hundreds of years before the canon was finally settled. But if the very early Church did not have a clear view of which

---

[10] Michael J. Kruger, *Canon Revisited: Establishing the Origins and Authority of the New Testament Books* (Wheaton, Ill.: Crossway, 2012), 290.

[11] Ibid., 289.

[12] Sawyer, "Evangelicals and the Canon", 45.

books belonged in the canon, how could the Church of the late fourth century have had one? As Roger Nicole states it, "If this principle were as simple as it is thought to be by its advocates it is difficult to understand why it took the Church some 300 years to make up its mind on the exact list of NT books."[13]

Given the above issues, theologian Herman Ridderbos concludes:

> The church did not begin by making formal decisions as to what was valid as canon, nor did it begin by setting specific criteria of canonicity.... As their artificiality indicates, these arguments are a posteriori in character.... If the canon is discovered by principles within the Bible then it is circular, and if by the Church (whatever its criteria) then it is not "biblical," but "traditional."[14]

New Testament scholar Bruce Metzger correctly states that "a basic prerequisite for canonicity was conformity to what was called the 'rule of faith' ... that is, the congruity of a given document with the basic Christian tradition recognized as normative by the Church."[15] What these scholars have discovered is that, at root, the Church knew which books belonged in the Bible because the Church knew which books she used as her Bible. These lists were not decrees based on popular fourth-century opinion; they were descriptions of what the Church already recognized as being true tradition.

> Now, in regard to the canonical Scriptures, he must follow the judgment of the greater number of Catholic churches; and among these, of course, a high place must be given to such as have been thought worthy to be the seat of an apostle and to receive epistles. Accordingly, among the canonical Scriptures he will judge according to the following standard: to prefer those that are received by all the Catholic churches to those which some do not receive. Among those, again, which are not received by all, he will prefer such as have the sanction of the greater number and those of greater authority.[16]

[13] Nicole, "The Canon of the New Testament", 203.

[14] Herman Ridderbos, *The Authority of the New Testament Scriptures* (Phillipsburg, N.J.: Presbyterian and Reformed Publishing, 1963), 45–46.

[15] Bruce M. Metzger, *The Canon of the New Testament: Its Origin, Development, and Significance* (Oxford: Clarendon, 1997), 251.

[16] Saint Augustine, *On Christian Doctrine* 2, 8.

What mattered, ultimately, was not whether the Church had an authoritative canon, but whether she had authoritative guidance. The Church could survive without the Bible, but not the Bible without the Church. The rule of faith (*regula fidei*) is that common faith handed down (*paradosis*) from the apostles to their successors (e.g., 2 Tim 2:2) and recognized from the very beginning as being the true faith (Jude 1:3). This explains why there seemed to be so little concern over the matter until heretics began making up their own canons in support of their private interpretations. It also makes sense of why some books could go in and out of favor—it is what they *taught* that mattered.

Providence or Power Play?

This historical explanation accommodates the best factors in the criteria-based theories previously discussed, but incorporates them into the life of the Church instead of making them out to be abstract factors existing outside the Church. The Church existed at least a decade before the earliest book of the New Testament was even begun, and it was four to six decades before the New Testament was completed. Because the Church already knew what the faith was, she could determine the canon of Scripture without ruling over it. It is not that Church tradition was an external standard, as some fear; rather, it is that both the Church's teaching and the Bible were part of the one Christian tradition.

A Church-determined canon makes some people uncomfortable, however. Besides the misguided concern that it places the Church above the Bible, there are skeptical issues raised as well. If the Church decided which books made it into the canon and which did not, then our faith in the biblical canon cannot be greater than our trust in the Church that determined it. Christians are left with either trust in God's providential guiding of the Church, or skepticism.

Popular scholar Bart Ehrman describes the situation this way:

The Christians who won the early conflicts and established their views as dominant by the fourth century not only gave us the creeds that have been handed down from antiquity, they also decided which books would belong to the Scriptures. Once their battles had been won, they succeeded in labeling themselves "orthodox" (i.e., those who hold to the "right beliefs") and marginalized their opponents as "heretics."[17]

Similarly, critical scholar Richard Carrier complains that until the fourth century, there were in fact many simultaneous literary traditions. The illusion that it was otherwise is created by the fact that the church that came out on top simply preserved texts in its favor and destroyed or let vanish opposing documents. Hence what we call "orthodoxy" is simply "the church that won".[18]

The Christian can, in good conscience, affirm the letter (if not the spirit) of these kinds of assertions with a few corrections. The first error is in assuming that a competing tradition was a church. Jesus established only one Church (which Paul called a "pillar and bulwark of the truth"). That Church was promised never to fail (Mt 16:18; Jn 16; 1 Tim 3:14–15). Being faith based, the Church cannot ultimately have lost the faith, or she would not only have failed but would have ceased to exist.

This leads to the error in the implicit conclusion that the canon is really not authoritative. Simply because fallible men made the determination or recognition of the biblical canon does not imply that it was a fallible process, any more than God's use of fallible authors necessitated fallibility in their writings. Since the biblical canon is certainly part of the faith that must be safeguarded to ensure the Church's existence, we can trust that, through God's providence, the Church did not err in her selection of the biblical canon. As J. P. Holding has stated it, "If we believe in the inspiration of the Bible, then it is also reasonable to assume God's hand in the matter of the compilation of the canon."[19]

---

[17] Bart D. Ehrman, *Lost Christianities: The Battles for Scripture and the Faiths We Never Knew* (New York: Oxford University Press, 2003), 13.

[18] Richard Carrier, "The Formation of the New Testament Canon", http://www.richard carrier.info/CanonNTSpecialEdit.pdf.

[19] James Patrick Holding, *Trusting the New Testament: Is the Bible Reliable?* (Maitland, Fla.: Xulon Press, 2009), 250.

Conclusion

If Christians cannot ground the authority of the Bible in its historical reality without violating their own principles, they will remain open for skeptical attack. Unfortunately, many ignore or misrepresent this history and end up with a Bible that is grounded firmly in midair. Making high claims about what the Bible teaches while misunderstanding its formation and nature can lead only to crisis when a believer learns the truth (often from the skeptics themselves). The number of ex-Evangelical atheists attests to the fact that most of the alleged criteria for a book's inclusion in the canon is either unhelpfully circular or ultimately relies on Christian tradition to be useful. "The conservative American Evangelical apologetic for the shape of the New Testament canon has been historically the weakest link in its bibliology. Arguments for the shape of the canon have been built upon unexamined theological assumptions and historical inaccuracies."[20]

In the end, to trust in the Bible is to trust in the Church that compiled it. Although this fact might upset skeptics or cause others illicitly to conclude that this places the Church in authority over the Bible, that is how it happened. "Those who accept the traditional canon of Scripture today cannot legitimately defend it with arguments which played no part in its formation."[21]

Only if God worked through the Church is this not a problem. If God infallibly guided the Church in her discernment of the canon, then the canon is infallible and trustworthy as a ground for the faith. If the Church cannot be trusted in her determination of the biblical canon, then the Bible is (at best) "a fallible collection of infallible books". Such a collection hardly provides legitimate grounds for faith in an infallible revelation, much less a faith allegedly based on it alone.

[20] Sawyer, "Evangelicals and the Canon", 29.
[21] Ellen Flesseman-van Leer, cited in Bruce, *Canon of Scripture*, 275.

APPENDIX 2

Facing the Issue of Christian Orthodoxy

Essentials of Orthodoxy

How seriously one takes the numerous theological disputes within Evangelicalism is supposed to correspond to whether any "essential doctrines" are threatened. If the disagreement is over essentials, division is required; if not, it is considered sinful. As Norman Geisler warns: "The truth is that if orthodoxy is to be preserved, then (a) there must be a standard, and (b) it must be possible to determine someone has fallen short of it, and (c) there must be consequences for falling short of it, and (d) these consequences should be feared (respected) by those desiring to be considered orthodox."[1]

Further, the importance of discerning the correct list of essentials can be clearly seen in the reasons given for why it is important to identify the essentials: (1) the essentials are the basis for Christian unity, (2) they "distinguish cults of Christianity from true Christianity", and (3) they are "the only truths over which we rightly can divide".[2] Thus, the ability to identify the essentials objectively becomes paramount to determining Evangelical orthodoxy.

The difficulty comes when one attempts to find a universal standard for Christian orthodoxy. Although Catholics and Eastern Orthodox have recourse to a living standard in the leaders of the Church, Protestants have rejected this authority. Sola scriptura demands that the Bible alone be the ultimate standard for orthodoxy, but there are serious problems with trying to hold to this standard.

---

[1] Norman L. Geisler, "The Essential Doctrines of the Christian Faith (Part One): A Historical Approach", *Christian Research Journal* 28, no. 5 (2005), Christian Research Institute, http://www.equip.org/articles/the-essential-doctrines-of-the-christian-faith-part-one-/.

[2] Ibid.

Can Scripture Alone Determine Orthodoxy?

Unbiblical Categories

First, if orthodoxy is discovered by the "essentials" of the faith, there is a glaring problem: the Bible nowhere marks off its teachings as "essential" or "nonessential" to the Christian faith. Thus, any categorizing of its teachings along those lines comes from a source that is necessarily outside the Bible. Although adherents of sola scriptura generally do not deny the legitimacy of extrabiblical authorities when dealing in nonultimate issues, they do not seem to consider them legitimate when it comes to determining orthodoxy.

One attempt to locate the essentials using the Bible alone is to orient them around the gospel message—basically deducing them logically from what is necessary for the gospel to be true as essential to the faith. Although the actual lists of essentials that this method produces are often respectable, it raises some notable concerns.

A rather glaring issue is that the same essentials are not deduced by different people, because they attach different significance to various salvific issues. For example, the popular Protestant writer John MacArthur comments, "The Gospel message itself must be acknowledged as a primary point of fundamental doctrine. But what message will determine the content of our gospel testimony?"[3] His response is to invoke Scripture: "We are dealing with matters that go to the very heart of the doctrines Scripture identifies as fundamental. Can we get more specific? Let's turn to Scripture itself and attempt to lay out some biblical principles for determining which articles of faith are truly essential to authentic Christianity."[4] MacArthur further claims that "the Fundamentals are clear in Scripture."[5]

MacArthur's list of essential doctrines includes faith, Jesus' divine Sonship and Messiahship, the bodily Resurrection of Christ, the Lordship of Christ, justification by faith alone, the absolute authority of Scripture over tradition, the deity of Christ, the Trinity,

---

[3] John MacArthur, "How Can We Determine What Doctrines Are Essential and What Are They?" Grace to You, http://www.gty.org/resources/questions/qa146/how-can-we -determine-what-doctrines-are-essential-and-what-are-they, adapted from John F. MacArthur, *Reckless Faith* (Wheaton, Ill.: Crossway, 1997), 108–17.

[4] Ibid.

[5] Ibid.

God's imputation of Christ's perfect righteousness to believers, anti-antinomianism, doctrinal and moral enlightenment, acknowledgment of our sinfulness, love for Christ, Jesus' Incarnation, the Virgin Birth, Christ's sinlessness, a lofty view of Scripture, and a sound method of Bible interpretation.[6] It is notable that he includes the specifically Protestant notions of sola scriptura and sola fide.

On the other hand, equally popular Evangelical author Norman Geisler produces a list different from MacArthur's essential doctrines: human depravity, Christ's Virgin Birth, Christ's sinlessness, Christ's deity, Christ's humanity, God's unity, God's triunity, the necessity of God's grace, the necessity of faith, Christ's atoning death, Christ's bodily Resurrection, Christ's bodily Ascension, Christ's present high-priestly service, and Christ's Second Coming, final judgment (heaven and hell), and reign.[7]

In addition to these soteriolological essentials, Geisler adds that the Bible as inerrant, infallible, and inspired Scripture is also an epistemological (or revelational) essential, because we would not be able to know the essentials without the Bible. Finally, he includes the hermeneutical (or interpretive) essential as the means by which we can properly derive the other essentials from Scripture.

Not only does Geisler's list not match MacArthur's; it does not match his own later list in his book *Conviction without Compromise*. There, Christ's Second Coming, final judgment (heaven and hell), and reign (originally one essential) was split into two items, and Christ's reign was dropped from the list altogether.[8] If this Bible-only process is truly a logical deduction from necessary doctrines related to salvation, it is troublesome that the results do not match.[9]

---

[6]MacArthur notes that his list is not "an exhaustive list of fundamental doctrines. Such a task is beyond the scope of this article. Furthermore, the attempt to precisely identify and number such a list of doctrines would be an extremely difficult thing to do." MacArthur, "How Can We Determine What Doctrines Are Essential and What Are They?"

[7]Geisler, "The Essential Doctrines of the Christian Faith (Part One): A Historical Approach".

[8]Norman Geisler and Ron Rhodes, *Conviction without Compromise: Standing Strong in the Core Beliefs of the Christian Faith* (Eugene, Ore.: Harvest House, 2008).

[9]Several popular Evangelical / Protestant writers have produced similarly dissimilar lists allegedly based on the same Bible-only method: Hank Hanegraaff (Christian Research Institute): "The essential tenets of the Christian faith are: Deity of Christ, Original sin, Canon, Trinity, Resurrection, Incarnation, New creation, Eschatology." Hank Hanegraaff, "What Is Essential Christian Doctrine?", Christian Research Institute, accessed May 28, 2015,

Two related problems remain: in both cases above, doctrines are included that are not *simply* deduced from the gospel (e.g., the Virgin Birth or sola scriptura[10]), and doctrines fail to be included that are clearly stated as being connected to salvation in the Bible (e.g., Jn 3:5; Acts 2:38; Rom 6:1; 1 Pet 3:21). Christ's burial and appearances are specifically stated by the apostle Paul to be part of the gospel message (1 Cor 15:1–5), yet neither appears in either MacArthur's or Geisler's essentials list. If the essentials of the faith are truly being deduced from the gospel, how could elements stated in *the gospel message itself* not be included?

---

http://www.equip.org/bible_answers/what-is-essential-christian-doctrine/#christian -books-4. Greg Koukl (founder of Stand to Reason): God's existence and the Trinity, Jesus' deity, the bodily Resurrection, man's fallenness and culpability, salvation is by grace through faith—substitutionary atonement. Koukl adds the inspiration of Scripture as a "functional necessity" but not an essential. Greg Koukl, "Essential Christian Doctrines", Stand to Reason, accessed May 28, 2015, http://www.str.org/articles/essential-christian-doctrines#.VWSBK cKh3IW. Matt Slick (founder of Christian Apologetics Research Ministry): "The Bible itself reveals those doctrines that are essential to the Christian faith. They are (1) the Deity of Christ, (2) Salvation by Grace, (3) Resurrection of Christ, (4) the gospel, and (5) monotheism. These are the doctrines the Bible says are necessary." Matt Slick, "Essential Doctrines of Christian- ity", Christian Apologetics and Research Ministry, accessed May 28, 2015, http://carm.org /essential-doctrines-of-christianity. S. Michael Houdmann (CEO of GotQuestions.org): "The Bible itself reveals what is important and essential to the Christian faith. These essentials are the deity of Christ, salvation by God's grace and not by works, salvation through Jesus Christ alone, the resurrection of Christ, the Gospel, monotheism and the Holy Trinity." "What Are the Essentials of the Christian Faith?" GotQuestions.org, accessed May 28, 2015, http://www.gotquestions.org/essentials-Christian-faith.html#ixzz3B2CBjXvR.

[10] In his article, MacArthur states, " 'The law of the Lord is perfect, restoring the soul' (Psalm 19:7). That means Scripture is sufficient. Apart from the truths revealed to us in Scripture, there is no essential spiritual truth, no fundamental doctrine, nothing essential to soul-restoration." Psalm 19:7–9 speaks of God's law (testimony, precepts, commandments, et cetera), not Scripture in general. Even though God's law is found in Scripture, this does not make the two wholly equivalent. There is plenty of Scripture that does not express God's law (e.g., poetry or the recounting of historical events). Even if the subject of each phrase were Scripture, David's descriptions ("perfect", "sure", "right", "clean", and "true") do not equate to "sufficient". Further, because this psalm was true at the time it was written, the Old Tes- tament (which was unfinished at the time) must have been "sufficient for every situation"— which, lacking even the Gospel, is plainly false. Even in the New Testament, God's revelation consisted in more than just what was written down (e.g., Jn 16:1–12; 21:25; 2 Thess 2:15). We know Scripture is sufficient in some way for some things (e.g., 2 Tim 3:16), but "sufficiency" can be said of a thing in more than one way. In the same way that ingredients can be materi- ally sufficient for making pancakes without being formally sufficient (i.e., having ingredients does not mean having pancakes), the Bible can be materially sufficient for the faith without being formally sufficient. The Bible might have the material we need for "all things that per- tain to life and godliness" (2 Pet 1:3), but we need to do something with it in order to achieve formal sufficiency (i.e., read it, understand it, live it).

In the end, it seems clear that these conclusions only have the appearance of being the result of a logical method. Since this method is one of the best attempts to ground Christian orthodoxy in the Bible alone (and not, for example, in some theologian's views, denominational confessions, or individual church doctrinal statements), this failure is significant.

Disagreeable Interpretations

Even if the Bible did list certain doctrines as essential, though, it would still fail to provide a guide for orthodoxy because orthodoxy is nearly always a matter of interpretation. In many cases of heresy, one affirms the words of Scripture without holding to the correct understanding of those words. To coin a term, one can be *orthovox* (affirming the right *words*) without being *orthodox* (holding the right *beliefs*). The science of hermeneutics (interpretation) thus becomes paramount in the debate.[11] This is necessary because, for the Protestant, no other authoritative safeguard to biblical interpretation exists.[12]

For the most part, Evangelicals are taught that the grammatical-historical method (GHM) is the type of interpretation one must use to be sure of arriving at the correct interpretation of Scripture.[13] The GHM purports to interpret the Bible according to its literal, or normal, sense (where "literal sense" is the grammatical-historical sense).[14]

---

[11] Remember that both MacArthur and Geisler included hermeneutics in their essentials lists.

[12] "The Bible alone is clear when a proper historical-grammatical hermeneutic is used apart from any necessary hermeneutical help from tradition or creeds. This does not exclude the supplementary, but non-essential, use of the early creeds in understanding the Scriptures. It merely insists that if the words 'sola Scriptura' are to have any real meaning, then it cannot mean the Bible plus tradition is necessary to understand God's revelation." Norman Geisler, "A Critical Review of *The Shape of Sola Scriptura* by Keith Mathison", *Christian Apologetics Journal* 4, no. 1 (Spring 2005): 120.

[13] See John MacArthur's ministry doctrinal statement, http://www.gty.org/connect/doctrine; Geisler and Rhodes' *Conviction without Compromise*, chap. 13; Hank Hanegraaff, "What Does It Mean to Interpret the Bible Literally?", Christian Research Institute, accessed May 28, 2015, http://www.equip.org/bible_answers/what-does-it-mean-to-interpret-the-bible-literally/; Greg Koukl's posts on whether the Bible is literal, at Stand to Reason, http://www.str.org/Search?q=Is+the+Bible+Literal%3F+; Matt Slick, "How to Interpret the Bible", Christian Apologetics and Research Ministry, accessed May 28, 2015, http://carm.org/how-interpret-bible; S. Michael Houdmann, "What Is Good Biblical Exegesis?", GotQuestions.org, accessed May 28, 2015, http://www.gotquestions.org/Biblical-exegesis.html.

[14] See the interpretation sections of International Council on Biblical Inerrancy, *The Chicago Statement on Inerrancy*, http://library.dts.edu/Pages/TL/Special/ICBI_1.pdf.

Because the Bible alone is considered a source trustworthy enough for doctrine, and the Bible must be interpreted in order to fulfill this function, using the GHM can be considered to be "the fundamental method that makes possible our knowledge of all the doctrinal essentials" without which "there is no orthodoxy."[15] Because sola scriptura itself can be seen as dependent on a correct hermeneutic procedure, the GHM is a sort of essential of essentials.

The first difficulty with this approach is that the GHM is not affirmed in Scripture. The best that one could hope to show are cases in which the Scripture "interprets itself" (a rarity), where its results are the same as those at which an interpreter using the GHM would have arrived. This would certainly not work in all cases, though—and fails in some determinative cases.[16]

A second, more important issue concerning this method has to do with the GHM's ability to promote unity, detect cults, and be useful for making divisive decisions. There is much disagreement among those who espouse the theological principle of sola scriptura and the hermeneutical principle of the GHM—yet this is the very problem this essential is supposed to solve. Further, these differences are not just over nonessential doctrine, as evidence by debate subjects often considered nonessential (including end-time issues such as the Rapture, the Millennium, and the book of Revelation[17]),

---

[15] Norman Geisler, "The Essential Doctrines of the Christian Faith (Part Two): The Logical Approach", *Christian Research Journal* 28, no. 6 (2005), Christian Research Institute, accessed May 28, 2015, http://www.equip.org/articles/the-essential-doctrines-of-the-christian-faith-part-two-/. See also Geisler and Rhodes, *Conviction without Compromise*, chap. 13.

[16] Consider the example of the prophetic fulfillments by Jesus Christ as listed by the apostle Matthew. Most of the fulfillments are more of the "fully filling" variety than confirmations of the miraculous predictive accuracy of the Old Testament. For example, the Virgin Birth prophecy of Isaiah 7 does not (if taken literally) seem to extend past the lifetime of the prophet, and thus would have been false had it been fulfilled only centuries later at the birth of Jesus. Moreover, Matthew's citing of Hosea's statement "out of Egypt I called my son" (Hos 11:1) is even stranger considering that it was originally a reference to a past event (i.e., the Exodus). Now, there are no real interpretive or theological problems here, for prophecies can have multiple referents—but these are not something that the GHM can ground or that it would have produced.

[17] One of the more ironic evidences of this problem comes from the fact that two of the most influential hermeneutics books affirming the GHM were written by Milton Terry and Bernard Ramm. These books have been cited as exemplars of the GHM. Terry's book was used as a textbook at Dallas Theological Seminary, and Robert Thomas cites both books approvingly in his book *Evangelical Hermeneutics* (see especially the notes in chapters 3 and 6).

there are also multiview books on essential doctrines such as justification, sanctification, and salvation itself.[18]

Further, there are also multiview books on doctrines often considered nonessential by Evangelicals but that could be considered essential given the teaching of the historical Church as well as salvation-linking statements from Scripture (e.g., baptism or Communion). Worse, many issues acknowledged to be secondary are often fought over more fiercely when they are said to be the product of one's denial of sola scriptura or the GHM.[19] These ongoing doctrinal disputes are serious evidence of the GHM's failure to enable Scripture to function as an authoritative source for discovering orthodoxy.[20] If the GHM can be believed, expounded upon, and taught by scholars with radically divergent views, how can it be trusted to deliver the consistent results required by a standard?[21]

The reason for the irony is that Terry is a preterist and Ramm is a millennial—two positions that schools such as Southern Evangelical Seminary and Dallas Theological Seminary as well as scholars such as Thomas and Geisler attack for not following the GHM!

[18]John MacArthur and Zane Hodges' long-standing debate over Lordship versus Free Grace is a good indication of how two theologians espousing the GHM can disagree over essential salvific doctrines.

[19]E.g., Norman L. Geisler, "Method Unorthodoxy", Dr. Norman L. Geisler, April 25, 2015, The "Licona Articles", http://normangeisler.com/licona-articles/; "Methodological Unorthodoxy", http://normangeisler.com/methodological-unorthodoxy/; and "The ETS Vote on Robert Gundry at their Annual Meeting in December 1983", http://normangeisler.com/the-ets-vote-on-robert-gundry-at-their-annual-meeting-in-december-1983-2/.

[20]Further evidence is supplied by the proliferation of "debate style" publications pitting scholars against one another—often (but not always) including those espousing adherence to the GHM (and usually sola scriptura as well). If adherence to these principles were sufficient for proving doctrinal truths, one would not expect so much disagreement. For examples, see Douglas Beaumont, "Theological Abstrusity", Douglas Beaumont, April 24, 2013, accessed May 28, 2015, http://douglasbeaumont.com/2013/04/24/on-protestant-abstrusity/.

[21]One could, of course, reply that others use the GHM inconsistently, but that would be very difficult to argue without begging the question. Further, hermeneutical inconsistency can also be found in the writings of champions of the GHM. A prime example comes from Geisler's handling of the abortion issue. In his 1971 book, *Ethics: Alternatives and Issues*, he argued that "the one clear thing which the Scriptures indicate about abortion is that it is not the same as murder ... [because] an unborn baby is not fully human ... (Ex. 21:22)." He went on to argue that abortion is not murder because life itself has not started and because the embryo is only potentially (or, in some cases "sub-") human. His conclusion was that abortion was justifiable for several reasons (therapeutic, eugenic, incestuous, et cetera). In 1989 Geisler published another ethics book in which he reversed most of his previous conclusions on abortion—using the same passages from Scripture. (E.g., although he based nearly his entire argument for abortion on Ex 21:22, he later said, "Exodus 21[:22–23] does not teach that

A third problem with attempting to use the GHM to discover orthodoxy is that, in addition to being unable to resolve doctrinal debates, the method can also be used to hide theological bias under the guise of "taking the Bible at its word". Consider the typical Evangelical handling of Jesus' words in John 6. There Jesus says, "The bread that I shall give for the life of the world is my flesh.... [U]nless you eat the flesh of the Son of man and drink his blood, you have no life in you.... [H]e who eats my flesh and drinks my blood has eternal life" (Jn 6:51, 53–54). The historic view of this passage is based on literal interpretation and teaches that Jesus is referring to the Eucharist (the Communion meal; cf. Mt 26:26–29; 1 Cor 11:23–25) and that in eating of it, one is literally consuming the flesh of Jesus (i.e., transubstantiation or, at the very least, the real presence of Jesus). The Evangelical position, on the other hand, is that Jesus' words are spiritual or symbolic here. The problem here is that whereas it is true that Jesus sometimes spoke in metaphors or figures of speech (even in John's writings; e.g., Jn 10:9; 15:1), there is nothing in the GHM that would lead to a nonliteral conclusion in this passage.[22]

Supporters of the GHM are quick to point out that it does not always have to deliver a literal interpretation. Rather, "a text should be taken figuratively (1) when it is obviously figurative ... (2) when the text itself authorizes the figurative sense ... or (3) when a literal interpretation would contradict other truths inside or outside the Bible."[23] Do these added considerations help the nonliteral interpretation of Jesus' words here? Certainly the grammar of the passage does not indicate that this is not a literal statement, nor does the context of the passage.[24] The text does not authorize taking the passage

---

a fetus is a potential person. Neither can this be legitimately inferred from the passage." He then went on to argue, based on Exodus 21, that the embryo is a human. A similar interpretive switch was made in his use of Psalm 139.) Although Geisler should be commended for admitting his error—the relevant question here is: On what basis did his viewpoint shift? He does not indicate that he switched hermeneutics, and any method that can justify two contrary interpretations cannot, by itself, be trusted to ground orthodoxy.

[22] See, for example, Norman L. Geisler and Ralph E. MacKenzie, *Roman Catholics and Evangelicals: Agreements and Differences* (Grand Rapids: Baker Academic, 1995), 261–62, and Norman L. Geisler, "Does the New Testament Support the Roman Catholic View of Communion?", Dr. Norman L. Geisler, http://www.normangeisler.com/.

[23] Geisler and Rhodes, *Conviction without Compromise*, 197.

[24] Note that Jn 10:9 and 15:1 are different speeches.

figuratively by calling out the fact that it is figurative, and taking the passage literally does not contradict other scriptural truths.[25] The only criterion left is that it is simply "obvious". But whatever reason one has for thinking this is "obviously figurative", it does not come from the grammar.

So much for the "grammatical" part of the GHM. What about the "historical"? Nothing in the historical interpretation of the passage indicates that it was not taken literally either. In fact, this is one of the rare instances in which we do know how the original recipients understood the words (made clear by the reactions of the disciples and Jesus' reaction to them). Further, a survey of the early Church's view of the Eucharist will show that taking Communion to be merely symbolic was not seriously put forth until about 1,500 years after the fact.[26]

Because the Bible does not mark out any of its teachings as essential or nonessential, and due to the GHM's not being taught in the Bible, its inability to resolve doctrinal disputes (even between its adherents), and its easy accommodation to theological bias, it clearly cannot be used to support sola scriptura in the discernment of orthodoxy. What, then, is left?

The Church Determined Orthodoxy

When Jesus ascended into heaven, he did not leave behind a book; he built a Church. Jesus said he would build the Church and that the gates of Hades would not overcome it (Mt 16:18). Therefore, the Church cannot cease to exist, and therefore it cannot teach falsehood as being of the faith. The canon of Scripture itself, along with the

[25] Some point to Jesus' statement that "the flesh is of no avail" (Jn 6:63) as an indication that "flesh" is not to be taken literally here. In response, not a single person listening to Jesus understood that as a factor when interpreting Jesus' words (nor did he correct them). Further, in the institution narrative, Jesus says that what he holds in his hand is going to be offered up ("this is my body which will be given up for you"). Obviously it was not bread that hung on the Cross.

[26] This doctrine was more of an Anabaptist position popularized by Zwingli but denied by Luther. For the early Church's view of the Eucharist, see "The Early Christians Believed in the Real Presence", Real Presence Eucharistic Education and Adoration Association, accessed May 28, 2015, http://www.therealpresence.org/eucharst/father/a5.html.

determinations of ecumenical councils and the Orthodox creeds, are products of that Church (Jn 16:13, cf. 1 Cor 11:2; 2 Thess 2:6; 3:15; 2 Tim 2:2). The Church, therefore, has been the guardian of orthodoxy for two thousand years.

In fact, it is entirely possible that Christianity's message could have been communicated verbally—and only verbally—forever.[27] First, there is nothing inherently problematic with such a thing occurring. A simple thought experiment will show that this is the case: suppose some atheistic world dictator succeeded in destroying every copy of the Bible in existence and then somehow made it impossible to create additional texts of any kind. Would Christianity disappear from the earth? Would men no longer have access to the saving gospel? Of course not. So, at least in theory, there is no problem with these two propositions being true at the same time: (1) Christianity exists, and (2) no Bible exists.

Second, the above theory has been shown to be true in reality. Receiving the gospel message is the requirement for becoming saved (1 Cor 15:1–5), and this message was not initially communicated in written form (1 Cor 15:1), yet those who heard it believed and became saved (becoming part of the Christian Church; 1 Cor 1:2). Thus, Christianity preceded the written message.

Third, it is a historical fact that Christianity preceded the writing of the New Testament. The earliest New Testament writings are typically considered to have been written in the mid-to-late '40s (whether the first book was the Gospel of Matthew, the letter of James, or Paul's letter to the Galatians is debated). This means that even with a late date of Christ's death and Pentecost (A.D. 33),

---

[27]Eusebius wrote, "Those great and truly divine men, I mean the apostles of Christ ... published the knowledge of the kingdom of heaven throughout the whole world, paying little attention to the composition of written works.... Paul ... committed to writing no more than the briefest epistles.... Of all the disciples of the Lord only Matthew and John have left us written memorials, and they, tradition says, were led to write only under the pressure of necessity." Eusebius, *Church History* 24. And Protestant theologian William Whitaker wrote that "Divine Providence can preserve from destruction whatever it chooses;... we may, in the same manner, infer that there is no need of the scriptures, that every thing should be trusted to Divine Providence, and nothing committed to writing, because God can preserve religion safe without the scriptures." William Whitaker, *A Disputation on Holy Scripture against the Papists, Especially Bellarmine and Stapleton* (Cambridge: Cambridge University Press, 1849), 652.

there is at *least* a decade gap between the beginning of the Church and the very first New Testament writing. The point is even more strongly made when we consider that Paul's writings (which are, at minimum, among the earliest New Testament writings) were letters addressed to already existing churches. Add to this decade more time for delivery and distribution, and I think it is easy to see that the Church had to go for quite some time with no (New Testament) Scriptures of her own.

Fourth, Christians existed and continue to exist without possessing the New Testament. Even when the New Testament started to be written, its contents were not in the possession of the average believer. Besides the delivery and distribution time lags, people simply did not have easy access to copies. Further, the New Testament was written at a time when most of the population was illiterate. Finally, it would be another 1,500 years or so before the invention of the printing press made the Bible widely accessible even to literate people. (Thus, this is not just an ancient, medieval, or Reformation-age issue). Even in our time, people from many parts of the world become Christians where the Bible is forbidden or inaccessible in their language. This certainly represents a hindrance to Christianity, but it is hardly destructive. So even if the skeptic were successful in showing the Bible to be untrustworthy, he has not really gained much ground—at least if he is using that untrustworthiness as an attack on Christianity itself. For even if we give up the entire Bible, Christianity remains.[28]

The significant point is that what kept the Church going during this time was her own teaching—orthodoxy. It can be found in a multitude of sources:

---

[28] Evangelical apologist Gary Habermas has an interesting method that he uses when defending the historicity of Christ's Resurrection; he calls it the Minimal Facts approach. Habermas agrees to use only the most academically respected sources (both Christian and secular) in support of his contention that Jesus Christ rose from the dead. In doing so, he avoids the Gospels, many of Paul's letters, and several other New Testament books that do not enjoy nearly universal "authentic status" among professional historians. Using only the minimal facts that can be gleaned from whatever historical documents are left, Habermas proceeds to argue that the Resurrection remains the best explanation of the data. It's a great approach, and his protégé Michael Licona has been very successful with his version of it as well. If we took the Minimal Facts approach to the absurd extreme of not relying on *anything* in the Bible (the "zero facts" approach?), what would we have left over from Christianity? As it turns out, pretty much everything—for it is all found in the traditions of the Church.

- the rule of faith (e.g., Rom 1:3–4; 1 Cor 11:23–36; 15:3–5; 1 Pet 3:18; 1 Jn 4:2)
- catechetical instructions (the Didache [first century])
- sermon messages (1 and 2 Clement [A.D. 95–97])
- post–New Testament epistles (letters of Ignatius [A.D. 98–117])
- baptismal confessions (the Old Roman Creed [second to third century])
- Bible commentaries (Theophilus, Diatessaron [second to third century])
- liturgical actions and language (Liturgies of Saint James and Saint Basil [fourth century])
- ecumenical councils, canons, creeds, and definitions (by the fifth century)

From the Jerusalem Council in Acts 15 to today, the Church has always determined orthodox doctrine by holding authoritative Church councils that, in turn, gave us the Creeds and the biblical canon. The difficulty for one who does not trust the Church to safeguard orthodoxy is that whatever other seemingly legitimate means one advances for Christianity, it is likely the product of the Church herself. If God kept the Church safe from error when she defined the canon of Scripture, why not when she wrote the orthodox creeds or when she has held her ecumenical councils?[29]

None of the above should be taken to suggest that we abandon the use of, devotion to, or defense of the Bible. Rather, what it shows

---

[29] In "The Essential Doctrines of the Christian Faith", Geisler admitted that his method is not the one the Church actually used (what he called the "historical approach"). Rather than adopt this method, though, he attempted to support his conclusions by noting that when his list is compared with "the list discovered by the historical approach, the same basic doctrines emerge". However, although it is true that many of his essentials also appear in the creeds, the reverse is not the case. First, Geisler occasionally takes a phrase (or even a single word) in a creed as equivalent to an entire doctrine (for example, equating the single word for "I believe" with the doctrine of the necessity of faith for salvation or taking the phrase "in accordance with the Scriptures" in reference to the Resurrection as counting toward making the Bible itself an essential). Second, Geisler leaves many creedal affirmations out (e.g., a single resurrection, a single visible Church, apostolic succession, and baptismal regeneration)—some of which are specifically connected to salvation in the creeds (such as "baptism for the forgiveness of sins" in the Nicene Creed or that belief in the content of the creeds is necessary for salvation in the Athanasian Creed). The question one must answer is: Why should one trust only certain parts of the creeds? To do so reduces this comparative support from the historical method to theological question begging.

is that God has used the Church to communicate his truths in many ways (1 Tim 3:15–16) and that the Bible—while holding the highest place as being the inspired words of God himself (2 Tim 3:15–17)— alone is insufficient for determining orthodoxy. This is not because it is insufficient for its purposes, but because such a thing is evidently not its purpose. This would be a problem only if the Bible proclaimed itself to be so, but it does not.

The Bible, being a book, must be interpreted. To prevent us from confusing our subjective interpretation with orthodox Christian teachings, God has given us his Church—the body of Christ.[30] It is united in belief, safeguarded from dogmatic error, and universal in scope, and it can be objectively identified by the historical fact of apostolic succession. Under the Church's guidance one need not worry over private interpretations or feel the need to redefine Christianity for every generation (or individual). Sincere seekers of truth have been given many aids in their pursuit—and each can be trusted as it rests on or works through the "pillar and bulwark of the truth": the Church (1 Tim 3:15).

Postscript: The Infallibility of the Church

Thomas Aquinas defined true faith in terms of one's willful adherence to a religious authority. Because supernatural truths of faith are not directly discoverable by the senses or reason, God must reveal them somehow. Because supernatural truths of faith must be revealed, questions concerning them cannot be resolved by other means (e.g., logic, science, philosophy, or history). God's revelation, in whatever form it takes, becomes the religious authority for believers. Christians typically insist that this authority must be infallible—after all, if we

---

[30] Saint Vincent of Lerins noted that "if one should ask one of the heretics,... 'What ground have you for saying that I ought to cast away the universal and ancient faith of the Catholic Church?' he has the answer ready: 'For it is written', and forthwith he produces a thousand testimonies, a thousand examples, a thousand authorities from the law, from the Psalms, from the apostles, from the prophets, by means of which, interpreted on a new and wrong principle, the unhappy soul may be precipitated from the height of Catholic truth to the lowest abyss of heresy.... Do heretics also appeal to Scripture? They do indeed, and with a vengeance.... Hardly ever do they bring forward anything of their own that they do not endeavor to shelter under words of Scripture ... an infinite heap of instances, hardly a single page, that does not bristle with plausible quotations from the New Testament or the Old." Saint Vincent of Lerins, *Commonitory* 25.

cannot really be sure what God has revealed, how can we submit ourselves wholly to it? Eternal salvation itself may be at stake.

When Jesus founded the Church on his apostles (cf. Eph 2:20; Rev 21:14), he made some rather startling assertions. He instructed the apostles to teach people all that he had taught them in order to make disciples (Mt 28:19–20). He also told the apostles they had the authority to judge sin (Mt 18:18) and said that whoever listened to them was listening to him, and whoever rejected them was rejecting him (Lk 10:16). These were no mere country preachers! The institution of the Church began with a transfer of divine authority to found a Church with the purpose of teaching doctrine and determining sin and salvation.

It is hard to imagine Jesus giving this kind of authority to the apostles, who served as the foundation of the Church, and then saying, "Of course, there is no guarantee that you will not mess it all up—but no worries." What good is divine, eternal, and immutable truth if its teacher can be in error? Would God entrust his Church with teachings connected to mankind's ultimate purpose (the reward of heaven or the penalty of damnation) without some means of guaranteeing she did not teach falsehood? Given this role, infallibility seems a necessity.[31]

The Church built on the apostles was tasked with the communication of Jesus' gospel, teachings, and forgiveness of sins (Mt 16:18; cf. Mt 28:18–20). She therefore could not fulfill her role if she fell into religious error—to do so would be to fail as the Church. Jesus, however, promised that his Church would not fail (Mt 16:18). If failure to accomplish her role as religious authority would constitute a failure of the Church, and the Church cannot fail, then the Church cannot teach religious error. Therefore, if the Church ever taught heresy, she

---

[31] It might be objected that Israel was under the religious authority of fallible leaders, and this might seem like a counterexample, given Judaism's close association with Christianity. But God did not just drop the Old Testament into the laps of the Israelites and leave them to try to figure out Judaism. Rather, he provided them with inspired and infallible prophets who spoke for him and who later even added to biblical revelation when needed. However, such things are not available to the Church because Jesus was the final revelation of God (Heb 1:1–2), and the New Testament was the final inspired revelation of God's Word. (These two points are fairly uncontested among the majority of Christians, so I will not argue for them here). So Israel does not function as a counterexample; rather it may point to the need for ongoing infallible guidance.

would not be the Church! Since this would entail a contradiction, the Church must be protected from teaching religious error (which is merely the negative way of expressing infallibility).

Further, we know from the Bible that Jesus did not give such a weighty role to the apostles without a means of accomplishing it. Rather, he promised the apostles the Holy Spirit to guide them into all truth (Jn 16:13), and their teachings (both written and verbal) were to be obeyed (2 Thess 2:15; 3:6). Thus, the Church's role, promises, and descriptions do not seem to leave room for religious error. That this is the Church's self-understanding is demonstrated by her actions. The first time a major doctrinal decision had to be made, the apostles talked it out and made their own judgment. In fact, they concluded that what they thought was what the Holy Spirit thought (Acts 15:28). If the promise of the Holy Spirit to lead the apostles into all truth did not confer on them some supernatural guidance, it is difficult to imagine how such a lofty claim could be made.

Finally, this protection does not end with the apostles. The Church's role did not change with the deaths of the apostles, and so the means necessary to accomplish her purpose can be expected to continue as well. In the Great Commission, Jesus told the apostles that he would be with them until the end (Mt 28:18–20). The Church Jesus founded was to become the "pillar and bulwark of the truth", and this did not cease in the first century of her existence. This implies that the apostles' roles and promised means would not cease with their deaths but would continue somehow. We know that the apostles, in fulfilling this Great Commission, did not simply start churches and leave them on their own. Rather, they ordained leaders to guide these groups as authoritative overseers (see, e.g., Titus and 2 Timothy). This provided for the continuation of the Church's identity, as well as continuing the Church's functions and means. History bears this out as well—for such was the Church's self-understanding from the earliest times, as reflected in the writings of the apostolic Fathers (some overlapping the lives of the apostles).[32]

---

[32]See, e.g., "The Early Church Fathers on Apostolic Succession—Catholic / Orthodox Caucus", Free Republic, accessed May 28, 2015, http://www.freerepublic.com/focus/f-religion/1775198/posts.

The above theoretical, theological, and biblical considerations point to the divine institution of a Church that God safeguards from authoritatively pronouncing religious error. Given her role as communicator of God's revelation unto salvation, and Christ's promises and examples of divine guidance, protection from failure seems necessary to guarantee the Church's very existence. Although this infallibility can and has been exercised through various means, there seems to remain a need for a single, infallible, apostolic office behind it all to provide an objective standard when necessary. Specific predictions and promises made to Peter, as well as the subsequent history of his successors, point to the office of the Bishop of Rome as the best fit for the "last line" of infallible doctrinal defense.[33] Thus can the Church's infallibility be grounded in both theory and practice.

---

[33] See David B. Currie, *Born Fundamentalist, Born Again Catholic* (San Francisco: Ignatius, 1996), 92–94.

APPENDIX 3

Facing the Issue of Sola Scriptura

Introduction

The doctrine of sola scriptura (Scripture alone) began as a concern for proper authority in religious matters. By *authority* is meant something like *that which has the right to compel agreement*. A religious authority would be one that has the right to compel faith (orthodoxy) and moral actions (orthopraxy). This does not mean that one cannot make free choices in these matters, but simply that in cases of faith and morals, a person's refusal to agree with the authority would signal an objective wrong on his part (should that person wish to remain in the religion at least).

It seems clear that all human authority in religious matters would be superseded by God's. Now, since God is clearly the authority for a Christian, and since the only record of God's communication that all Christian bodies believe to be inspired is the Bible, the Bible must have the top spot as far as authorities go. This was the original sense of sola scriptura—the Bible is the ultimate authority in matters of faith and morals—not that it was the only authority. Sola scriptura meant that Scripture alone was the ultimate authority in religious matters, as opposed to including Church tradition or the teachings of men.[1]

---

[1] See Keith Mathison, *The Shape of Sola Scriptura* (Moscow, Ida.: Canon Press, 2001), or James R. Payton Jr., *Getting the Reformation Wrong: Correcting Some Misunderstandings* (Downers Grove, Ill.: InterVarsity Press, 2010). For a critical response to this idea, see Bryan Cross, "Solo Scriptura, Sola Scriptura, and the Question of Interpretive Authority", Called to Communion, November 4, 2009, accessed May 28, 2015, http://www.calledtocommunion.com/2009/11/solo-scriptura-sola-scriptura-and-the-question-of-interpretive-authority/.

Considering the number of angles one could take in responding to sola scriptura, sufficient response to it could easily become an entire book, and covering all those angles is not the purpose of the present writing.[2] However, given that the issue of sola scriptura weighs so heavily in one's consideration of Catholicism, it deserves some comment.

Sola Scriptura and Biblical Sufficiency

"Is the Bible sufficient?" This question lies at the heart of many Catholic-Protestant debates. A major roadblock to coming to agreement is that a thing can be said to be sufficient in more than one way. Here I would like to explain two meanings: formal and material sufficiency. Grasping the distinction between these two types of sufficiency is critical to understanding the debate. *Material* sufficiency concerns whether the Bible contains all the information one needs to learn the faith, and *formal* sufficiency relates to whether the Bible can be properly interpreted all by itself.

A helpful analogy is that of a recipe and a dish's ingredients. Although one might have all the ingredients ("materials") necessary to prepare a certain dish, one must also have the recipe for cooking ("forming") them into the right kind of food. In this case, neither the recipe nor the ingredients are sufficient to prepare the dish—both are required. The real debate over sola scriptura is whether the Bible is both materially and formally sufficient for the faith, or whether it is only materially sufficient. Based on verses that extol the Scriptures (such as Ps 19 or 2 Tim 3:16–17), some argue that the Bible alone is sufficient in both senses, thus requiring no extrabiblical interpretive authority. The problem for this view is explaining the numerous disagreements and divisions among the very groups who make that claim.[3]

---

[2] One such book weighs in at over 650 pages: Robert A. Sungenis, ed., *Not by Scripture Alone: A Catholic Critique of the Protestant Doctrine of Sola Scriptura* (Goleta, Cal.: Queenship, 1998).

[3] See Douglas Beaumont, "Theological Abstrusity", Douglas Beaumont, April 24, 2013, accessed May 28, 2015, http://douglasbeaumont.com/2013/04/24/on-protestant-abstrusity/.

Now, it is clear that the Bible is interpreted in many ways. This is not to say that the Bible is 100 percent wide open for anybody's interpretation (just as a given collection of ingredients cannot make *any* kind of food), but it does seem to accommodate more than one interpretation in many cases. Since the Bible must be interpreted in order to function as an authority in the life of the believer, some principle must be in play to ensure that we get out of it what we are supposed to get out of it. Whatever that is (philosophy, science, theology, inspiration, angelic explanation) would be the formal principle or principles. Understood this way, it seems clear that the Bible is not formally sufficient on its own. If it were, there would not be disagreement over its meaning (or at least not nearly as much as there is).

This is no attack on the Bible. It is no more wrong or demeaning to say that the Bible is only materially sufficient than it is ridiculous to complain that milk and eggs and bread are not sufficient to make french toast. Only if the Bible were actually both materially and formally sufficient would such a statement be wrong or demeaning. Further, it seems pretty clear from the Bible itself that more is required than the text alone (e.g., Lk 24:27; Acts 8:26–31; 17:1–3; 18:24–26; 2 Pet 3:16). At the very least, knowledge of reality is needed—for words merely point to things in reality. So our understanding of reality will clearly affect our interpretation. This is just an issue with texts—not the Bible in particular. And it is not an issue that goes away just because a book is inspired.

Sola Scriptura and Unity

Unity among Christians was clearly one of the chief concerns of Christ (Jn 17) and the apostles (e.g., 1 Cor 1; Eph 4). This unity is not only a spiritual reality but a physical one as well, for Jesus taught that the oneness of the Church would be a witness to the world (Jn 17:23). Protestantism, in principle and in practice, cannot unify Christians. Sola scriptura effectively makes unity in moral code, doctrinal creed, and liturgical practice impossible, for every appeal to Scripture is an appeal to an interpretation of Scripture, and men interpret the Scriptures in radically different ways. Would Christ set up his Church in such a way that would necessarily lead to division and dissent? In fact, the principle of sola scriptura makes answering the question "What is the Christian view of _____?" difficult if not impossible; hence, Christians divide.

To resolve the interpretative problem, the Protestant has recourse to one of two options: (1) appeal to the perspicuity of Scripture or (2) attempt to establish the leaders of the church as the authoritative interpreters of Scripture. The sheer number of denominations clearly indicates that the former is false (i.e., the Bible is not so clear). The latter cannot escape the initial problem of interpretive authority because the individual believer must decide which church has teaching authority. In order to decide this, he must find which church he believes interprets the Scriptures correctly. Hence, the individual is still the authority on the true teaching of the church. An excellent essay that develops the latent problems in the second attempt to resolve Protestant theology's interpretive mess is written by Bryan Cross. In this essay, well worth a careful reading, Cross responds to Keith Mathison's book *The Shape of Sola Scriptura*. Further, Michael Liccione has written a follow-up essay that poignantly spells out the fundamental philosophical issues in the debate.[4]

One could object that the Catholic convert is in the same predicament as the Protestant, for he seems to be doing the same thing he accuses the Protestant of doing (tu quoque fallacy)—that is, interpreting the Scriptures and then deciding that the Catholic Church is interpreting the Scriptures correctly. In reality, however, the Catholic convert is not doing what the Protestant does. The Catholic Church does not ask converts to read the Scriptures and decide for themselves if Catholic teaching is true; rather, the Catholic Church makes a historical claim that the interpretive authority she has is clearly evident from a study of Church history. Christ received his authority from the Father and then conferred that authority on Peter and the apostles, who in turn conferred their authority on their successors on

---

[4]See Cross, "Solo Scriptura, Sola Scriptura, and the Question of Interpretive Authority", and Michael Liccione, "Mathison's Reply to Cross and Judisch: A Largely Philosophical Critique", Called to Communion, February 18, 2011, accessed September 1, 2014, http://www.calledtocommunion.com/2011/02/mathisons-reply-to-cross-and-judisch-a-largely-philosophical-critique/.

down to the present day. The Catholic stance is not rationalistic, for the Church does not attempt to prove she has this authority (rational proofs for articles of faith are impossible, for if proof were possible, faith would be superfluous). Rather, the convert embraces the Catholic teaching by faith, for without faith it is impossible to please God (Heb 11:6).[5]

Sola Scriptura and the Bible

One of the biggest issues with sola scriptura is that the Bible says nowhere that it alone functions as the ultimate authority for faith and morals (or anything else—see below). This makes sola scriptura an authoritative extrabiblical *tradition* (the very thing it was supposed to rule out). There are, however, many texts that indicate that both the written word of the apostles and the spoken word of the apostles ("tradition" in Catholic theology) are equally authoritative (Mt 28:19; Mk 16:15; Jn 21:24–25; 1 Cor 11:2; 15:3, 11; 2 Thess 2:15; 3:6; 2 Tim 1:13; 2:2). Furthermore, the Scriptures do not teach that the Bible is the pillar of truth; rather, the Church is called the "pillar and bulwark of the truth" (1 Tim 3:15).

The book of Acts gives a clear example of how the Church is supposed to handle doctrinal disputes. In Acts 15, Luke records a doctrinal dispute over the status of Gentiles in the Church. A council is called, and the leaders of the early Church convene to give an authoritative pronouncement of correct faith and practice for the whole Church. The last word on the debate is given by Peter, and then James stands up to confirm Peter's pronouncement by quoting an obscure passage from Amos that seems to have nothing to do with the matter at hand. However, James explains that the passage in Amos indicates the full membership of Gentiles in the Church. What is most interesting about the passage in Acts is the role that the Bible plays at the council. The Bible is not the judge of the dispute at hand, which one would expect if sola scriptura were true. Rather, the Bible is the witness to an authoritative pronouncement of the

[5] For further reading, see Bryan Cross, "The *Tu Quoque*", Called to Communion, May 24, 2010, accessed May 28, 2015, http://www.calledtocommunion.com/2010/05/the-tu-quoque/.

teaching body of the Church, which is what one would expect if the Catholic teaching on authority is true.[6]

Recognizing that direct biblical support for sola scriptura is not to be found, Protestants have tried to find biblical justification for the doctrine by arguing indirectly from other passages (which is a legitimate method). These will be briefly addressed below.

2 Timothy 3:16–17

The Scripture passages that are most commonly referenced to defend sola scriptura are, at best, evidence of the principle or simply do not contradict it, but the Scriptures in no way establish the principle. For example, Protestants routinely appeal to 2 Timothy 3:16–17—"All Scripture is inspired by God and profitable for teaching, for reproof, for correction, and for training in righteousness, that the man of God may be complete, equipped for every good work"—as evidence of sola scriptura, but this passage in no way endorses this position. Paul is certainly pointing out that the Scriptures are the preeminent guide for the moral life, but he is in no way claiming that Scripture supplies one with a comprehensive view of doctrine, worship, ecclesial government, et cetera.

Further, Protestant apologists usually attempt to poke holes in the Catholic view of authority without addressing the numerous facts of Church history that do not make sense if sola scriptura is true. For example, how should one understand the bizarre situation in which the early Church would find herself if sola scriptura were true? Would the authoritative spoken word of the apostles become non-authoritative once the apostles died? Must the Christians in the churches that Paul established forget what he taught them about the sacraments, worship, Church structure, discipline, et cetera once he died? How could early Christians limit their authority to the New Testament when the first list of New Testament books is found in the writing of Saint Athanasius (A.D. 367) and the debate on the canon extended beyond the time of the Protestant Reformation?

---

[6]See Jason Stellman, "I Fought the Church, and the Church Won", Called to Communion, September 23, 2012, accessed May 28, 2015, http://www.calledtocommunion.com/2012/09/i-fought-the-church-and-the-church-won/.

In addition, how does one explain that when heretical groups based their positions on the Bible the Church Fathers also referenced used apostolic succession, and not the Bible alone, as the measuring stick of Orthodoxy?[7] How does the principle of sola scriptura consistently line up with the historical fact that the Scriptures are the effect of true apostolic teaching (correct orthodox doctrine) and not the cause of orthodox teaching? These and many other problems arise when one accepts sola scriptura, while the Catholic paradigm on authority has no problem in explaining this fact.

Psalm 19

In his article "The Sufficiency of Scripture", John MacArthur argues that Scripture alone is sufficient for every situation. He states, "Psalm 19:7–9 is the most monumental and concise statement on the sufficiency of Scripture ever made. Penned by David under the inspiration of the Holy Spirit, these three verses offer unwavering testimony from God Himself about the sufficiency of His Word for every situation."[8] MacArthur's equation of "God's glorious revelation" and "Scripture" is questionable, though, and there are several issues with his use of this psalm to argue this "total sufficiency" position.

First, Psalm 19:7–9 is speaking of God's *law*—not Scripture in general. There is more to Scripture than God's law (which was originally spoken—not written, and could have remained so forever), so they are not necessarily the same thing. Here is what the text says in the translation MacArthur cites:

> The *law* of the Lord is perfect, restoring the soul;
> The *testimony* of the Lord is sure, making wise the simple.
> The *precepts* of the Lord are right, rejoicing the heart;
> The *commandment* of the Lord is pure, enlightening the eyes.

---

[7] See Pope Saint Clement I (A.D. 70), Saint Irenaeus of Lyons (A.D. 189), Tertullian of Carthage (A.D. 200), and Saint Cyprian of Carthage (A.D. 254). For quotations from these and other Church Fathers regarding authority and the early Church, see Jimmy Akin, "Apostolic Tradition", in *The Fathers Know Best* (San Diego: Catholic Answers, 2010), 166–74.

[8] See John MacArthur, "The Sufficiency of Scripture", Grace to You, accessed May 28, 2015, http://www.gty.org/resources/Distinctives/DD11/The-Sufficiency-of-Scripture; adapted from John MacArthur, *Our Sufficiency in Christ* (Wheaton, Ill.: Crossway, 1998).

The *fear* of the Lord is clean, enduring forever;
The *judgments* of the Lord are true; they are righteous altogether.[9]

None of the subjects in this passage is Scripture, yet that is the subject of MacArthur's alleged proof. The only way the argument can be made to appear sound is for MacArthur to expand the words' definitions and add his own commentary to those expanded definitions.[10]

Second, even if the subject of each phrase were Scripture, David's descriptions ("perfect", "sure", "right", "clean", and "true") do not equate with "sufficient". Again, the only way the argument can be supported is by substituting MacArthur's commentary for the plain text.

Third, what David said when he wrote this psalm had to be true *at the time he wrote it*. Following MacArthur's argument, then, the Old Testament (which was unfinished at the time) must have been "sufficient for every situation". But was it? Where does the Old Testament (even after completion) explain the gospel message or reveal the Church? Where does Scripture explain how we should view stem cell research or what kinds of music to listen to? Where, in fact, does Scripture indicate its own table of contents?

It seems that the "most monumental and concise statement ever made" on scriptural sufficiency requires more extrapolation than it should, and that something more is needed has certainly not been disproven from this passage.[11]

1 Corinthians 4:6

One verse that is sometimes cited as a definitive biblical statement on sola scriptura is a small infinitive phrase in 1 Corinthians 4:6: "not to go beyond what is written".[12] That this small phrase is a difficult text to nail down is indicated by its numerous interpretations (both Protestant and Catholic), but if there is a single proof text for sola scriptura, this is it. The first problem with using 1 Corinthians 4:6 as

---

[9] New American Standard Bible (NASB); emphasis added.

[10] MacArthur does indeed do this; e.g., *fear* is said to be a synonym for *God's Word*.

[11] MacArthur's commentary was seventeen times longer than the passage itself!

[12] The New International Version (NIV), alone among the major translations, phrases this as a distinct command: "Do not go beyond what is written."

proof of sola scriptura is that many prominent Protestant thinkers did not see it as such, even though they affirmed sola scriptura.[13]

Second, although Paul does not mention Scripture or the Bible in this passage, every time Paul uses the Greek word translated "written" here, he is referring to the Old Testament—but limiting it to the Old Testament would mean that 1 Corinthians 4:6 did not apply to itself!

Third, generalizing "what is written" to include only the Old and New Testament writings would be contrary to Paul's command to "stand firm and hold to the *traditions* which you were taught by us, either by *word of mouth* or by letter" (2 Thess 2:15; emphasis added; cf. 2 Thess 3:61; 1 Cor 11:2). The idea that everything an apostle taught orally was eventually reduced to writing is itself an extrabiblical idea (cf. 1 Cor 11:34; 2 Cor 2:4; cf. 2 Cor 7:8; 3 Jn 13). And what of the apostles (or Jesus himself!) who never wrote any Scripture?

Fourth, the apostles themselves taught from sources outside the Bible (e.g., Acts 7:53; 17:28; 26:14; Jude 9, 14–15). If they could use extrabiblical writings to write the Bible, then the principle that one cannot go beyond the Bible seems awkward at best.

Finally, given that the primary concern of 1 Corinthians is clearly that of *unity*, and that in the letter's opening section Paul addresses disunity caused by *unbiblical assessments of ministers* (cf. the textual connection between Paul and Apollos in 1 Cor 1:12; 3:4; 3:22; and 4:6, along with his mention of "numerous guides" both in 1 Cor 1:10 and 4:14), plus the judgment theme leading right up to 4:6, it seems best to me to take "not to go beyond what is written" to be referring to the proper biblical standards of ministerial judgment.

Sola Scriptura and the Biblical Canon

An odd issue for sola scriptura adherents is that, even if one could find sufficient biblical support for the idea, one would first have to prove that his proof texts are really in the Bible in the first place—for the

---

[13] See Douglas Beaumont, "Does 1 Corinthians 4:6 Teach Sola Scriptura?", Douglas Beaumont, April 20, 2015, accessed May 28, 2015, http://douglasbeaumont.com/2015/04/20/does-1-corinthians-46-teach-sola-scriptura/.

principle of sola scriptura cannot give one a list of the authoritative books that belong in the Bible. Protestants usually attempt to resolve this problem in one of two ways: (1) appeal to the testimony of the Holy Spirit to confirm which books are canonical or (2) make theological arguments for the list of books that belong in the canon.

The first way cannot explain how it is that many godly, Spirit-led Christians throughout history have disagreed on the canon, so the testimony of the Holy Spirit to the human heart is not sufficient. The latter attempt also fails to produce an authoritative canon for any list of criteria that a book must meet to be included in the Bible; it either leaves out books that Christians agree are canonical or includes books that are not canonical. Moreover, a list of criteria can be made only after one knows which books are canonical. Finally, a criteria list fails the historical test, for this was not the way the canon was initially formed. (See appendix 1.)

Sola Scriptura and Church Tradition

It is often claimed that adding anything to the Bible to interpret it authoritatively puts those things "above Scripture". In many ways, though, trust in the Bible itself requires trust in extrabiblical traditions. Now, if the Bible itself depends on extrabiblical traditions, how can one claim that no extrabiblical traditions may be added to the Bible? Here are some of the important things tradition must support if the New Testament is to be identified and trusted.[14]

---

[14] A related problem for Protestants is that if the Church was still trustworthy (however this is explained) by the time she defined the canon (in the fourth century at the earliest), why was she not trustworthy when she defined these doctrines?

A.D. 90—the Lord's Supper as a sacrifice
A.D. 95—apostolic succession
A.D. 110—the real presence of Jesus in the Eucharist
A.D. 110—the necessity of authoritative bishops to the Church
A.D. 150—baptismal regeneration and the necessity of baptism for salvation
A.D. 150—the basic structure of the Mass as Christian worship
A.D. 155—veneration of saints and their relics
A.D. 160—Mary as the New Eve
A.D. 170—the use of the word *Trinity*
A.D. 180—the primacy of the Bishop of Rome
A.D. 200—"Trinity", "Person", "substance" formula

Table of Contents

Because the Bible has no inspired contents page, one must go outside the Bible to discover which books make it up. Because the Church compiled these books, the Church is trusted to identify the Bible (whether acknowledged or not).

Authorship

Although some take apostolic origin as the test for inclusion in the Bible, many New Testament books do not identify their authors. None of the Gospels identifies its author in the text, nor does Acts or Hebrews. James and John are not identified, and several candidates have been suggested. Both Pauline and Petrine epistles name their authors, but both authors have letters whose authenticity has been questioned *by Christians* since the early centuries of Christianity (Martin Luther himself discredited several New Testament books in the sixteenth century). In the end, it is the Church that determined which books were considered part of the biblical canon.

Autographa

Since we have none of the original New Testament writings (the autographa), our entire New Testament tradition is based on trust in tradition. Although the textual history for the New Testament is incredibly strong, small errors in the beginning would never be caught later. Thus, we give implicit trust in the Church to keep the text stream clear.

None of this should be upsetting, since nonscriptural traditions are trusted by the New Testament writers in many places,[15]

---

[15] For example:

Mt 2:23—The prophecy "He shall be called a Nazarene" is oral tradition. It is not found in the Old Testament.

Mt 23:2—Jesus relies on the oral tradition of acknowledging Moses' seat of authority (which passed from Moses to Joshua to the Sanhedrin). This is not recorded in the Old Testament.

Acts 15:1–14—Peter resolves the Church's first doctrinal issue regarding circumcision without referring to Scriptures.

Acts 17:28—Paul quotes the writings of the pagan poets when he teaches at the Areopagus. Thus, Paul appeals to sources outside of Scripture to teach about God.

oral traditions were often trusted as authoritative,[16] and the writers even record that authoritative aid is often needed for proper

---

Acts 20:7—As for meeting on Sunday, already in the New Testament we seem to find Christians meeting together as a Church on the first day of the week (i.e., Sunday). Although not a watertight case, it does seem that Acts 20:7 and possibly 1 Corinthians 16:2 refer to Christians' gathering as a Church on Sunday. But by A.D. 115, Ignatius, a bishop, was telling Christians to meet not on the Sabbath but on Sunday (what he calls the "Lord's Day"—the day when Jesus rose from the dead).

Acts 20:35—Paul relies on the oral tradition of the apostles for this statement ("it is more blessed to give than to receive") of Jesus. It is not recorded in the Gospels.

1 Cor 7:10—Paul relies on the oral tradition of the apostles to give the charge of Jesus that a wife should not separate from her husband.

1 Cor 10:4—Paul relies on the oral tradition of the rock following Moses. It is not recorded in the Old Testament. See Exodus 17:1–17 and Numbers 20:2–13.

Eph 5:14—Paul relies on oral tradition to quote an early Christian hymn—"Awake, O sleeper, and arise from the dead, and Christ shall give you light."

Heb 11:37—The author of Hebrews relies on the oral tradition of the martyrs being sawed in two. This is not recorded in the Old Testament.

Jas 4:5—James even appeals to Scripture outside of the Old Testament canon ("He yearns jealously over the spirit which He has made").

2 Pet 1:20—Interpreting Scripture is not a matter of one's private interpretation. Therefore, it must be a matter of "public" interpretation of the Church.

Jude 9—Jude relies on the oral tradition of the Archangel Michael's dispute with Satan over Moses' body. This is not found in the Old Testament.

Jude 14–15—Jude relies on the oral tradition of Enoch's prophecy, which is not recorded in the Old Testament.

[16] For example:

Mt 28:19 (cf. Mk 16:15)—Some who preached the gospel to all creation did not write the Gospel.

Mk 16:15—Jesus commands the apostles to "preach", not write, and only three apostles wrote. The others who did not write were not less faithful to Jesus, because Jesus gave them no directive to write. There is no evidence in the Bible or elsewhere that Jesus intended the Bible to be the sole authority of the Christian faith.

Lk 1:1–4—Luke acknowledges that the faithful have already received the teachings of Christ and writes his Gospel only so that they "know the truth concerning the things of which you have been informed". Luke writes to verify the oral tradition they already received.

Jn 8:6–8—Jesus Christ taught orally, the "spoken word". He did not write a book. The only record that he wrote anything at all is in, "Jesus bent down and wrote with his finger on the ground." We do not even know what he wrote.

Jn 20:30; 21:25—Jesus did many other things not written in the Scriptures.

1 Cor 5:9–11 and Col 4:16; cf. 2 Pet 3:15–16—Peter says Paul's letters are inspired, but not all his letters are in the New Testament canon; Paul wrote two other letters to Corinth and one to Laodicea that we no longer have.

1 Cor 11:2—Paul commends the faithful to obey apostolic tradition.

1 Cor 11:34—Paul says that "[a]bout the other things I will give directions when I come." We do not have "3 Corinthians" so we do not know what those things were, even if he did write them down.

interpretation.[17] Given all this trust in extrabiblical tradition and its eventual authoritative role, one wonders why it is so strenuously objected to by Protestants long after the fact.

Solo Scriptura and Authority

Although sola scriptura is still sometimes expressed along the lines of Scripture (alone) as being the "supreme and final authority in faith and life",[18] many Evangelical Christians follow the early Anabaptists in couching sola scriptura more in terms of *"solo* scriptura"—denying *any* authority outside of the Bible.[19] If Scripture alone is the ultimate authority, then it is thought that to follow a Bible-only methodology regarding theology, ethics, science, et cetera will keep one safe from the errors of fallible human thinking.[20]

Phil 4:9—Paul says, "What you have learned and received and heard and seen in me, do."

1 Thess 2:13—Paul says, "when you received the word of God, which you heard from us".

1 Thess 3:10—Paul wants to see the Thessalonians face-to-face and supply what is lacking. His letter is not enough.

2 Thess 2:14–15—Paul says that God has called us "through our gospel". The fullness of the gospel before the Gospels are written is the apostolic tradition that includes teaching either by word of mouth or by letter.

2 Thess 3:6—Paul instructs us to obey apostolic tradition.

1 Tim 3:14–15—Paul prefers to speak and not write and is writing only in the event that he is delayed and cannot be with Timothy.

2 Tim 2:2—Paul says apostolic tradition is passed on to future generations, but he says nothing about all apostolic traditions being eventually committed to the Bible.

2 Tim 3:14—"[C]ontinue in what you have learned and have firmly believed, knowing from whom you learned it."

[17] For example:

Acts 8:30—"Philip ran to him, and heard him reading Isaiah the prophet, and asked, 'Do you understand what you are reading?'"

Heb 5:12—"For though by this time you ought to be teachers, you need some one to teach you again the first principles of God's word."

2 Pet 3:16—The Scriptures are difficult to understand and can be distorted by the ignorant to their destruction. God did not guarantee that the Holy Spirit would lead each of us to interpret the Scriptures infallibly.

[18] This is the language used by Southern Evangelical Seminary's doctrinal statement: http://ses.edu/about-us/doctrinal-statement.

[19] For example, Norman Geisler, "A Critical Review of The Shape of Sola Scriptura by Keith Mathison", *Christian Apologetics Journal* 4:1 (Spring 2005).

[20] The first page of a Google search brought up two representative statements of this popular understanding of sola scriptura: "Scripture alone is called God's word (cf. Jn.10:35; 2 Tim.3:16; 2 Pt.1:20), and in 1 Cor. 4:6 we are specifically told 'not to go beyond what is

Bible-alone theology may sound very fine when constrained to an abstract ideal, but as has been said, a good hypothesis can "be killed by inches, the death by a thousand qualifications."[21] Even allowing that the Bible is the final and ultimate authority for Christian faith and practice, the Bible still must be *understood*. That is, the Bible's authoritative teaching resides in the *message* it conveys—not the physical *book* itself. And discovering the message of the Bible requires navigating through many layers of human interaction first.

The Bible was written in three ancient languages: Hebrew, Aramaic, and (Koine) Greek. Since the average Christian does not understand these ancient languages thoroughly, the Bible he holds is almost certainly a *translation* of the words of God. But there is a plethora of Bible translation "versions" on the shelf of the average bookstore, and translation issues are not always minor. Choosing any one of them is to rely on the linguistic authority of the translator. One might think this issue could be resolved by learning the original languages—but that would introduce another authority, that of the language instructors.

Even after one learned the original biblical languages, interpretation still enters in. Translation involves far more than simple word replacement. To translate correctly, one must be familiar with how that language was used at the time of the original writing (grammar, cultural context, linguistic innovation, et cetera). In order to master all the elements involved in learning these languages, several additional authorities would have to be relied on.

Even if this arduous task were accomplished, language and translation study give one only knowledge of what ancient texts

---

written.'... Not once did Jesus speak well about traditions. Neither did Peter nor Paul as he states in Col. 2:8 'Beware lest anyone cheat you through philosophy and empty deceit, according to the tradition of men, according to the basic principles of the world, and not according to Christ.'" "The Bible's Tradition of God's Word Only", Let Us Reason Ministries, accessed May 28, 2015, http://www.letusreason.org/rc23.htm. "The only way to know for sure what God expects of us is to stay true to what we know He has revealed—the Bible. We can know, beyond the shadow of any doubt, that Scripture is true, authoritative, and reliable. The same cannot be said of tradition. The Word of God is the only authority for the Christian faith. Traditions are valid only when they are based on Scripture and are in full agreement with Scripture. Traditions that contradict the Bible are not of God and are not a valid aspect of the Christian faith. *Sola scriptura* is the only way to avoid subjectivity and keep personal opinion from taking priority over the teachings of the Bible." "What Is *Sola Scriptura*?", GotQuestions .org, accessed May 27, 2015, http://www.gotquestions.org/sola-scriptura.html.

[21] Antony Flew, "Theology and Falsification", in Anthony Flew and Alasdair McIntyre, *New Essays in Philosophical Theology* (London: SCM Press, 1955), 97, http://www.stephenjay gould.org/ctrl/flew_falsification.html.

say—understanding what they *mean* is another issue. Thus, one must also deal with the hermeneutic layer. This is made all the more difficult because there is no overarching hermeneutic that works for the whole Bible. At least some of the Bible is poetry, metaphor, parable (or proverb), and so forth—and recognition of these things requires extrabiblical knowledge. Recognizing literary devices such as hyperbole and metaphor depends on one's experience of reality; thus, correct notions of metaphysics are necessary if we are to avoid subjectivity in biblical interpretation.[22] Either philosophical field could easily take up a lifetime, and the authorities involved in such pursuits are mostly (if not entirely) extrabiblical.

Worse, philosophical knowledge of reality is often insufficient for issues of history and culture. Language meaning might be objectively understood via a proper hermeneutic, but its specific referents can remain unknown. The particular realities that words pick out are not shared by the biblical writers and our average Christian, for they are thousands of years, and thousands of miles, removed from one another—and sometimes important cultural details are lost to history. A thorough knowledge of history and culture is necessary to avoid anachronism and other such errors and to catch subtle remarks that the original readers would have recognized. The Bible causes these issues; it does not solve them. To penetrate this historical-cultural layer, one must once again rely on extrabiblical authorities.

Even if a reader could somehow (miraculously?) manage to meet the above criteria, the job is still not done. For once he knows what a text says and what it means, he must then grasp what it *teaches*. Here we run into more examples of how Scripture does not supply easy answers. Do the stories of people speaking in tongues in the book of Acts teach us that believers today must do likewise? Is the head covering in 1 Corinthians 11 a practice that has some parallel today? Does the acceptance of slavery throughout the Bible indicate that it has an acceptable place in the world today? Why do we practice the Lord's Supper but not foot washing when Jesus commanded both during the same talk? These sorts of questions cannot be answered simply by knowing what the Bible says or means. Issues of cultural relevance, proper dispensations, audience similarity, general versus

---

[22] See Thomas A. Howe, *Objectivity in Biblical Interpretation* (Altamonte Springs, Fla.: Advantage Inspirational, 2005).

particular commands, and so forth all remain. Now subjects such as ethics, moral philosophy, theology, and others come into play. And since it is the Bible that seems to raise these issues, it seems that once again extrabiblical information is required.

Now, even if all of these tremendous extrabiblical interpretive issues were somehow overcome, the biggest challenge yet remains— for before the Bible can be interpreted, it must be identified. One must first choose which "original Bible" to read. For the New Testament alone one must choose between the Minority and the Majority Text traditions (and there are different versions of each of these forms, such as the Nestle-Aland, or the United Bible Society's, or the Textus Receptus—each having had numerous revisions). The Old Testament, too, has some textual issues—the most notable being that the Hebrew manuscript copies, the Masoretic text, that we have are much later than the original writings. There is also the Greek translation of the Old Testament, known as the Septuagint, or "LXX", which is quoted more in the New Testament than the Masoretic text yet sometimes differs considerably from the Hebrew texts we have. As skeptics are happy to point out, few of these manuscripts agree completely. Now, this is not such a huge problem, since, given thousands of comparisons, we can arrive at a pretty solid understanding of what the original must have said. But differences, or variants, remain, and questions need to be answered when it comes to deciding which variants to use when producing the "original" edition. How is an average Christian to choose between them? Unless he is willing to trust in the text-critical authorities, he will have to learn text criticism himself. Worse, unless he wants to trust the people who typed up what is found on these ancient manuscripts, he will have to gain access to all of them directly, from all over the world, and make his own copies. To do otherwise would be to trust extrabiblical authorities.

Complicating this task is the fact that the Bible is not *a book*. Rather, it is a collection of various writings that are bound together for convenience. But who decided which books are in this collection? We know from history that the canon of the New Testament was determined by councils—but these are extrabiblical authorities. Is the average Christian just as free to jettison the biblical canon as he is the traditional Church creeds and councils? And if he is, on what biblical basis would he do so? How can sola scriptura survive if we cannot be sure of what counts as "scriptura" in the first place? But

many claim that the whole point of sola scriptura is to avoid traditions! This introduces yet another authority layer to be overcome—
that of tradition.

The Bible warns of following false traditions, but as with false philosophy and false religion, it is the *false* part that is important.[23] Now,
to be absolutely sure of one's understanding of Christian doctrine
from the Bible alone (i.e., apart from tradition), at least three things
must be the case. First, authoritative tradition must have ceased with
the apostles (to avoid the self-defeating proposition that the Bible—
which teaches that traditions must be trusted—alone is trustworthy).
Second, the Bible would have to be perfectly clear in what it teaches
(to avoid any possible misunderstanding, each part would have to
have this clarity—for if it did not, it may be the case that one part
would alter another). Third, everything the apostles wanted taught
must have been recorded in Scripture (because the slightest bit of
additional information could radically alter our understanding of anything else we read).

The first point begs the question and is self-defeating because the
Bible does not teach that authoritative tradition ceased with the apostles. As to the second criterion, the numerous and disparate interpretations of Scripture offered by the very people who proclaim its
clarity seem to argue against that position. The third point is even
more problematic for sola scriptura as it has been popularly defined,
for even if Church tradition after the apostles is not authoritative, and
even if Scriptures are perfectly clear, it would have taken only one
extra sentence to change everything.[24]

---

[23] To be consistent in affirming Scripture's alleged negative outlook on tradition, one must
ignore certain verses (e.g., 2 Thess 2:15; 3:6; or 1 Cor 11:2)—a practice that is made easier by
the NIV translators who purposefully translated the Greek term *paradosis* as "traditions" in its
negative contexts and as "teachings" in its positive references!

[24] As an example, let's consider Communion (the Lord's Supper / the Eucharist). Paul told
the Corinthians concerning Communion, "About the other things I will give directions when
I come" (1 Cor 11:34). Suppose that what he later said to them was, "By the way, Jesus Christ
is physically present in the Communion bread and wine." That one sentence would be a
game changer for interpretation of not only 1 Corinthians 11, but John 6 and Matthew 26
as well! Now, we do not seem to know what directions Paul gave concerning Communion
when he came to them later. 2 Corinthians says nothing about it. Paul does mention two
other letters to the Corinthians that we do not have, so perhaps it was in those. Or maybe in
the epistle that he sent to the church at Laodicea (Col 4:16) he said something of interpretive
importance. Either way, it did not make it into the Bible—and to be 100 percent certain of
his Bible-only understandings, our average Christian would have to know for sure.

Finally, since the Bible does not say that it alone is trustworthy or authoritative, the idea that it is so is a theological one. In many areas, holding to theological positions that are not clearly stated in the Bible is not necessarily a big problem, since many positions are based on theological speculation. Here, however, it becomes a bigger issue, for it would be incoherent to claim that the Bible alone is a trustworthy source of theological information when the Bible itself does not say that it alone is a trustworthy source of theological information. In addition, it would also turn out to be self-defeating since the Bible itself teaches that other sources of revelation exist (e.g., the principles of natural theology and the moral law found in Romans 1 and 2). And, since the Bible actually commands believers to hold to "traditions" that they "heard" (see above), it simply cannot be the case that the Bible's position is that traditions do not become authoritative until they are written down.

In conclusion, Bible-only theology sounds fine as long as it remains an abstract principle (or slogan). The reality is much messier. At least the following authoritative layers would need to be peeled back before a strict Bible-only theological method could succeed:

- *linguistic*—to avoid having to trust nonauthoritative translators
- *translational-interpretational*—to avoid having to trust nonauthoritative interpreters
- *hermeneutical-philosophical*—to avoid having to trust nonauthoritative philosophers
- *historical-cultural*—to avoid having to trust nonauthoritative historians
- *applicational*—to avoid having to trust nonauthoritative teachers
- *mystical*—to avoid having to trust nonauthoritative personal views
- *textual*—to avoid having to trust nonauthoritative text critics
- *canonical*—to avoid having to trust nonauthoritative Church decisions
- *traditional*—to avoid having to trust nonauthoritative traditions
- *theological*—to avoid having to trust nonauthoritative theologians

These layers of human interaction are like lenses through which the Bible's message is seen—and to whatever degree these interpretive layers influence how one understands the Bible's message, to that degree they have a practical authoritative function. Thus, it seems clear that the Bible in our hands can be depended on to deliver authoritative truth only to the degree that the authorities at each layer can be trusted to deliver authoritative truth—and in the real world, reliance on extrabiblical authority is found at nearly every step of Bible study. Even if the average Christian had the time, materials, and intellect for such an endeavor, he would still realistically have to rely on a host of extrabiblical authorities (teachers, authors, researchers, principles, et cetera) to learn all that he would need to know to become a trustworthy (yet extrabiblical and thus still fallible!) authority himself.[25]

[25] See Douglas Beaumont, "Sola Scriptura: Death by a Thousand (or Ten) Qualifications?", Douglas Beaumont, July 3, 2011, accessed May 28, 2015, http://douglasbeaumont .com/2011/07/03/sola-scriptura-death-by-a-thousand-or-ten-qualifications/.

APPENDIX 4

Facing the Issue of Sola Fide

Salvation by Faith Alone

Martin Luther is famous for propagating the dictum of sola fide: that sinners are saved ("justified") by faith alone (i.e., apart from works). Among the reasons that works supposedly play no causal role in justification is that, according to Luther, justification consists solely in the imputation of the alien righteousness of Jesus Christ, who perfectly fulfilled the righteous demands of the law on our behalf. The person justified by faith in Christ remains intrinsically unrighteous, so that his own works can contribute nothing to his justification (contra Catholicism).[1] The person is nevertheless "set right" with God through faith alone in Christ's righteousness alone.[2]

Luther described sola fide as being the article by which the church stands or falls.[3] This doctrine came to be known as the "material principle" (i.e., the distinctive and essential doctrinal content) of the Reformation. Sola fide was not simply one among others of Luther's doctrines—it was paradigmatic for his view of Scripture and therefore

[1] It is important to bear in mind throughout the following discussion that according to Catholic theology the principle or root of all good works acceptable to God is the theological virtue of love, which is a gift of grace bestowed by the Holy Spirit (Rom 5:5). See Saint Thomas Aquinas, *Summa Theologiae* II-II, 27–33.

[2] Alister E. McGrath, *Iustitia Dei: A History of the Christian Doctrine of Justification*, 3rd ed. (Cambridge: Cambridge University Press, 2005), 226–28.

[3] See Justin Taylor, "Luther's Saying: Justification Is the Article by Which the Church Stands and Falls", The Gospel Coalition, August 31, 2011, accessed May 28, 2015, http://thegospelcoalition.org/blogs/justintaylor/2011/08/31/luthers-saying/.

the entirety of Christian faith and life.[4] As will be shown below, the biblical doctrine of salvation as well as the contents of the Bible itself were at stake—and the doctrine of sola fide (whether true or false) was used by Luther to justify questionable Bible translations, to question the content of the canon of Scripture, and to reject the Church of his day.

Considering the several important facets of the Protestant doctrine of sola fide, sufficient response to this doctrine could easily become an entire book. Such a detailed response is not the purpose of the writing.[5] Instead, we will here focus on the relation of sola fide to the other major principle of the Protestant Reformation—namely, sola scriptura.[6] In this connection, we will consider the following: (1) whether Luther's doctrine of justification by faith alone originated from Scripture alone, (2) whether Scripture clearly teaches justification by faith alone, and (3) whether the teaching of Scripture on faith, works, and justification can be successfully harmonized in light of the teaching of the Catholic Church.

Luther and Sola Fide

Martin Luther is often pictured as a champion of biblical theology, a man who brought the Church back under the authority of the

---

[4]Concerning the doctrine of sola fide as the material principle of the Protestant Reformation, the popular Evangelical Anglican theologian J. I. Packer writes:

> It has been common since Melanchthon to speak of justification by faith as the *material* principle of the Reformation, corresponding to biblical authority as its *formal* principle. That is right. Of all the Reformers' many biblical elucidations, the rediscovery of justification as a present reality, and of the nature of the faith which secures it, was undoubtedly the most formative and fundamental. For the doctrine of justification by faith is like Atlas. It bears a whole world on its shoulders, the entire evangelical knowledge of God the Saviour. The doctrines of election, of effectual calling, regeneration, and repentance, of adoption, of prayer, of the Church, the ministry, and the sacraments, are all to be interpreted and understood in the light of justification by faith, for this is how the Bible views them.

J. I. Packer, "Sola Fide: The Reformed Doctrine of Justification", Ligonier Ministries, accessed May 28, 2015, http://www.ligonier.org/learn/articles/sola-fide-the-reformed-doctrine -of-justification/.

[5]For an extended response, see Robert Sungenis, ed., *Not by Faith Alone: A Biblical Study of the Catholic Doctrine of Justification* (Goleta, Cal.: Queenship, 1997).

[6]For more on the Protestant principle of sola scriptura, see appendix 3.

Bible. What many do not realize is that Luther rather self-consciously brought Scripture under his own authority, as revealed by his handling of key biblical texts that did not comport with his own theology. Three examples from three key "sola fide" texts are found in the books of James, Romans, and Ephesians.

Luther versus James

James 2:24 is a rather large problem for sola fide adherents. It is the only verse in Scripture that includes the words *justified, faith*, and *alone*, and it says a person is "justified by works and not by faith alone."[7] A clearer contradiction of sola fide would be difficult to produce. How did Luther handle this?

Luther was so convinced of his sola fide insight that he called the epistle of James an "epistle of straw" and implied that it was not properly part of Scripture. Luther considered this epistle to be nonapostolic and thought it did not communicate the gospel.

The tension between Luther's theology and James' letter is evidenced by Luther's *Preface to James*, where he says, "It is flatly against Saint Paul and all the rest of Scripture in ascribing justification to works." As German-educated Protestant theologian and Church historian Philip Schaff notes in his *History of the Christian Church*, Luther "brought Paul into direct *verbal* conflict with James, who says (James 2:24), 'by works a man is justified, and *not only* by faith.'... It is well known that Luther deemed it impossible to harmonize the two apostles in this article, and characterized the Epistle of James as an 'epistle of straw,' because it had no Evangelical character."[8]

Thus, Luther's understanding of salvation became such an overriding factor that it affected his belief in the canon of Scripture itself.

Luther versus Paul

Another means of avoiding the fact that no verse of Scripture teaches sola fide is reflected in one of Luther's more infamous moves: his deliberate addition of the word *alone* (German: *allein*) to Romans 3:28. When Luther translated the Bible into German, he made this

---

[7] This is true across translations. See http://biblehub.com/james/2-24.htm.

[8] Philip Schaff, *History of the Christian Church* (New York: Charles Scribner's Sons, 1910), posted at Bible Research, accessed May 28, 2015, http://www.bible-researcher.com/luther02.html; emphasis in the original.

verse say, "So now we hold, that man is justified without the help of the works of the law, alone through faith." Concerning this addition, Schaff writes, "The most important example of dogmatic influence in Luther's version is the famous interpolation of the word *alone* in Rom. 3:28, by which he intended to emphasize his sola fide doctrine of justification, on the plea that the German idiom required the insertion for the sake of clearness."[9]

This is not just Schaff's attempt to explain what seems to be a mistranslation—it reflects Luther's own explanation. In *An Open Letter on Translating*, Luther defends his addition of *alone* to the text:

> I know very well that in Romans 3 the word *solum* is not in the Greek or Latin text—the papists did not have to teach me that. It is fact that the letters s-o-l-a are not there. And these blockheads stare at them like cows at a new gate, while at the same time they do not recognize that it conveys the sense of the text—if the translation is to be clear and vigorous, it belongs there.[10]

Now, there are other Protestant German Bibles, such as the Elberfelder and the Hoffnung für Alle, that do not insert the word *allein* in Romans 3:28, so it would seem that the German translation does not actually require the addition of that word to make sense.[11] But Luther continues:

> I was not depending upon or following the nature of the languages alone when I inserted the word *solum* in Romans 3. The text itself, and Saint Paul's meaning, urgently require and demand it. For in that passage he is dealing with the main point of Christian doctrine, namely, that we are justified by faith in Christ without any works of the Law.[12]

Luther has also been accused of making other textual changes to fit his theology.[13] Now, although it is certainly a feature of translation

---

[9] Ibid.

[10] Martin Luther, "An Open Letter on Translating", Bible Research, accessed May 28, 2015, http://www.bible-researcher.com/luther01.html.

[11] Note that Romans 3:28 lacks the word for *alone* in both the Latin translation Luther used (i.e., *sola*) and the original Greek manuscripts (i.e., μόνον; cf. Jas 2:24).

[12] Luther, "An Open Letter on Translating".

[13] See Bob Thiel, PhD, "*Sola Scriptura* or *Prima Luther*? What Did Martin Luther Really Believe about the Bible?", Cogwriter, accessed May 28, 2015, http://www.cogwriter.com /luther.htm.

that sometimes words must be added for clarity, what is clear here is that it is Luther's *theology* that is being inserted into the text.[14] Luther's understanding of salvation was such an overriding factor that it led not only to his subtraction of entire books but to his addition of words to the text. This is certainly not what one would expect from someone claiming to uphold sola scriptura!

Luther versus Works

A major issue for Luther's theology is that he excludes *all works* from the conditions for salvation based on verses that mention only qualified works. For instance, he uses verses that speak of works of the law to argue against *any* works. This move by Luther reflects a classic logical fallacy: simply because all *works of the law* are *works*, that does not mean that all *works* are *works of the law*.[15]

Thus, the addition of *alone* to Romans 3:28 is not only erroneous as a translation; it is also an interpretive error based on an unjustified conflation of "works" with certain "works of the law". This can be seen when Luther points out Paul's example of Abraham's faith. Notice how Luther moves from "works of the law" to an unqualified use of "works":

> Paul excludes all works so completely as to say that the works of the law, though it is God's law and word, do not aid us in justification.... All works are so completely rejected—which must mean faith alone justifies—whoever would speak plainly and clearly about this rejection of works will have to say, 'Faith alone justifies and not works.' The matter itself and the nature of language require it.[16]

Luther's own cross-reference to Galatians 2:16 in Romans 3:28 makes it clear that *works* there should be qualified, for there Paul writes, "yet [we] know that a person is not justified by works *of the law* but through faith in Jesus Christ, even we have believed in Christ Jesus" (emphasis added).

---

[14] This type of argument is rejected by Evangelical Protestants when it is used to counter their theology. See, for example, James White, "Germans, JW's and John 1:1", Alpha and Omega Ministries, accessed May 28, 2015, http://vintage.aomin.org/GERM_JWS.html; or "Is the New World Translation a Valid Version of the Bible?" GotQuestions.org, accessed May 28, 2015, http://www.gotquestions.org/New-World-Translation.html.

[15] This is known as the fallacy of converting a universal affirmative statement.

[16] Martin Luther, "An Open Letter on Translating".

Paul uses Abraham's faith as an example in Galatians as well as Romans—but note which works of "the law" Paul is speaking of: "the law, *which came four hundred and thirty years afterward*, does not annul a covenant previously ratified by God" (Gal 3:17; emphasis added). Here, *works of the law* clearly refers to the *law of Moses* (cf. Ex 25 and Heb 8:13—9:1)—not to works of the *law of Christ* (cf. Gal 6:2; Mk 12:28–33).

When Paul contrasts faith and works, he qualifies "works" in the text. For example, he speaks of "works of the law" (Gal 2:16; 3:2, 5, 10; Rom 3:20, 28), "works of darkness" (Rom 13:12; Eph 5:11), and "works of the flesh" (Gal 5:19). Even when there is not a direct verbal qualifier, context makes clear what kinds of works Paul means (e.g., works done for *illegitimate boasting* [Rom 3:27; 4:2; cf. Gal 6:4]). To ignore these important qualifications would bring Paul not only into conflict with James but with himself—for throughout his writings Paul commanded Christians to do good works (see the next section).

Luther versus Sola Scriptura

We have seen that sola fide was used by Luther both to mistranslate the content and to question the canon of Scripture—the very Scripture he claimed to stand upon against the Church of his day. It seems Luther himself was guilty of doing the very thing he accused the Catholic Church of doing: elevating theology above the Bible. Luther's doctrine had huge implications for his life as well.

The other major "sola" to drive the Reformation was sola scriptura—the belief that the Bible alone was the final court of appeal in doctrinal matters. It was to this "formal principle" that Luther and other Reformers appealed when they came into conflict with Catholic teachings.[17] In 1521, Luther was called to defend his doctrinal views at the Diet of Worms. In his defense he is said to have made this famous statement: "I consider myself convicted by the testimony of Holy Scripture, which is my basis; my conscience is captive to the Word of God. Thus I cannot and will not recant, because

---

[17]For more on the distinction between material and formal principles, see Douglas Beaumont, "The Bible and Legos", Douglas Beaumont, April 20, 2015, accessed May 28, 2015, http://douglasbeaumont.com/2015/04/20/the-bible-and-legos/.

acting against one's conscience is neither safe nor sound. God help me. Amen."[18]

Now, Luther's translation of the Bible was made shortly after he spoke these words. One wonders if he had them in mind while adding the word *alone* to Romans 3:28. What is to be made of sola scriptura or Luther's "captivity to the Word of God" if he adds his own theology to the Scriptures? Although Luther at times sounds like (and has been portrayed as) a simple, pious expositor and disciple of Scripture, it seems that at times he was simply captive to his own mind. So confident was Luther in his views that he once claimed, "I for my part am certain that the words I speak are not mine, but Christ's. Then my mouth also must be his whose words it speaks."[19]

At face value, these do not sound like the words of a man who has set aside "the traditions of men" in favor of the sole authority of the written Word of God, but rather of someone who has tacitly appointed himself the Magisterium of the Church. Although Luther says the same of "every man ... who speaks the word of Christ", his handling of the biblical canon, his translation of the Bible, and his other writings seem to confirm this suspicion. In the same place he wrote the above statement, Luther added, "I ask that men make no reference to my name, and call themselves not Lutherans, but Christians. What is Luther? My doctrine, I am sure, is not mine (John 7:16)."[20]

Scripture and Sola Fide

Many of those who follow the tradition of Luther regarding justification by faith alone maintain that the teaching of Scripture is so clear on this point that anyone who simply reads the relevant texts without bias and using common sense will see the truth of the doctrine of sola

---

[18] Elesha Coffman, "What Luther Said", *Christianity Today*, August 8, 2008, accessed May 28, 2015, http://www.christianitytoday.com/ch/news/2002/apr12.html.

[19] Martin Luther, "A Sincere Admonition by Martin Luther to All Christians to Guard against All Insurrection and Rebellion", in *Works* 3:174, http://media.sabda.org/alkitab-8/library/lut_wrk3.pdf.

[20] Luther, "A Sincere Admonition", in *Works* 3:176.

fide. On this view, no extrinsic or self-appropriated religious authority is needed to justify taking a stance like Luther's. This is essentially the claim that Scripture is "perspicuous" on matters pertaining to salvation, which further refines Luther's application of the material principle to the formal principle of the Reformation—some things in Scripture are hard to understand, but anything you need to know in order to be saved is easy to understand.

Of course, one of the reasons the Protestant Reformation became a movement apart from the Catholic Church is that Luther and the Church could not agree on the interpretation of the Bible concerning matters pertaining to salvation. Not only that, but to this day conservative Protestants disagree among themselves on the interpretation of the Bible regarding matters that they mutually agree pertain to salvation in a vital way. Although it is theoretically possible that all persons on the wrong side of the disputed soteriological questions are either so stupid that they cannot understand the plain meaning of Scripture, or so immoral that they refuse to accept the plain meaning of Scripture, or just so addled by their own tradition as to be rendered nonculpably confused about the plain meaning of Scripture, it is also possible that the meaning of Scripture as a whole on matters pertaining to salvation is not plain or "perspicuous" in the sense that all persons of goodwill using common sense and seeking to understand the Bible on its own terms will come to the same conclusions.

Private Interpretation

A little experience among people with other views is sufficient to dispel the notion that everyone with whom one disagrees about matters pertaining to salvation is either stupid, ignorant, or immoral. Rather, it seems to be the case that even among those who accept the formal principle of the Reformation—sola scriptura—theological paradigms invariably inform Bible interpretation. When a Bible verse seems to teach something that someone does not agree with, that verse gets relegated to the category of "unclear" and is then "explained" by referring to a different "clear" verse (namely, one that sounds like the interpreter's view).

The trouble is that many verses deemed unclear have the same form as those that are considered clear. One verse says, "Salvation is by X", and another says, "Salvation is by Y." Yet, one is seen as clear and the other unclear. Nothing in the text seems to blame for this distinction, though. The alleged unclear verses often end up being simply those that seem to teach most strongly against one's theology.

Nor is this only a problem for nonsalvific passages. In fact, the problem is *especially* evident when it comes to salvation verses. Someone new to Christianity and the Bible, who knew no theology or specialized theological terminology, could do a Bible search on the words *salvation* and *saved* and discover a long and varied list of "clear" requirements to be saved. Cross-referencing words such as *faith, belief, grace, works, repent, endure,* and others that pop up regularly in these salvation passages would generate a "salvation summary" twenty pages long![21] Grammatically speaking, few of these would seem unclear—they would become difficult only if the new Christian was later taught what not to believe: Women saved by *childbirth*? Having to *endure* to the end? How can *persecution* save?

What makes one verse clear and another unclear seems to have more to do with one's prior theological position than with biblical wording, and of course theologians are at odds with one another. To one who believes in baptismal regeneration, verses such as Mark 16:16, Acts 2:38, and 1 Peter 3:21 seem quite clear. To those who believe repentance must be part of faith, a host of verses from the Gospels are considered the "main, plain" ones. Those who believe that faith saves apart from good works find passages such as Luke 7:50, Romans 3, Ephesians 2:8–9, and Galatians 2 obvious. Those who think works must accompany faith can point to Matthew 5, Ephesians 2:10, James 2, and Revelation 14.

Now, these interpretive difficulties are all resolvable, but the resolutions are inevitably theological and not merely exegetical, precisely because some verses are hermeneutically prioritized as being "clear" from the start. That is, theology is doing the grouping, categorizing, and explaining of the biblical data. The end result is that the "clear" verses are held both "theologically" and "biblically" (i.e., taken at face value), whereas the "unclear" verses are held only "theologically" (i.e., as carefully qualified). But using theology to

---

[21] See the partial summary of one such search at the end of this essay.

explain the "unclear" verses easily results in a circular argument for one's position.

There are in fact "clear" verses for almost every understanding of salvation, and similar results are produced in other areas as well. Good, smart, faithful people disagree over nearly every theological position imaginable—and all attempt to gain support from the Bible and more or less successfully harmonize the biblical data. The idea that these various conflicting theologies can be concluded by appealing to the "clear, main, plain" verses is therefore simply an invitation to beg the question.

Authoritative Interpretation

The reality is that most people learn Christianity in a particular theological context and simply absorb whatever they are taught until they are able to do their own study. By then, their default theology is often so ingrained that they forget they are still interpreting the Bible they are reading. Verses that seem to teach their views clearly are trotted out as proof texts, while contrary passages are labeled "unclear" and then understood by the "clear" ones.[22] Unless a theological paradigm shift occurs, this will likely remain the case—and disagreements will often be seen as signs of ignorance or even sin.

This problem is not limited to Protestants, which is why Catholics read Scripture in light of the tradition of the Church and her living Magisterium as a matter of principle. Catholics do not subject the teaching authority of the Church to the rule of private interpretation of Scripture, such that they "submit" to the former only when it agrees with the latter, which is the Protestant modus operandi (i.e., sola scriptura). From a Catholic point of view, to contradict or disregard these authorities when interpreting the Bible would be to take the Bible out of context, whereas submitting to and learning from them is to read Scripture for what it is in reality: the Word of God given by inspiration to, through, and for the Church.

---

[22] This idea that "Scripture interprets Scripture" is often erroneously referred to as the *analogia fide*—the "analogy of faith", which originally referred to the rule of faith (regula fidei)—the core set of Christian teachings that determine orthodoxy. See Daniel H. Williams, *Evangelicals and Tradition: The Formative Influence of the Early Church* (Grand Rapids: Baker Academic, 2005).

For Catholics, the Bible does not exist in a theological vacuum apart from interpretive authority. Instead, the meaning of Scripture is made clear by the teaching of the Church, so that various disputes can be and have been definitively settled by the Church's God-given authority (cf. Mt 16:18–19). Thus, orthodoxy is established and believers are given an interpretive key, the genuine tradition, by which to perceive and discover further the authentic harmony of Sacred Scripture.

Catholics and Sola Fide

Catholics believe that by means of good works rooted in love we can grow in the righteousness of God and in this sense be justified by works as well as by faith. Thus, we are justified by faith because faith is the beginning of justification, but justification is not by faith *alone* because dead faith does not justify; rather, justifying faith is faith animated by love (Rom 2:6–16; Jas 2:14–26). The difficulty is that it is also stated several times in the New Testament that we are *not* justified by works (e.g., Gal 3:11 and Eph 2:8–9). All interpreters of Scripture must find a way to harmonize these teachings. We saw above how Luther attempted to do it and why it is problematic. The Catholic position on justification does not depend on there being only one possible way to harmonize the biblical data, but it is helpful to see how the biblical data can be harmonized in a manner consistent with the Catholic doctrine of justification.[23]

The most famous of these seeming discrepancies in the biblical data on justification is between James and Paul. The alleged contradiction between their views on faith and works is exemplified by the following statements:

James: "You see that a man is justified by works and not by faith alone" (Jas 2:24).

Paul: "For we hold that a man is justified by faith apart from works of the law" (Rom 3:28).

---

[23] Because no amount of dogma can exhaust the depths of the Word of God, Catholics can and do explore various ways of harmonizing the biblical data in keeping with the Church's tradition. Such exegetical efforts are spiritually rewarding in themselves, and they can also serve as an indirect confirmation of the Church's dogma.

In these two verses we come very close to finding a contradiction in the Bible. James and Paul use the same words (*justified, faith, works*) in the same context (salvation) and even using the same illustration (Abraham's righteousness; cf. Rom 4:3 and Jas 2:21–23) to make seemingly conflicting points.

What is the solution? It might be that Paul and James are using the word *faith* differently. Thus, while Paul is talking about the kind of faith that saves (genuine faith), James is talking about the kind of faith that does not save (spurious or merely nominal faith). Usually the difference is reckoned to be that the former faith has works as its product ("fruit"), whereas the latter does not (we are saved by faith alone, but not a faith that is alone).

On the other hand, it might be that Paul and James are using the word *justification* differently. That is, whereas Paul is equating justification with salvation itself, James means something like proof of one's salvation. Sometimes it is said that Paul is speaking of justification before God (a one-time act whereby God declares a person to be just), and James is speaking of justification before men (i.e., one's faith being proved genuine to others).

A better possibility is that the difference between James and Paul on this point comes down to an equivocation on the word *works*. This solution is established by the actual wording of the texts in question and not a theological retooling of their definitions.

Works of Law

The term *legalism* is given to views of salvation in which salvation relies on works. It is a view rejected by both sola fide Protestants and faithful Catholics—but for different reasons.[24] One of these reasons is that Catholics recognize distinctions among works in the Bible that Protestants often conflate.

When Paul is discussing things such as faith, works, and law, he nearly always qualifies his terms. For example, he speaks positively of following the "law of the Spirit of life" (Rom 8:2) and "faith working through love" (Gal 5:6) but speaks negatively of "works of the law" (Gal 2:16; 3:2, 5, 10; Rom 3:20, 28), "works of darkness"

---

[24] See Joe Heschmeyer, "The Catholic View on Justification (and Sanctification)", Shameless Popery, November 9, 2010, accessed May 28, 2015, http://catholicdefense.blogspot.com/2010/11/catholic-view-on-justification-and.html.

(Rom 13:12; Eph 5:11), and "works of the flesh" (Gal 5:19). Even when there is not a direct qualification, context indicates what Paul means, such as with works done for illegitimate boasting (Rom 3:27, 4:2; cf. Gal 6:4).

James differs from Paul in that his letter does not include negative references to either works or the law. When James references obedience to the law, he refers to the "law of liberty". This is established in the very first chapter:

> For if any one is a hearer of the word and not a doer, he is like a man who looks intently at his natural face in a mirror; for he observes himself and goes away and at once forgets what he was like. But he who looks into the perfect law, the law of liberty, and perseveres, being no hearer that forgets but a doer that acts, he will be blessed in his doing. (Jas 1:23–25)

James defines this "law of liberty" (which he also refers to as the "royal law") in chapter 2: it is the great commandment of Jesus (cf. Mt 22:37; cf. Deut 6:5):

> If you really fulfil the royal law, according to the Scripture, "You shall love your neighbor as yourself," you do well. But if you show partiality, you commit sin, and are convicted by the law as transgressors. For whoever keeps the whole law but fails in one point has become guilty of all of it. For he who said, "Do not commit adultery," said also, "Do not kill." If you do not commit adultery but do kill, you have become a transgressor of the law. So speak and so act as those who are to be judged under the law of liberty. For judgment is without mercy to one who has shown no mercy. (Jas 2:8–13)

James is speaking of the *law of love* to those who will be judged under the *law of liberty*. James, then, is affirming something that Paul affirms—namely, the spiritual law that sets us free for good works by which we are justified. Thus, James is not contradicting Paul by affirming that anyone will be justified by works *apart from grace and the Spirit*. Paul, in fact, parallels James' words when he writes:

> For in Christ Jesus neither circumcision nor uncircumcision is of any avail, but faith working through love.... For you were called to freedom, brethren. Only do not use your freedom as an opportunity for

the flesh, but through love be servants of one another. For the whole
law is fulfilled in one word: "You shall love your neighbor as yourself." (Gal 5:6, 13–14)

This harmony also helps explain why Paul connects faith, hope,
and love more than he contrasts faith and works.[25] When we consider
that Paul (in his negative statements about salvation by works and the
law) and James (in his positive statements about salvation by works
and the law) speak of different senses of the word *works*, the perceived
contradiction disappears, and the objective textual harmony that
results is neither legalistic nor licentious (even if it is not Protestant).

Works of Love

One of the most important doctrinal implications of this way of
harmonizing the texts on faith, works, and justification is that faith
and charity (love), although they are different theological virtues,
are necessarily joined together *in justification*. Faith can exist without
love, but *justifying* faith is always faith formed by love—that is to
say, *living* faith.[26] Thus, when Saint Paul speaks of justification by
faith, he is referring to living faith. Living faith is not opposed to

---

[25] For example, in Gal 5:6 Paul says, "For in Christ Jesus neither circumcision nor uncircumcision is of any avail, but faith working through love." But if circumcision is a work,
then how could "faith working" be the only thing that "is of any avail"? Galatians is one of
the go-to books of the New Testament for showing the antithesis of faith and works, but
note that in this section Paul again qualifies the works he is railing against: they are "works *of
the law*" (e.g., Gal 2:16; 3:2, 5, 10; emphasis added), not just any good work—and especially
not faithful works done in love. This joining of faith and love also occurs early in Romans—
another favorite book for sola fide adherents. Yet again, though, Paul qualifies the works he is
referring to as "works *of the law*" (e.g., Rom 3:20, 28; 9:32 [implied]; emphasis added). He also
mentions boasting about one's works as being a problem—not simply doing them. Although
not a heavyweight in the antiworks sections of the New Testament, the book of Ephesians
provides the most single famous sola fide proof text: "For by grace you have been saved
through faith; and this is not your own doing, it is the gift of God—not because of works,
lest any man should boast" (Eph 2:8–9). Here we have Paul clearly distinguishing between
grace (*by which* we are saved), faith (*through which* we are saved), and works (*by which* we are *not*
saved). Interestingly, though, if we read to the end of the passage—"For we are his workmanship, created in Christ Jesus for good works, which God prepared beforehand, that we should
walk in them" (Eph 2:10)—works are mentioned again (as that *for which* we are saved—cf.
1 Thess 1:3 and 2 Thess 1:11).

[26] This principle is dogmatically defined by Trent, session 6, chaps. 7 and 8, http://www
.americancatholictruthsociety.com/docs/trent/trent6.htm.

Spirit-enabled good works as a cooperating cause of justification (Jas 2:22), because what makes faith alive is love, which is the principle of all good works.

Sample Bible search on the words "saved", "repent", and "salvation":

Mt 3:2 (cf. Mt 4:17)—"Repent, for the kingdom of heaven is at hand."

Mt 5:3 (Sermon on the Mount; cf. Lk 6:20)—"Blessed are the poor in spirit, for theirs is the kingdom of heaven."

Mt 5:10—"Blessed are those who are persecuted for righteousness' sake, for theirs is the kingdom of heaven."

Mt 5:20—"For I tell you, unless your righteousness exceeds that of the scribes and Pharisees, you will never enter the kingdom of heaven."

Mt 6:33—"But seek first his kingdom and his righteousness, and all these things shall be yours as well."

Mt 7:21—"Not every one who says to me, 'Lord, Lord,' shall enter the kingdom of heaven, but he who does the will of my Father who is in heaven."

Mt 10:22 (Mt 24:13; Mk 13:13)—"But he who endures to the end will be saved."

Mk 1:15—"The time is fulfilled, and the kingdom of God is at hand; repent, and believe in the gospel."

Mk 2:5—"And when Jesus saw their faith, he said to the paralytic, 'Child, your sins are forgiven.'"

Mk 8:35 (Mt 16:25; Lk 9:24)—"[W]hoever loses his life for my sake and the gospel's will save it."

Mk 16:16—"He who believes and is baptized will be saved; but he who does not believe will be condemned."

Lk 3:3—"And he went into all the region about the Jordan, preaching a baptism of repentance for the forgiveness of sins."

Lk 7:50—"And he said to the woman, 'Your faith has saved you; go in peace.'"

Lk 8:12—"[B]elieve and be saved."

Lk 13:3 (Lk 13:5)—"I tell you, No; but unless you repent, you will all likewise perish."

Lk 15:7, 10—"Just so, I tell you, there will be more joy in heaven over one sinner who repents than over ninety-nine righteous persons who need no repentance.... Just so, I tell you, there is joy before the angels of God over one sinner who repents."

Lk 24:47—"and that repentance and forgiveness of sins should be proclaimed in his name to all nations, beginning from Jerusalem".

Jn 5:24—"Truly, truly, I say to you, he who hears my word and believes him who sent me, has eternal life."

Jn 6:29—"Jesus answered them, 'This is the work of God, that you believe in him whom he has sent.'"

Jn 6:35—"Jesus said to them, 'I am the bread of life; he who comes to me shall not hunger, and he who believes in me shall never thirst.'"

Jn 6:40—"[E]very one who sees the Son and believes in him should have eternal life, and I will raise him up at the last day."

Jn 6:47—"Truly, truly, I say to you, he who believes has eternal life."

Jn 8:24—"I told you that you would die in your sins, for you will die in your sins unless you believe that I am he."

Acts 2:21—"And it shall be that whoever calls upon the name of the Lord shall be saved."

Acts 2:38, 40—"Repent and be baptized every one of you in the name of Jesus Christ for the forgiveness of your sins, and you shall receive the gift of the Holy Spirit.... Save yourselves."

Acts 3:19—"Repent therefore, and turn again, that your sins may be blotted out."

Acts 5:31—"God exalted him at his right hand as Leader and Savior, to give repentance to Israel and forgiveness of sins."

Acts 8:22—"Repent, therefore, of this wickedness of yours, and pray to the Lord that, if possible, the intent of your heart may be forgiven you."

Acts 15:11—"But we believe that we shall be saved through the grace of the Lord Jesus, just as they will."

Acts 16:31—"Believe in the Lord Jesus, and you will be saved, you and your household."

Rom 5:9—"Since, therefore, we are now justified by his blood, much more shall we be saved by him from the wrath of God."

Rom 10:9—"[I]f you confess with your lips that Jesus is Lord and believe in your heart that God raised him from the dead, you will be saved."

1 Cor 1:18, 21—"For the word of the cross is folly to those who are perishing, but to us who are being saved it is the power of God.... For since, in the wisdom of God, the world did not know God through wisdom, it pleased God through the folly of what we preach to save those who believe."

1 Cor 3:15—"If anyone's work is burned up, he will suffer loss, though he himself will be saved, but only as through fire."

1 Cor 5:5—"[Y]ou are to deliver this man to Satan for the destruction of the flesh, that his spirit may be saved in the day of the Lord Jesus."

1 Cor 7:16—"Wife, how do you know whether you will save your husband? Husband, how do you know whether you will save your wife?"

1 Cor 15:2—"by which you are saved, if you hold it fast—unless you believed in vain".

2 Cor 7:10—"For godly grief produces a repentance that leads to salvation and brings regret, but worldly grief produces death."

Rom 3:25–28—"whom God put forward as an expiation by his blood, to be received by faith. This was to show God's righteousness, because in his divine forbearance he had passed over former sins; it was to prove at the present time that he himself is righteousness and that justifies him who has faith in Jesus. Then what becomes of our boasting? It is excluded. On what principle? On the principle of works? No, but on the principle of faith. For we hold that a man is justified by faith apart from works of the law."

Gal 2:16—"yet who know that a man is not justified by works of the law but through faith in Jesus Christ, even we have believed in Christ Jesus, in order to be justified by faith in Christ, and not by works of the law, because by works of the law shall no flesh be justified".

Gal 3:11—"Now it is evident that no one is justified before God by the law; for 'He who through faith is righteous shall live.'"

Eph 2:5—"even when we were dead through our trespasses, made us alive together with Christ (by grace you have been saved)".

Eph 2:8–10—"For by grace you have been saved through faith; and this is not your own doing; it is the gift of God—not because of works, lest any man should boast. For we are his workmanship, created in Christ Jesus for good works, which God prepared beforehand, that we should walk in them."

Phil 2:12—"Therefore, my beloved, as you have always obeyed, so now, not only as in my presence but much more in my absence, work out your own salvation with fear and trembling."

2 Thess 2:10—"those who are to perish, because they refused to love the truth and so be saved".

2 Thess 2:13—"But we are bound to give thanks to God always for you, brethren beloved by the Lord, because God chose you from the beginning to be saved through sanctification by the Spirit and belief in the truth."

1 Tim 2:15—"Yet woman will be saved through bearing children, if she continues in faith and love and holiness, with modesty."

1 Tim 4:7–10—"Have nothing to do with godless and silly myths. Train yourself in godliness; for while bodily training is of some value, godliness is of value in every way, as it holds promise for the present life and also for the life to come. The saying is sure and worthy of full acceptance. For to this end we toil and strive, because we have our hope set on the living God, who is the Savior of all men, especially of those who believe."

1 Tim 4:16—"Take heed of yourself and of your teaching; hold to that, for by doing so you will save both yourself and your hearers."

2 Tim 1:9—"who saved us and called us to a holy calling, not in virtue of our works but in virtue of his own purpose and the grace which he gave us in Christ Jesus ages ago".

Titus 3:5—"[H]e saved us, not because of deeds done by us in righteousness, but in virtue of his own mercy, by the washing of regeneration and renewal of the Holy Spirit."

Heb 5:9—"[A]nd being made perfect, he became the source of eternal salvation to all who obey him."

Heb 7:25—"Consequently he is able for all time to save those who draw near to God through him, since he always lives to make intercession for them."

Heb 9:28—"[S]o Christ, having been offered once to bear the sins of many, will appear a second time, not to deal with sin but to save those who are eagerly waiting for him."

Jas 1:21—"Therefore put away all filthiness and rank growth of wickedness and receive with meekness the implanted word, which is able to save your souls."

Jas 2:14, 17–18, 20–22, 24–26—"What does it profit, my brethren, if a man says he has faith but has not works? Can that faith save him? ... So faith by itself, if it has no works, is dead.... But some one will say, 'You have faith and I have works.' Show me your faith apart from your works, and I by my works will show you my faith.... Do you want to be shown, you foolish fellow, that faith apart from works is barren? Was not Abraham our father justified by works when he offered up his son Isaac on the altar? You see that faith was active along with his works, and faith was completed by his works.... You see that a man is justified by works and not by faith alone. And in the same way was not also Rahab the harlot justified by works when she received the messengers and sent them out another way? For as the body apart from the spirit is dead, so faith apart from works is dead."

Jas 5:15—"And the prayer of faith will save the sick man, and the Lord will raise him up; and if he has committed sins, he will be forgiven."

1 Pet 2:2—"Like newborn infants, long for the pure spiritual milk, that by it you may grow up to salvation."

1 Pet 3:21—"Baptism, which corresponds to this, now saves you, not as a removal of dirt from the body but as an appeal to God for a clear conscience, through the resurrection of Jesus Christ."

2 Pet 2:20—"For if, after they have escaped the defilements of the world through the knowledge of our Lord and Savior Jesus Christ, they are again entangled in them and overpowered, the last state has become worse for them than the first."

1 Jn 3:23—"And this is his commandment, that we should believe in the name of his Son Jesus Christ and love one another, just as he has commanded us."

1 Jn 4:16—"So we know and believe the love that God has for us. God is love, and he who abides in love abides in God, and God abides in him."

1 Jn 5:1—"Every one who believes that Jesus is the Christ has been born of God, and every one who loves the parent loves the one begotten by him."

1 Jn 5:5—"Who is it that overcomes the world but he who believes that Jesus is the Son of God?"

1 Jn 5:13—"I write this to you who believe in the name of the Son of God that you may know that you have eternal life."

Jude 5—"Now I desire to remind you, though you were once for all fully informed, that he who saved the people out of the land of Egypt, afterward destroyed those who did not believe."

Jude 23—"save some by snatching them out of the fire; on some have mercy with fear, hating even the garment spotted by the flesh".

Rev 2:19—"I know your works, your love and faith and service and patient endurance, and that your latter works exceed the first."

Rev 14:12—"Here is a call for the endurance of the saints, those who keep the commandments of God and the faith of Jesus."